VICTORIAN PUBLISHING AND
MRS. GASKELL'S WORK

Victorian Literature and Culture Series

Karen Chase, Jerome J. McGann, *and* Herbert Tucker, *Editors*

VICTORIAN PUBLISHING AND MRS. GASKELL'S WORK

Linda K. Hughes

and

Michael Lund

UNIVERSITY PRESS OF VIRGINIA

Charlottesville and London

The University Press of Virginia
© 1999 by the Rector and Visitors of the University of Virginia
All rights reserved
Printed in the United States of America

First published 1999

♾ The paper used in this publication meets the minimum requirements of the
American National Standard for Information Sciences—Permanence of Paper
for Printed Library Materials, ANSI z39.48-1984.

Library of Congress Cataloging-in-Publication Data
Hughes, Linda K.
    Victorian publishing and Mrs. Gaskell's work / Linda K. Hughes and
Michael Lund.
        p.   cm. — (Victorian literature and culture series)
    Includes bibliographical references and index.
    ISBN 0-8139-1875-8 (alk. paper)
    1. Gaskell, Elizabeth Cleghorn, 1810–1865—Relations with publishers.
2. Authors and publishers—Great Britain—History—19th century.
3. Literature publishing—Great Britain—History—19th century.
I. Lund, Michael, 1945–   . II. Title. III. Series.
PR4711.H84   1999
823'.8—dc21   98-53634
                                                      CIP

Contents

Acknowledgments

AN ABBREVIATED VERSION OF chapter 4 was published as "Textual/Sexual Pleasure and Serial Publication" in *Literature in the Marketplace: Nineteenth-Century British Publishing and Reading Practices,* ed. John O. Jordan and Robert L. Patten (Cambridge: Cambridge Univ. Press, 1995), 143–64. Portions of "Elizabeth Gaskell's Virgins," *Australasian Victorian Studies Annual* 1 (1995): 51–57, also appear here.

We are grateful to students at Longwood College and Texas Christian University, who have helped us learn to appreciate the work of Elizabeth Gaskell. We specifically acknowledge the research assistance of Nancy Myers, Julianne Smith, and Stacia Dunn Neeley. Pubali Ray Chaudhuri also provided editorial assistance.

For permission to reproduce the Samuel Laurence portrait of Elizabeth Gaskell on the cover, we are grateful to Mrs. Trevor Dabbs. We also express warm thanks to Mrs. Joan Leach, Hon. Secretary of the Gaskell Society, for her assistance.

Abbreviations

1882	*Thomas Carlyle: A History of the First Forty Years of His Life, 1795–1835*
1884	*Thomas Carlyle: A History of His Life in London, 1834–1881*
A	*Athenaeum*
B	*Blackwood's Edinburgh Magazine*
C	*Cornhill Magazine*
CB	"The Crooked Branch"
CH	*Elizabeth Gaskell: The Critical Heritage*
CP	"Cousin Phillis"
CR	*Cranford*
CSS	"Christmas Storms and Sunshine"
DG	"The Doom of the Griffiths"
DNW	"A Dark Night's Work"
F	*Fraser's Magazine*
FR	*Fortnightly Review*
HJ	*Harper's New Monthly Magazine*
HJM	"The Heart of John Middleton"
HW	*Household Words*
ILN	*Illustrated London News*
LCB	*The Life of Charlotte Brontë*
LG	*Literary Gazette*
LL	"Lizzie Leigh"
LMG	*The Letters of Mrs. Gaskell*
MB	*Mary Barton*
MC	"The Moorland Cottage"
MG	*Manchester Guardian*
MLL	*My Lady Ludlow*
MM	*Macmillan's Magazine*
NS	*North and South*

ONS   "The Old Nurse's Story"
PC   "The Poor Clare"
PR   Press
R   Ruth
RT   Round Table
S   Sharpe's London Magazine
SL   Sylvia's Lovers
SP   Spectator
SR   Saturday Review
T   Times
TB   Temple Bar
TR   The Reader
UH   Unitarian Herald
WD   Wives and Daughters
WR   Westminster Review

VICTORIAN PUBLISHING AND
MRS. GASKELL'S WORK

Introduction: Virgin Spaces
in Victorian Forms

A CHARACTER IN one of Elizabeth Gaskell's earliest stories, "Christmas Storms and Sunshine" (*Howitt's Journal,* 1848), is Mr. Hodgson: "He was chief compositor, or whatever title may be given to the head-man in the mechanical part of a newspaper. He hardly confined himself to that department. Once or twice, unknown to the editor, when the manuscript had fallen short, he had filled up the vacant space by compositions of his own; announcements of a forthcoming crop of green peas in December; a gray thrush having been seen, or a white hare, or such interesting phenomena; invented for the occasion, I must confess; but what of that?" (CSS, 111). Unlike the rigid bed of Procrustes, which sometimes required stretching his guests or lopping off their legs to make them fit, Mr. Hodgson's galleys provide a comfortable place of expression for the compositor. We shall take the sly Mr. Hodgson and his frames as a model for his creator and her work. Throughout her career this eminent Victorian was finding "vacant spaces" in the ideology of her day, spaces into which she could slide things of value: "announcements . . . of such interesting phenomena." Her "invention" was capable of using the mechanical limits of her world's newspaper to subtle ends; and her compositions clearly pleased those who, like the narrator in this story, discovered them.

But precisely identifying Elizabeth Gaskell's distinctive qualities without reference to the frame of the culture that surrounded her is difficult. Just as one of her most memorable characters—Molly Gibson in her final novel, *Wives and Daughters*—borrowed from all the people important in her life to find her own identity, so Gaskell spoke by taking up and altering the voices of other prominent figures in her world. She could write the industrial novel in *Mary Barton,* the historical tale in *Sylvia's Lovers,* the idyll in "Cousin Phillis," yet she always altered the tropes that generated these forms so as to make the final product uniquely her own. We will even risk a pun on her protagonist's name in *Wives and Daughters* by suggesting that mollification is a central technique of her writing. Taking on some of the fixed formulas of her culture in her narrative voice and novel structures, Gaskell softened their nature and reduced the rigidity of their application, just as she might be said to mollify readers hostile to change by relying on (or resorting to) these familiar forms.

In the study that follows, then, we take Gaskell's particular style as our cue, not trying to fit her work into preexisting critical frames but instead documenting how she used spaces within and beside such frames to special advantage. What is important about her work is her openness to a many-sided reality that includes oppression, harm, suffering, ambition, opportunity, and even opportunism, but an openness that also makes room for sweetness and compassion. Her vision subverts but also bridges, relies on form and yet formally innovates.

As a consequence of embodying so much of her culture's values in her fiction, Elizabeth Gaskell (1810–65) was recognized for much of her own century as a voice of Victorian convention: the loyal wife, the good mother, the respected woman writer. But this reputation as "Mrs. Gaskell" inspired a steady decline in her standing among twentieth-century literary critics. Both F. R. Leavis and Frederick Karl dubbed her a "minor novelist," and Yvonne Ffrench, though devoting a slim volume to her work, termed her an "unassuming yet steadfast luminary . . . dimmed by the proximity of the great surrounding planets, her contemporaries."[1] As late as 1980 Gaskell's fiction had received little serious attention from scholars, though her biography of Charlotte Brontë was regularly cited as a helpful historical document. Recently, however, she has been rediscovered by biographers (see Jenny Uglow's superb 1993 critical biography *Elizabeth Gaskell: A Habit of Stories*), by feminists (Felicia Bonaparte's 1992 *The Gypsy-Bachelor of Manchester: The Life of Mrs. Gaskell's Demon*), by literary historians (Hilary Schor's critical study of 1993, *Scheherezade in the Marketplace: Elizabeth Gaskell and the Victorian Novel*), and by general readers (as evinced by the new paperback editions of her major novels and short fiction).

Although the post-Victorian reaction to the stereotypical "Mrs. Gaskell" obscured key elements of her accomplishments for many twentieth-century critics, the perspectives she opened were not completely lost on her original readers. We hope, therefore, to model ourselves after Mrs. Hodgson from "Christmas Storms and Sunshine," who listened carefully when her husband read aloud from the newspaper he worked for: "His wife always knew when to expect a little specimen of her husband's literary talent by a peculiar cough, which served as prelude; and, judging from this encouraging sign, and the high-pitched and emphatic voice in which he read them, she was inclined to think, that an 'Ode to an early Rose-bud,' in the corner devoted to original poetry, and a letter in the correspondence department, signed 'Pro Bono Publico,' were her husband's writing, and to hold up her head accordingly" (CSS, 111). Like her character, Gaskell was an author who understood the mechanics of book production, the business of publication, and the nature of reception. Thus she realized where the unclaimed spaces in the literary industry lay and knew how to use her own distinctive voice to reach certain audiences. We like to think, as we reread contributions to the firm of Smith, Elder, or to *Household Words* or the *Cornhill,* that we hear in turn a "peculiar cough." We hold up our heads accordingly and hope to register the particular voice also heard by her contemporaries.

Elizabeth Gaskell cannot be contained in a single critical category because she is too attuned to the material realities that are central to her writing—the body, the marketplace, and the book qua book. If any critical methodologies were to be singled out as appropriate for studying Gaskell right now, they might be those associated with publishing history. But as John O. Jordan and Robert L. Patten point out, "publishing history, 'literary sociology,' the history of the book, or the 'sociology of texts,' as the field is variously denominated, 'lacks binding theoretical coherence'" because of its "interdisciplinarity" and must begin by recognizing "the impossibility of composing a single metanarrative." Yet we can endorse the general goal of such study as identified by Jordan and Patten: "to know more about how books were produced and consumed [in the past], and to understand how that knowledge directs as well as contributes to our interpretations of culture and history."[2]

Elizabeth Gaskell's books especially appropriated Victorian literary form and narrative rhythms to represent, explicitly or implicitly, things previously unsaid about women's lives, such as unwed motherhood, menses, pregnancy, and sexual desire. In taking on this work, Gaskell repeatedly confronted challenges embedded in Victorian ideas of gender and authorship. Like Mr. Hodgson, she was forced to discover and use "vacant space" within existing structures as well as to invent new forms. In part these challenges arose because she was female and women authors were seen in fixed ways by editors, publishers, and readers. She altered such dominant Victorian forms as the serial novel and the biography so as to complicate and refine the vision of her mostly masculine contemporaries. At the same time, she created a body of work that has survived deliberate efforts to confine it within limits comfortable to specific audiences.

One of the often unrecognized features of Gaskell's art we emphasize is that characters and characteristics minimized by other Victorian authors are often given substantial presence in her work. In Victorian society in general, of course, too many females were thought of as surplus; their bodies did not count in any significant census. In the first chapter of *North and South,* for instance, Margaret Hale seems to be only "the blank" (*NS,* 37) on which to hang her cousin Edith's wedding clothes. But though no one in her aunt's house "thought about it," Margaret's "tall, finely made figure" (39) represents a more physical heroine than someone like Edith—for whom the "great kitchen tea-kettle" is "too heavy" (45). To a degree surprising for Victorian fiction, Gaskell's narrative frequently draws attention to Margaret's material presence, as in her "wide mouth," which is "one soft curve of rich red lips" (48). A bracelet "on one taper arm" is fascinating to industrialist John Thornton, especially when it "would fall down over her round wrist" then be pushed "up impatiently, until it tightened her soft flesh" (120). Clichéd accounts of Victorian fiction suggest that one of the favorite principles of the Cranford ladies would guide "Mrs. Gaskell": they "felt it would be better to consider [an unpopular engagement] in the same light as the Queen of Spain's legs—facts which certainly existed, but the less said about the better" (117). Legs, arms, feet, and hands, however, insistently constitute the foundation of Elizabeth Gaskell's fictional world; she was an author who acknowledged the materiality of human beings as readily as she negotiated the material conditions of publication. And she was more careful than many not to chop off the legs of her characters in order to keep them within Mrs. Grundy's limits.

As the bodies of her young women are presented in powerful detail, so the men of Gaskell's work possess distinct material identities. In the three-volume *Sylvia's Lovers* (1863), for instance, Charley Kinraid's body is a primary subject. It is shot "through t' side" and "kicked . . . aside for dead" (*SL*, 55) when he tries to protect Monkshaven whale fishermen from a press-gang during the Napoleonic wars. Charley later loses control over his own body when he is captured by a press-gang: after a "hand-to-hand struggle" he is bound lying "still as any hedgehog . . . as if it cost him more effort to be passive, wooden, and stiff in their hands than it had done to fight and struggle with all his might" (216–17). Gaskell's work reveals a conviction that the physical world where such violence to the human form occurs can be understood if adequately represented in language, and that language used effectively can alter the shape of material reality. This principle of representation is underscored in her recurring use of letters, diaries, legal documents, and newspapers to embody fictional characters in her imagined world.

Another important distinction of Gaskell's world is that even the weakest or seemingly least important bodies matter more than art, including the art of novels, though this affirmation of materiality is necessarily conveyed through linguistic signs that are simultaneously material forms and abstractions removed from the palpability to which they refer. In one installment of the later *My Lady Ludlow* (3 July 1858) the narrator explains how, at least for the title character of this novella, representation must lie at one remove from the material reality of life. Arranging a lifetime's memorabilia, the narrator compares Lady Ludlow's pictures to locks of hair:

> *I don't think that looking at these made my lady seem so melancholy, as the seeing and touching of the hair did. But, to be sure, the hair was, as it were, a part of some beloved body which she might never touch and caress again, but which lay beneath the turf, all faded and disfigured, except perhaps the very hair, from which the lock she held had been dissevered; whereas the pictures were but pictures after all—likenesses, but not the very things themselves. This is only my own conjecture, mind. My lady rarely spoke out her feelings.* (MLL, 37)

Margaret Dawson's conjecture is played out in Mrs. Gaskell's work, as the objective of her fiction is a changed (sometimes melancholy) audience, the fellow Victorians who have held in their hands the "likenesses, but not the very things themselves" of their own world and discovered new value in what they represent. We use the term "Mrs. Gaskell's work" in our title and throughout this book, then, to signify not just what she wrote but also what she wrought—the effects of her fiction on her contemporaries.

Another of Gaskell's insufficiently appreciated distinctions is her fusion (not merely counterpointing) of decorum and daring until both become something other than they first seemed. By this means she opens, beneath a surface of extraordinary sweetness and wry wit, spaces within contemporary ideology for her readers to explore. The opening sentences of *Cranford* are a famous case in point for such gentle provocativeness, as apparently empty space yields surprising substance: "In the first place, Cranford is in possession of the Amazons; all the holders of houses, above a certain rent, are women. If a married couple come to settle in the town, somehow the gentleman disappears; he is either frightened to death by being the only man in the Cranford evening parties, or he is accounted for by being with his regiment, his ship, or loosely engaged in business all the week" (*CR,* 1). What appears as humor that gently mocks the ridiculousness (even horror) of an all-female society also presents itself as an aggressive threat (the Amazon reference) or as a marginalizing of the male within a deliberately female-centered fictive world. Cranford is mostly populated by old women and most usually (as indicated by the recurrent appellation "Miss") virginal old women. Old age and virginity are related concepts within patriarchal discourse, for both are defined negatively, relative to men, by empty, unused spaces within female bodies. Yet virgin space, reconceived within a female-centered world, can also function as a guarantor of physical (and social) liberty; what might be thought an empty, invisible, unproductive space can be seized on and used productively as a form of agency. Again, these "old maids" (the patriarchal term) are also Amazons. And "Mrs. Gaskell" is more than the conventional chronicler of her age.

Another place we hear a cough is near the end of that first chapter of *Cranford.* The elder Miss Jenkyns (Deborah), who champions the literary merits of Dr. Johnson over the talents of popular upstarts, opines, "I consider it vulgar, and below the dignity of literature, to publish in numbers" (*CR,* 9). Here Gaskell's wit is self-directed, since she herself, like Hood and Dickens, published in numbers. Serialization was often censured for being cheap (commercial rather than whole and artistic) and fragmented. A form that seemed tainted to many, however, has also been reconceived in recent scholarly work, including our own *The Victorian Serial*. The intervals between parts created enormous gaps, both spatial and temporal. Within author-centered studies these spaces are sometimes unproductive and even vicious, destroying artistic integrity. But these spaces that from one point of view were thought unused ("virgin") were found by readers to be highly productive, granting them increased agency in forecasting, interpreting, and discussing an ongoing literary work. Elizabeth Gaskell offered her readers unique opportunities in the spaces of serial publication.

We explore the serial structure of her last novel, *Wives and Daughters* (1864–66), in chapter 1 to found our study on the more practical, nuts and bolts business of publishing practices in her time. In chapter 2 we contrast the early *Mary Barton* (1848) with the late *Sylvia's Lovers* (1863) in order to specify how over the course of her career she developed the voice of narrative authority that enabled her to choose among established publishers (Chapman and Hall; Smith, Elder) in presenting her work to a wide audience. In chapter 3 we show how social documents define and restrict human identity in "Lizzie Leigh" (1850), *Ruth* (1853), and *Cranford* (1851–53); yet with these works of her own Gaskell reconceived the body of "the fallen woman" in ways no other Victorian author attempted. In chapter 4 we document in more detail the innovative and subversive narratives she wrought on the material ground of Victorian publishing through her well-known industrial novel *North and South* (1854–55). In that work Gaskell offered alternative patterns for installment publication that, though frustrating such influential figures as her frequent editor Charles Dickens, had designs made more visible by new tenets of literary theory. And in our final chapter we argue that, in *The Life of Charlotte Brontë* (1857), the one work whose reputation has remained high from her own time to the present, she not only reshaped the public memory of a friend and fellow author but also established a new role for herself and other women in the Victorian present and the modern future.

Although it angered some in her own time, Gaskell's art has survived to our day, where it is increasingly seen to point out fault lines in Victorian complacency. Gaskell thus resembles another character from her novella *My Lady Ludlow* (*Household Words,* 19 June to 15 September

1858), the eccentric and active Miss Galindo. Known for skill at "fine sewing, and stitching, and button-holing," Miss Galindo also is the "ostensible manager" of the town "repository" for "Works of Art" (*MLL*, 124), a place where "small manufactures of ladies of little or no fortune" can be sold. As one who produces her own art, then, and who draws on and advances the art of other women, Miss Galindo is an aggressive examiner of the human community: "Out of doors, and in the village, she was not popular, although she would have been sorely missed had she left the place. But she asked too many home questions (not to say impertinent) respecting the domestic economies (for even the very poor like to spend their bit of money their own way), and would open cupboards to find out hidden extravagances, and question closely respecting the weekly amount of butter" (125). Through her fiction-writing career, Gaskell asked home questions and opened cupboards hiding secrets (often to her cost in the "village" of Manchester), pushing on fragile points of Victorian ideology including the subject of "the writer," especially "the woman author," in order gradually to offer her own versions of these entities.

Even as she inspired strong reaction from some, Elizabeth Gaskell, with an effortlessly disarming style, never lost her reading public. Jenny Uglow is "intrigued by her notorious 'charm'—a word which, when applied to her writing, at once praises and diminishes, and partly explains why such an original, passionate and sometimes rather strange writer is so often taken for granted."[3] While expressing subtly unconventional ideas, Gaskell spoke in a voice interesting and distinctive enough to be heard and heeded among competing voices. In her correspondence with literary giants such as Thomas Carlyle, John Forster, and William Makepeace Thackeray, Gaskell often acknowledged their superior experience, knowledge, and achievement. (She requested that all her letters be destroyed after her death, but many survived and have been expertly collected and edited by J. A. V. Chapple and Arthur Pollard.) In more private letters to family and friends—and even more dramatically in her own fiction—we sometimes hear another voice, something Felicia Bonaparte cites as evidence of her "demon" of repressed anger.

Bonaparte finds Miss Galindo an expression of Gaskell's demon, noting that this character must sometimes act like a man.[4] To serve as Mr. Horner's clerk, for instance, Miss Galindo admits to Margaret Dawson that she must put on certain disguises: "I try to make him [Mr. Horner] forget I'm a woman. . . .I have gone good lengths to set his mind at ease. I have stuck my pen behind my ear, I have made him a bow instead of a curtsy, I have whistled—not a tune, I can't pipe up that—nay, if you won't tell my lady, I don't mind telling you that I have said 'Confound it!' and 'Zounds!'" (*MLL,* 137). In dealing with Lady Ludlow's lawyer, Smithson, Miss Galindo must also hide her true nature: "But my greatest triumph has been holding my tongue. He would have thought nothing of my books, or my sums, or my black silk gown, if I had spoken unasked. I have buried more sense in my bosom these ten days than ever I have uttered in the whole course of my life before" (167). Mrs. Gaskell, too, desisted from open rebellion but, like Miss Galindo, thereby gained access to the public sphere and posted telling signs in her texts (the counterparts of Miss Galindo's bows) for all to see.

As is evident in such passages from her work, of course, another key to the continuing success of both character and author was humor. Miss Galindo tells Lady Ludlow, "You know, perhaps, that I was nearly being an authoress once, and that seems as if I was destined to 'employ my time in writing'. . . .it ended in my having nothing to say, when I sat down to write. But sometimes, when I get hold of a book, I wonder why I let such a poor reason stop me. It does not others" (*MLL,* 130–31). Gaskell's humor, as well as her struggle with the forms of Victorian publishing, triumphed in her famous last work, *Wives and Daughters.*

When we view that final novel within the context of other major works of the age, such as novels by Thackeray, Anthony Trollope, George Eliot, and Wilkie Collins also appearing on the pages of the 1860s *Cornhill* (perhaps the premier literary magazine of the time), we begin to recognize her contributions to literary history. Her creation of a distinctive style on that central stage is best seen in the enduring narrative structure of the whole work and in her main character, whose life is extended by the sudden death of her creator before the last chapter of that masterpiece was written. Molly Gibson lives on beyond her last appearance in *Wives and Daughters,* waiting to be seen "as she really is" in the unwritten final pages: "Molly stood out against the new gown for herself, and urged that if Cynthia and Walter were to come to visit them often, they had better see them as they really were, in dress, habits, and appointments" (*WD,* 683).

In her fiction Elizabeth Gaskell achieved the stature and the continuing power to advance her vision of people in her day "as they really were." Yet the nature of that vision was reshaped by her contemporaries in the public discussion of her life and works at the time of her death. When "Cousin Phillis" was declared Gaskell's masterpiece in some obituaries, elements of her greatest achievements were obscured. Her work, that is, was shortened and narrowed until it fit into a comfortable framework, something like the editorial restraint of Mr. Hodgson's conservative counterpart in "Christmas Storms and Sunshine," the Procrustean Mr. Jenkins: "He would as soon have thought of borrowing the king's crown for a nightcap, or the king's sceptre for a walking-stick, as he would have thought of filling up any spare corner [of his paper] with any production of his own" (CSS, 112). Our effort here is to recover what we can of Elizabeth Gaskell's effort—her work to fill the empty spaces of Victorian literary forms.

I

Standing in the *Cornhill*— Authorial Voice in Periodical Context: *Wives and Daughters*

SCHOLARS HAVE FREQUENTLY examined part endings of serial fiction in periodicals to assess their role in retaining readers through suspense and anticipation. Little attention, however, has been bestowed on the beginnings of serial parts. To do so is to engage immediately the issues of authority, voice, and readership. For in opening any periodical contribution and certainly each part of a serial novel, authors had to create a position and stance from which to speak as well as points of entry for readers. They had, that is, to construct authorial identities and the identities of implied readers as well as fashioning openings onto the worlds of their fictions.[1]

At the same time, narrative beginnings in print were always mediated by a number of other forces, including the impact of competing novels and discourses on the novelist's own reception, editorial policy, the standing of a serial novel within a given issue (at the head, in the middle, or at the end), and the publisher who negotiated with authors for manuscripts.[2] George Smith, for instance, supported Trollope's close involvement in proofreading the text of *Framley Parsonage* through its serialization in the *Cornhill*.[3] Other authors would have exerted less agency in the publishing process, as we will show in chapter 4 regarding Gaskell and her frequent editor, Charles Dickens. "Standing," then, as we are using it, at once implies narrative stance, location within the material text of the periodical, and cultural authority.

We begin with the openings of Elizabeth Gaskell's installments of *Wives and Daughters* in the *Cornhill Magazine* (August 1864 to January 1866), examining her innovative establishment of authorial voice and identity amid the competing discourses of other novels serialized in the magazine just before (George Eliot's *Romola,* Trollope's *Framley Parsonage,* Thackeray's *Denis Duval*), simultaneously with (Frederick Greenwood's *Margaret Denzil's History,* Wilkie Collins's *Armadale*), and soon after *Wives and Daughters* (Trollope's *The Claverings,* George Meredith's *The Adventures of Harry Richmond,* Thomas Hardy's *Far from the Madding Crowd*). Gaskell's distinctive voice emerges from her adopting conventional plots and discourses while also rewriting them, apparently reinforcing convention yet gently interrogating it as well.[4] We then complicate Gaskell's authorial role by examining two forms of editorial oversight carried out by Frederick Greenwood, editor of the *Cornhill* from 1864 to 1868: his choice of serial parts to open each number, and his organizing of fiction, poems, and essays within each issue. These arrangements created a distinctive structure within which the fiction would have been read and understood.

Once we have acknowledged the context in which Gaskell asserted her authorial voice in the *Cornhill,* we consider how the same principles are embodied in a fictional heroine, Molly Gibson in *Wives and Daughters*. This young Victorian woman must imitate her author in determining the many voices that describe and define her world, then establish an independent stance from which to speak for herself. Finally, because the novel in which Molly appears was cut short by the author's death at the next-to-last installment, we briefly consider the impact of her death on its reception, a process we will return to in the epilogue.

Elizabeth Gaskell's first task as serial author was to inaugurate her novel as a whole. *Wives and Daughters: An Every-Day Story* opened in the August 1864 *Cornhill* with a deliberately evasive tone: "To begin with the old rigmarole of childhood." The author's voice assumes a familiar center of narrative beginning, childhood, but prefaces it with a blatant announcement of beginning[5] and swiftly moves past it in the word "rigmarole." The rest of the novel's first paragraph (cited below) is similarly decentering. The mature author had sufficient standing in the Victorian literary marketplace (especially with *Cornhill* publisher George Smith) to alter traditional modes of narration inherent in nineteenth-century periodical publication and often adopted by male (as well as some female) writers. Indeed, when we compare the tone of this narrative opening with that of a serial that immediately preceded *Wives and Daughters* in the *Cornhill,* we can see more precisely how Gaskell's technique offered to alter established practice.

Four parts of William Makepeace Thackeray's unfinished novel *Denis Duval* were featured from March to June 1864 by the magazine for which he served, with much public fanfare, as the first editor. The magazine's decision to publish the fragment *Denis Duval* and Thackeray's narrative stance itself suggest the norms from which Gaskell's text deliberately strayed: "To plague my wife, who does not understand pleasantries in the matter of pedigree, I once drew a fine family tree of my ancestors, with Claude Duval, captain and highwayman, *sus. per coll.* in the reign of Charles II., dangling from a top branch" (*C,* March 1864, 257). Claiming to be above his wife's petty pride in (his) family history, this narrator directs his attention toward the *Cornhill's* readers, assuming more shared values with them than with his wife.

The lines of connection suggested by Thackeray's beginning were neatly confirmed at the end of his posthumous novel when the magazine's editor, Frederick Greenwood, provided a continuation and a conclusion of sorts to the famous author's text: "The readers of the *Cornhill Magazine* have now read the last lines written by William Makepeace Thackeray. The story breaks off as his life ended—full of vigour, and blooming with new promise like the apple-trees in this month of May: the only difference between the work and the life is this, that the last chapters of the one have their little pathetical gaps and breaks of unfinished effort, the last chapters of the other were fulfilled and complete" (*C,* June 1864, 655). The insistence on authorial integrity here—"vigour," "blooming," "promise," "fulfilled," "complete"—is embodied in the *Cornhill's* continuation of text from Thackeray's *Denis Duval* "Chapter VIII" through Greenwood's "Notes on *Denis Duval.*" And as they held in their hands "the last lines written by William Makepeace Thackeray," the body of *Cornhill* subscribers implicitly set the standard of literary achievement within which Gaskell would attempt in *Wives and Daughters* to position herself in new relationships to past *Cornhill* authors and to these same readers.

Ironically, the same voice sustaining Thackeray's creative energy also took over Elizabeth Gaskell's novel at its conclusion, and for the same reason—the author's untimely death: "Here the story is broken off, and it can never be finished. What promised to be the crowning work of a life is a memorial of death. A few days longer, and it would have been a triumphal column, crowned with a capital of festal leaves and flowers: now it is another sort of column—one of those sad white pillars which stand broken in the churchyard" (*C*, January 1866, 705). Greenwood's conclusion to an author's text begins here much less confidently than it had with Thackeray's work, which may indicate the role of gender, since in Greenwood's remarks on Gaskell the continuum between the bodily Thackeray and the body of his works shifts to a careful separation of authorial production from the female body.[6] Editorial presences in these two places, however, converge insofar as both reveal the infrequently acknowledged center of Victorian literary history, the powerful but generally invisible voice of magazine editor that surrounded and shaped nineteenth-century manifestations of authorship. Greenwood's next sentence in his "conclusion" to *Wives and Daughters* implied the presence of editors and subscribers that completed Victorian literary history: "But if the work is not quite complete, little remains to be added to it, and that little has been distinctly reflected in our minds" (706). Although Greenwood pays homage to the author's distinctive gifts, he also insists on the active role of readers and (as we see through his own assertion of voice and perspective) literary editors.

The strength of Gaskell's efforts to build new centers for narrative in the major monthlies edited by powerful figures like Greenwood might be measured against another important novel appearing in the early 1860s *Cornhill*. George Eliot's *Romola* began its serialization in July 1862 (just two years before *Wives and Daughters*) with the comfortable tone of a first-person plural narrative: "More than three centuries and a half ago, in the mid spring-time of 1492, we are sure that the star-quenching angel of the dawn, as he travelled with broad slow wing from the Levant to the Pillars of Hercules, and from the summits of the Caucasus across all the snowy Alpine ridges to the dark nakedness of the western isles, saw nearly the same outline of firm land and unstable sea—saw the same great mountain shadows on the same valleys as he has seen to-day" (*C*, July 1862, 1). The assumption of an eternal human landscape and the communal voice of this text confirm rather than challenge existing relationships among author, periodical, and audience (though these expectations were to undergo considerable revision as the novel developed).

Similar authorial stances are visible in other important literary texts of the early 1860s *Cornhill*: Trollope's *The Small House at Allington*, which ended in April 1864, four months before the first installment of *Wives and Daughters,* and Wilkie Collins's *Armadale,* which began in the issue presenting Gaskell's fourth part (November 1864) and ran five months later to June 1866. Collins opened his thriller using a familiar authorial stance, organizing a scene around men who are preparing for action:

> *It was the opening of the season of eighteen hundred and thirty-two, at the Baths of Wildbad.*
>
> *The evening shadows were beginning to gather over the quiet little German town; and the diligence was expected every minute. Before the door of the principal inn, waiting the arrival of the first visitors of the year, were assembled the three notable personages of Wildbad, accompanied by their wives—the mayor, representing the inhabitants; the doctor, representing the waters; the landlord, representing his own establishment.*

(*C,* November 1864, 513)

Although the women in this scene are clearly positioned in the background, the novel's plot will later include one of the most fascinating female characters of 1860s fiction, Lydia Gwilt. Not only does her personality take over the story in this sensation novel, but her voice (in letters and a diary) dominates many installments, frequently opening the latest monthly part of Collins's novel (see especially the consecutive installments from December 1865 to February 1866 and the three parts from April to June 1866). But for the beginning of his novel Collins was content to direct readers to conventional structures of society and narration.

Besides orchestrating the opening of her novel as a whole, Gaskell—like Eliot, Trollope, and Collins—also had to devise beginnings for each monthly installment of the novel's eighteen-month serial run. That beginnings were a crucial Victorian site for negotiating authority, or standing, is evident from an article published in the *Cornhill* during the novel's serialization: "The Ethics of Friendship," in the September 1864 issue. Although the essay is concerned mostly with protecting confidences even if it means lying for a friend, the writer also notes the problem of inconsiderate interruption and the resulting importance of beginnings, when one can be assured of a hearing: "We do indeed point and polish the beginnings of our sentences, but take little care or thought for the fashion of an ending which we are instinctively conscious we shall never achieve" (*C,* September 1864, 301).

The *Cornhill*'s editor, Frederick Greenwood, also attested to the importance of beginnings through the voice of his fictional narrator in *Margaret Denzil's History*. The initial installment of this work (the conclusion of which ran concurrently with the first two parts of *Wives and Daughters*) began with a statement later echoed by "The Ethics of Friendship": "How my history was begun for me—that is to say, where I was born and who were my parents—is doubtful still, I sometimes think. Only this I have found out for certain—that in life as well as in storytelling the beginning is very important, and that a good ending can scarcely come of a bad beginning" (*C,* November 1863, 582). Initiating her long novel in the same magazine some months later, Gaskell could be expected to recognize this principle of the importance of beginnings.

In Gaskell's case, however, such authority in storytelling had to be worked out in relation to expectations of female authorial voice and plots relating the domestic lives of women. (Note that Greenwood placed Margaret Denzil's narrative within the editorial frame provided by the voice of her older, more experienced husband.) Like *Framley Parsonage,* which had appeared in the *Cornhill* from January 1860 to April 1861, Gaskell's novel involves the subjects of domesticity and debt, secrecy and money. Yet Gaskell and Trollope approach these issues from markedly different starting points in their individual installments, constructing their authorial identity in divergent ways. Most typically Trollope begins each part with a highly authoritative cultural stance, asserting cultural truths while assuming readers' concurrence or generalizing about his characters or story before he proceeds to specific events, details, and nuances. He works inward from the public stance of authoritative author to the domestic scene, as in the opening to his second part: "It is no doubt very wrong to long after a naughty thing. But nevertheless we all do so. One may say that hankering after naughty things is the very essence of the evil into which we have been precipitated by Adam's fall. When we confess that we are all sinners, we confess that we all long after naughty things" (*C,* February 1860, 150).

Gaskell, in contrast, generally centers each part in specific and safely domestic detail before moving to representations of behavior involving economics, social status, and public mores or generalizing about events and characters. She thus typically works outward from the domestic scene to the public sphere. Trollope's openings are grounded in a rhetoric of cultural authority, Gaskell's in the rhetoric of domesticity. Even in her beginning of the second installment, when she must jump over a five-year time span, Gaskell assumes a broad authorial perspective only momentarily (in her reference to her own writing) before quickly centering her narrative within the specific, and private (domestic), subjectivity of Molly Gibson: "Molly grew up among these quiet people in calm monotony of life, without any greater event than that which has been recorded,—the being left behind at the Towers, until she was nearly seventeen. She had become a visitor at the school, but she had never gone again to the annual festival at the great house; it was easy to find some excuse for keeping away, and the recollection of that day was not a pleasant one on the whole, though she often thought how much she should like to see the gardens again" (*WD,* 34).

The contrast between Gaskell's and Trollope's beginnings of serial parts is even more pronounced in the opening paragraphs of their inaugural installments. Here is Trollope's beginning to *Framley Parsonage,* in which he encapsulates the character of Mark Robarts and turns his attention to money:

> *When young Mark Robarts was leaving college, his father might well declare that all men began to say all good things to him, and to extol his fortune in that he had a son blessed with so excellent a disposition.*
>
> *This father was a physician living at Exeter. He was a gentleman possessed of no private means, but enjoying a lucrative practice, which had enabled him to maintain and educate a family with all the advantages which money can give in this country.*

(*C,* January 1860, 1)

The opening paragraph of *Wives and Daughters* relinquishes a retrospective viewpoint, which grants the novelist omniscient authority, and privileges a domestic perspective and psychological process over character assessment and external constraints on individual experience (such as status and money). Gaskell structures her opening after the nursery rhymes long associated with women's domestic roles. But while echoing "The House That Jack Built," she reverses its momentum and direction, moving not from a domestic commodity (a bag of malt) to the larger social context of marriage and lands, but moving ever inward from shire to village to private room until the narrative arrives at Molly's subjectivity.

To begin with the old rigmarole of childhood. In a country there was a shire, and in that shire there was a town, and in that town there was a house, and in that house there was a room, and in that room there was a bed, and in that bed there lay a little girl; wide awake and longing to get up, but not daring to do so for fear of the unseen power in the next room; a certain Betty, whose slumbers must not be disturbed until six o'clock struck, when she wakened of herself "as sure as clockwork," and left the household very little peace afterwards. It was a June morning, and early as it was, the room was full of sunny warmth and light.

(WD, 1)

This passage is brilliantly attuned to the sensibility of the twelve-year-old Molly, whose consciousness will govern what materials can be admitted in early parts[7] until her maturation allows for confronting the complexities of class, secrets, pain, death, and small betrayals as well as the more reassuring experiences of love, nurturing, and loyalty. Gaskell's chosen entrée to the display of authorial power, then, is through the childish, the domestic, the particular. Yet the throwaway quality of her first line (mere "rigmarole") suggests power so firmly, yet lightly, assumed that it can afford to play with conventions. The most frequent observation about the narrator's authorial voice here, as in *Sylvia's Lovers,* is its confidence. It is through abnegating claims to authority or appearing to submit to the conventions of feminine domesticity that Gaskell acquires and demonstrates cultural standing.

Gaskell's strategy for constructing authorial identity underlies the differences in style between her novel and the second serial running in the *Cornhill* during the same months of 1864–66, Wilkie Collins's *Armadale.* This novel revolved around traditional British concepts of identity (Who is the true Allan Armadale?) and property (Who is to inherit Thorpe-Ambrose?). If Gaskell began most of her monthly installments in the domestic sphere, Collins almost always fixed his story at the outset within the social matrices of time and place. Of the novel's twenty installments, seventeen begin with identification of a specific temporal or spatial setting (twelve of those mention both time and place; four begin with letters or diary entries marked by address and hour). Once this larger social frame is acknowledged, the personal situations of individual characters are explored as plot develops. Gaskell's method, by contrast, is generally to describe a particular psychological condition: Molly's feelings at her father's second marriage (January 1865); the strained relations between Squire Hamley and his son (May 1865); Molly's concern for Cynthia (November 1865). Then she continues her exploration of these emotional states.

Beginning each part with a particular situation illustrating the emotional states of her characters, then moving outward through the installment to discover general rules or guidelines revealed by such conditions, allowed Gaskell to probe and bring into question the social matrices within which individuals are confined—especially those related to gender. Collins, on the other hand, did not desire to challenge the tenets of a patriarchal society that granted authority to only one of the Armadales and never to Lydia Gwilt. Hence his installments can begin grounded in established social constructs of time-progress and place-property. His characters may occasionally strain but must always in the end conform to enduring Victorian principles of social organization.

One example will help to show Gaskell's method: the October 1865 installment in which a range of social types were represented. This installment began with Molly situated in the familiar plot of romantic comedy: "'My dear Molly, why didn't you come and dine with us? . . . Oh, Mr Osborne Hamley, is that you?' and a look of mistaken intelligence at the *tête-à-tête* she had disturbed came so perceptibly over Miss Phoebe's face that Molly caught Osborne's sympathetic eye, and both smiled at the notion" (*WD*, 520). The first two chapter titles of the part further alluded to stereotypical female characters and behavior: "Hollingford Gossips" and "Scandal and Its Victims"; but other chapter titles ("An Innocent Culprit," "Molly Gibson Finds a Champion") revealed how Gaskell would subtly alter conventional constructs. One of the candidates for the role of Molly's "champion," for instance, is Lord Cumnor, "a very good-natured old woman [who] rode about on his stout old cob with his pockets full of halfpence for the children, and little packets of snuff for the old people. Like an old woman, too, he enjoyed an afternoon cup of tea in his wife's sitting-room, and over his gossip's beverage he would repeat all that he had learnt in the day" (*WD*, 552). Molly is the installment's "culprit" in that she has secretly met Mr. Preston in the woods and passed a letter to him at Grinstead's store; but she is also "innocent" in that she has come in contact with him only in the effort to help Cynthia. More important, Molly has appropriated agency where money is concerned

(Preston's loan to Cynthia), defied her father (who demands to know why she met Preston), and interfered in a pledged courtship—all actions that generally lie beyond a Victorian woman's sphere.

If authors like Gaskell and Collins attempted to shape their own distinctive discourses, editorial power was a vital part of literary production and serialization as well. This was especially true of the editor's positioning of competing serial novels within each issue of a magazine. As *Armadale* vied with *Wives and Daughters* for the position of pride in subsequent issues of the *Cornhill,* we can trace editorial preferences for authorial, periodical, and reader identity.

One place stands out in the parallel serial runs of *Wives and Daughters* and *Armadale:* July 1865, when Gaskell's text supplanted Collins's as the first feature of the *Cornhill'*s monthly issue. *Armadale* had logically taken the magazine's first position at its beginning in November 1864; and it kept Gaskell's text at the magazine's fourth or fifth spot for eight months. In the last issue with this arrangement, June 1865, *Armadale'*s story resumed with the protagonist's taking Neelie Milroy, the woman he professes to love, on a picnic; yet the installment concluded with the powerful, mysterious appearance of Lydia Gwilt out on the lonely Broads of Norfolk. At a place that Miss Milroy, the typical heroine of Victorian fiction, considers "the most lonely, dreary, hideous place I ever saw in my life!" (*C,* June 1865, 658), the protagonist Allan Armadale meets a woman of nearly paralyzing beauty; but she is a character Collins's readers already recognized as an adulteress and a murderer. This scene is an ominous fulfillment of Armadale's dream from the February 1865 installment: near "a broad, lonely pool, surrounded by open ground" under "the cloudless western sky, red with the light of sunset . . . stood the Shadow of a Woman" (*C,* February 1865, 662). Perhaps because this powerful and dangerous shadow of a woman dominated the story from this point to the novel's end, Greenwood placed it in the middle of each issue, not at the beginning. Chapters 8 and 9 of book 2, then—the July 1865 installment—marked the turning point of Wilkie Collins's plot, with Lydia becoming the object of Allan's romantic desire and of readers' narrative interest. Yet Frederick Greenwood turned to Elizabeth Gaskell as the first voice in the next seven issues of the *Cornhill.*

The July 1865 part of *Wives and Daughters* might also be seen as a transitional moment in Gaskell's whole novel, at this point just over half published. The June installment had focused on the affairs of male characters: Squire Hamley's and Lord Cumnor's efforts to drain wastelands, Osborne's fragile health and difficult financial situation, Roger's improving professional prospects. The tone of this masculine-centered installment was set in the first sentence of the initial chapter ("Old Ways and New Ways"): "Mr Preston was now installed in his new house in Hollingford; Mr Sheepshanks having entered into dignified idleness at the house of his married daughter, who lived in the country town" (*WD*, 349). Molly remained for most of the part offstage—at the Miss Brownings, for instance—when it was learned that Roger would undertake a several years' scientific expedition abroad. The July installment, however, was dominated by romantic developments, especially Molly's struggle to accept the fact that Roger had proposed to Cynthia, a typical act of self-denial for Victorian heroines and Victorian women. The August part's beginning then stressed the theme of accepting romantic disappointment: "The honour and glory of having a lover of her own was soon to fall to Molly's share; though to be sure it was a little deduction to the honour that the man who came with the full intention of proposing to her, ended by making Cynthia an offer" (*WD*, 420). The *Cornhill*'s editor allowed this note of conventional feminine duty to introduce the magazine contents for the concluding six months of 1865. Whether or not the decision to front issues with Gaskell's or Collins's serial fiction rested specifically on conformity to gender norms, it is clear that competing fictions vied for primacy of place and that the editor's decision to privilege one novel over the other depended on his notions of authorial appeal and the magazine's readers.

In composing the contents of each issue, however, Frederick Greenwood not only had to decide which serial chapters constituted the most effective beginning but also had to fashion a sequence for the whole issue. In effect, his editorial task was to create an issue's intertextuality, the relation and dovetailing of text with text for readers who might choose to read an issue straight through. Although many readers doubtless picked and chose from among a month's contents and read at random,[8] some editorial principle was at work in each month's layout, an index to the editor's sense of how fiction, nonfiction, and poetry related to each other. This editorial hand in the production of a monthly issue in turn complicates our sense of what constitutes the beginning of an essay or a novel's serial part because a preceding entry could serve as lead-in or backdrop for the next item. These juxtapositions brought to the fore issues of cultural authority and gender and remind us how brilliantly Gaskell's own interplay between convention and its displacement was attuned to the interplay of perspectives within each periodical issue as a whole.

The contents of the August 1864 number, for example, led to a many-sided debate related to Gaskell's subtitle, "An Every-Day Story"; successive contributions take up the question of what constitutes the groundwork of reality, the quotidian level of life. Gaskell's first part seems to ally the everyday with domestic culture in which both women and men participate (even those of scientific bent like Mr. Gibson). Lord Cumnor and Mr. Gibson, as well as female principals, are generally glimpsed as they surface at home or pursue family relationships. The larger social world of class and prestige exists, to be sure, and is a potent influence. But it is subordinated to a child's domestic history and key moments in her development. Gaskell's unsigned serial part was immediately followed by Matthew Arnold's signed essay "The Literary Influence of Academies." He too, like Gaskell (who alluded to a nursery rhyme), opened with a reference to the literature available for reading, but unlike Gaskell's story, his essay invoked the public world of affairs accessible only to those who had received formal education—that is, men: "It is impossible to put down a book like the history of the French Academy, by Pellisson and D'Olivet, which M. Charles Livet has lately reedited, without being led to reflect upon the absence, in our own country, of any institution like the French Academy, upon the probable causes of that absence, and upon its results" (*C*, August 1864, 154). When Arnold went on to identify the strengths of English culture as "energy and honesty" versus the "quick and flexible intelligence" (157) of the French and to name the English as essentially a provincial culture, the French as essentially urban and urbane (162–63), he immediately exposed the arbitrary boundaries of Gaskell's "everyday" story rather than the novel's universality. The brunt of his argument was the desirability of cultural authority, of having clear standards of excellence established by a cultural elite. Since Arnold wrote under a patronymic—his signature— and from the position of Professor of Poetry at Oxford,[9] he in one sense overtook Gaskell's authority and offered an entirely different representation of what should be the everyday grounds of social formations.

Yet Gaskell was given primacy of place before Arnold, and her novel introduced his essay. Putting the two side by side constrained Arnold's authority insofar as Gaskell's portrait of provincial life and compelling representation of domestic and inner lives identifies all that is left out in Arnold's scenario. Gaskell's Molly even implicitly argues for solid English character versus "foreign" cultures when a houseguest at the Towers speaks to Molly in French, inferring that nationality from Molly's "wild and strange" appearance. Molly returns only a blank stare and then remarks, "I don't understand French. I'm only Molly Gibson, ma'am" (*WD*, 19).

Frederick Greenwood appears to have savored the juxtaposition of Molly's and Arnold's respective command of French and to have extended the joke when he immediately followed Arnold's essay with a travel article on "Monaco": "Every morning, Sundays not excepted, a small white steamer may be seen feebly paddling out of the Port of Nice, and rounding the lighthouse of Villefranche" (*C*, August 1864, 173). "Sundays not excepted" immediately called into question the probity of things French, especially when it became apparent that the feeble steamer originating from France was taking passengers to gambling tables in Monaco even on the Sabbath. The world of tourism and gambling was altogether another thing from the clarity and intellectual flexibility with which Arnold had just associated French culture. And his elevation of French over English prose was pointedly countered by the succeeding essay's single quotation of French, drawn not from high culture but from Monaco's newspaper, the *Journal de Monaco,* on the rather uninspiringly urbane subject of the price and abundance of oranges (183).

The third item, a two-part Irish story called "The Lovers of Bally-vookan," further expanded the role of erotic relations and provinciality in the issue and in the definition of the "everyday." In this (not very successful) story, however, the public, masculine realm of politics also constituted an important element, since the narrator mentioned Gladstone's tax on Irish whiskey in the opening sentence (foreshadowing the smuggling that figures in the story's plot). Two essays on social policy and philosophy followed. The first ("The Limited Enlistment Act") considered how to increase reenlistment in the military and dovetailed with the previous story insofar as a disproportionate number of Irishmen were reported to reenlist because too few Englishmen did so. The essay was also an implicit commentary on *Wives and Daughters:* the masculine spheres of the military and government and the backdrop of the Indian Mutiny that propelled the writer's anxiety about sufficient preparedness again pointed to the narrowness of Gaskell's world, just as hers questioned the exclusive realm of action assigned to men in surrounding essays and fiction.

The issue's next essay, "Morality of the Doctrine of Averages," investigated the claims of statistics versus ethics and affection as a means of explaining marriages, murders, and suicides, thus juxtaposing, like *Wives and Daughters,* the competing paradigms of science and domestic affection. As the writer contemplated with anxiety the prospect of construing marriages or love for children as "cyclic [statistical] recurrences" (*C,* August 1864, 218), the countervailing world of Molly Gibson was available to enact what might be lost in an alienating mathematical model of reality (a representational strategy associated with the masculine academy and scientific societies).

Another essay on tourism ("The Tyrol Jubilee in 1863") again looked briefly to Continental culture, as had Arnold and the Monaco piece, before ushering in the other serial, Greenwood's own *Margaret Denzil's History (Annotated by Her Husband).* If this too focused on a female protagonist, its sensationalism—including suicide, hints at white slavery, and marital separation—contrasted markedly with the quiet domestic realism of *Wives and Daughters.* The stance of Greenwood's novel on women's discourse and cultural authority also diverged from Gaskell's, since a woman's attempt to write her own history was represented as subject to emendation and editing by her husband—in fact, much the same situation as Gaskell's implicit and (at her death) ultimate authorial relation to Greenwood. The two novels in juxtaposition seemed to ask which was the norm, the placidity of domestic life or its sensational cataclysms, its potential for success or its frequent failures. Greenwood's novel was also framed, at least potentially, by the previous essay on statistics, which served to raise the question whether the suicide of John Denzil's first wife was a personal tragedy or part of a larger social phenomenon.

The August number then concluded with an obituary notice of Nassau Senior written by Thackeray's daughter Annie under the initials A. I. T. Besides gesturing toward the whole story a completed life might tell, in contrast to a novel's serial parts, Thackeray's essay was also notable for drawing together domesticity and public action, science and affection, into a single discourse, suggesting they need not function as oppositions. Thus she opened by reviving a picture of Nassau Senior at home: "To many of those who but a few weeks ago were sitting in the shady garden at the back of Mr. Senior's house at Kensington, it must have seemed as if his last words of welcome were sounding almost yet, his kindly greeting still their own, when they heard that their old friend was gone from amongst them" (*C,* August 1864, 253). Thackeray's opening sentence is remarkably close to Gaskell's strategy for beginning parts, since it also began by situating author and reader within the private, enclosed spaces of a home made gracious by ties of domestic affection. The obituary hence validated Gaskell's own choice of entrée by repeating it and perhaps indicates that the women writers participated in a specifically gendered approach to writing. Thackeray, like Gaskell, also focused on a single person or character from a stance of affectionate detachment. Unlike the narrator of the novel, however, Thackeray ranged more widely across a spectrum of discourses, invoking Arnold's world of the academy in discussing Senior's time at Oxford, the realms of social policy, the military, and social sciences in recounting his work on social reform. Like Greenwood in his novel, Thackeray also supplanted her own female language with the capstone of masculine commentary, ending the notice with her father's words from *De juventate.*

The openings of Gaskell's *Wives and Daughters* and beginnings of other texts that surrounded it thus tell a story that is at once simple and very complex. In part they substantiate the eminent standing Gaskell enjoys today as an important Victorian novelist and an intriguing woman writer whose negotiations of gender helped spur her innovations in fiction. They also provide further evidence of the strongly gendered codes of writing that governed much of the material Victorians consumed in the literary marketplace. Yet these openings also demonstrate that Gaskell's own efforts were intertwined with other novelists' attempts to open a space in public discourse and attract readers, with editorial interventions that regulated where and when readers might encounter her texts, and with the intertextual dynamics of individual issues of the *Cornhill.* Although she achieved preeminence through her standing in the *Cornhill,* that positioning was far more mobile and actively negotiated than has often been acknowledged.

A story parallel to her own struggle for authorial standing is embodied in the narrative of Gaskell's last novel. More than her earlier serial novels, *Wives and Daughters* made a female's development from childhood to womanhood a central focus of the plot as well as driving force behind it. This emphasis on development and domesticity has elicited charges that Gaskell reinforces conservative ideologies of womanhood. There is truth to such accusations, yet they seem to miss the more interesting point of what she aims for and achieves. Take the title, for example. At a glance it seems to inscribe obligatory marriage, reproduction, and descent, a far cry from the Amazon world of *Cranford* or the revised model of courtship presented in *North and South*.[10] But read carefully, with due attention to plurals, the title points in other directions. The title refers to Mr. Gibson's two wives, of course, each with her own daughter, but also to Hyacinth (the second Mrs. Gibson) as mother and stepmother. The range of reference includes Fanny Hamley, the beloved daughter whom Molly comes to replace for the dying Mrs. Hamley, and Mrs. Hamley, wife of the Squire, who is a spiritual mother to Molly amid preparations for Mr. Gibson's second marriage. In these respects the function of the title, rather than instating biological determinism, is to loosen the connection between biology and motherhood, gender and essence, replacing identities with multiplicities of being and social roles.

A similar opening of traditional roles to new possibilities characterizes the novel itself. Just as each issue of the *Cornhill* offered various voices with which readers could inaugurate relationships, so the central character of *Wives and Daughters* encountered multiple figures of authority who offered to guide her to maturity. As readers watched Molly grow physically, emotionally, and intellectually in the course of this long novel, various models presented themselves to her.[11] And in her responses and assertions Molly in turn offered Gaskell's readers a subtle new guide for the future.

Given her father's medical practice, one of the models offered Molly is female invalidism, a reminder not only of actual illnesses to which women's bodies were vulnerable in the nineteenth century but also of invalidism as a subversive (if also self-defeating) protest against enforced socialization into domestic roles.[12] Lady Cumnor seems to resort to invalidism out of sheer boredom when her daughters are fully grown and time weighs heavily. Gaskell is far more evasive in her representation of

Mrs. Hamley. When told that "possibly Mrs Hamley would not have sunk into the condition of a chronic invalid, if her husband had cared a little more for her various tastes, or allowed her the companionship of those who did" (*WD,* 41), readers might well conclude that hers was a reaction to the Squire's tyranny or insensitivity within marriage. Yet within a few paragraphs Gaskell remarks that Mr. Gibson "knew there was real secret harm going on all this time" (43), and eventually she dies of her illness. Neither possibility seems to cancel out the other; in the story of Mrs. Hamley both her body and her social position as a woman matter.

Molly's resistance to or emulation of the model presented by Mrs. Hamley helps chart her own course in the novel. For the most part Molly is irrepressibly healthy and vigorous, climbing cherry trees to read books (*WD,* 247) or digging up roots until she is dirty and presumably sweaty to boot (*WD,* 343). Near the novel's end, however, we see the danger she is exposed to by induction into feminine roles. Exhausted from putting others' needs before her own, serving as repository for their secrets, comforting their griefs rather than pursuing her own happiness, she lapses into an extended illness "until at last her father feared that she might become a permanent invalid" (*WD,* 614). By the time the novel breaks off Molly is on the mend and seems on her way back to health; if she is still affected by her brush with invalidism, Molly has moved beyond this threat.

Her stepmother, Hyacinth, is the foremost model of women who are attractive yet calculating, who secure masculine attention while concealing their own inclinations from others and themselves.[13] Although Cynthia at times rebels against Hyacinth, she is ultimately her mother's daughter. Ranged against these women are models of perpetual virginhood as seen in Phoebe and Sally Browning. Molly threads her way amid all these possibilities without settling definitively into any one of them, just as her creator artfully positions her story within alternatives created by Collins and Trollope, Greenwood and Eliot.

Perhaps one reason Gaskell is so successful at thwarting Molly's socialization into conventional femininity, while hinting at it,[14] is that Gaskell also resorts to unconventional models for the growing girl—Osborne and Roger Hamley. She suggests that female types imposed on women can also be discerned in men and that sons, like daughters, can perpetuate a mother's influence—though only men can pass on a father's legacy or leave home to pursue an education. The contrast between virile men and passive, delicate women favored by the crudest ideologies of gender relations in the nineteenth century is here played out between brothers.[15] Like a stereotypical woman Osborne Hamley has, according to his father, "a girl's delicate face, and a slight make, and hands and feet as small as a lady's. He takes after madam's side" (*WD,* 74). Like a woman as well, Osborne is given education that provides him with finished graces but unfits him to earn a living;[16] and Osborne ultimately reproduces his mother's invalidism (and early death). Osborne continues the pattern (discussed in chapter 3) established by Peter Jenkyns, Frederick Hale, and Charley Kinraid of the exiled or imprisoned man in Gaskell's fiction whose problematic story has no appropriate form.

Osborne Hamley also gives to *Wives and Daughters* an indirect representation of Gaskell's negotiation with editors and publishers in the Victorian marketplace. Having taken a French wife from the servant class, the next "Hamley of Hamley" cannot find a way to confess his marriage to his very traditional father and thus resolve his perilous financial condition. Desperate for money and approval—and physically more ill than he knows—Osborne thinks of trying "the fate of his poems with a publisher, with the direct expectation of getting money for them" (*WD,* 272). He is aware of a periodical context for literary activity, imagining his poems "praised in *Blackwood* and the *Quarterly*" (272). And he suspects a structure for the whole: "in their order" they "were almost equivalent to an autobiographical passage in his life" (270). He even analyzes audiences and potential reviewers when he speculates that his work would be recognized "if I called [my wife] 'Lucy' in these sonnets" (272).

Osborne, however, is dismayed to find that "there's no one like a publisher for taking the conceit out of one. Not a man among them would take [the poems] as a gift" (*WD,* 339). Osborne is advised by Molly's father to work in other modes: "Try your hand at prose, if you can't manage to please the publishers with poetry" (340). Meanwhile his brother's mastery of newer Victorian forms is evident when Roger publishes "a paper in some scientific periodical, which [excites] considerable attention" (*WD,* 311). Dr. Gibson links Roger's promise as a writer to bodily strength: "Now I, being a doctor, trace a good deal of his superiority to the material cause of a thoroughly good constitution, which

Osborne has not got" (*WD,* 386). Osborne's love lyrics, like his weakened body, are not substantial enough to demand the recognition of payment from the Victorian marketplace; and just as important, his literary output is not steady, sustained, and ongoing, as was the work most valued by this age's expansive reach.

What Osborne Hamley lacks is the chance to build his life little by little, day by day within the national structure he assumes to be his inheritance. He more specifically would have to work within the dominant temporal framework of Victorian life: the regular, steady beat of industrial time, which can be felt in the periodic issue of installment literature. At the time *Wives and Daughters* was published, for example, Tennyson's lifelong project was almost precisely between its two important volumes (the 1859 *Idylls of the King* and *Holy Grail and Other Poems* in 1869). And Robert Browning would soon issue *The Ring and the Book* in four separate volumes (from November 1868 through February 1869). In her own fiction, Elizabeth Gaskell had also achieved both the stature and the continuing power to advance her vision.

Roger, in contrast to Osborne, is a "tall powerfully-made young man, giving the impression of strength more than elegance" (*WD,* 87). Intellectual, apt to muck about with snakes, insects, and plants in pursuit of knowledge, he at first appears to reproduce his father's lack of refinement and strikes Molly as "heavy-looking, clumsy" (87). Roger's education is not only more successful than Osborne's but also more instrumental, providing income and access to knowledge. Curiously, however, Osborne and Roger are alike subjected to some of the same parental plotting as Molly. Early on the Squire gives thought to protecting them from unwise marital options (that is, Molly herself), just as Molly shows up at Hamley Hall because Mr. Gibson is intent on extending the duration of her virginity.

This blurring of ostensible boundaries between male and female social roles also applies to subjectivities. Osborne combines his femininity with masculinity, acting out the role of erotic hero to "rescue" the French governess he secretly marries. Roger, more like Molly in this, seems oblivious to sexual attraction until Cynthia arrives. If Osborne perpetuates his mother's aesthetic and physical delicacy, Roger perpetuates her genius for comfort and conciliation. In part 1, when Hyacinth finds Molly crying on the grounds of Cumnor Towers, the former governess performs the role of domestic comforter but quickly abandons the performance to pursue self-interest. In part 4, when Roger finds Molly sobbing on the grounds next to Hamley Hall after Mr. Gibson announces his engagement, he brings Molly genuine comfort. He may prate of putting others' needs before her own (a modeling of feminine behavior Molly successfully resists at this point [*WD*, 120]), but he also nurtures her intellect, bringing her books and encouraging her to gaze through a microscope (124).

By part 8 Roger is adopting roles of male gallantry after meeting Cynthia, but he also enacts the role of domestic comforter as his mother— "the ruling spirit of the house as long as she lived" (*WD*, 257)—did before him. After a sad, desolate encounter between the Squire and Osborne at dinnertime, with all amiss and raw edged after Osborne's creditors have assessed the property and gauged the length of his father's life, Roger arrives. He promptly takes charge of the Squire and, in a charming scene that ends the part, soothes and comforts him by first listening, then telling a funny story to distract him from his griefs (276–77). As Molly faces her future, then, both women and men work as potential models in Gaskell's world; and as with Gaskell's choice of title, her characterization loosens the ties that bind gender and identity.

Another feature of Roger Hamley connects him closely to Molly and links both to the novel's serial format. Gaskell's further achievement in her last work is adapting the serial form to her theme, and vice versa. As the Squire remarks in part 8, "He may be slow, but he's steady, is old Roger" (*WD*, 268), while Osborne is "quick and clever" (276). In the preceding installment Cynthia draws a similar contrast between herself and Molly, terming Molly good, herself capable only of being a heroine: "I'm capable of a great jerk, an effort, and then a relaxation—but steady every-day goodness is beyond me" (*WD*, 229). When we recall that the subtitle of Gaskell's novel is *An Every-Day Story,* the effect, as many note, is to align Molly with the novel itself, which also succeeds by its slow, steady unfolding over time. Cynthia's definition of a heroine—one capable of a jerk, effort, then relaxation—as well as invoking masculine sexual rhythms, is congruent with some conceptions of serial parts, each building to a peak of interest through some striking incident that leaves readers hanging while the author "relaxes" between installments and gears up for another jerk of the plot (see chapter 3).

But as we will argue in the case of *North and South*'s serialization in *Household Words* (chapter 4), Gaskell's handling of *Cornhill* installments differs markedly from this model, more often concluding on quiet moments of relationship or characterization such as the scene described above between Roger and his father. In defining her own conception of heroine in contrast to the conventional romance plot Cynthia invokes, Gaskell was demonstrating her awareness of and faith in her own mode of serial writing, her confidence that she could define new ways for women writers and characters to work in the world of letters.

The changes in Molly, then, come slowly, almost imperceptibly, as physical change in women's and men's bodies does in experience—though in sum they are momentous. Reading the novel in parts, with the "virgin spaces" between parts enacting the passage of time represented in the novel itself, reinforces the minute but significant changes registered in Molly, which themselves drive the plot.[17] Molly's passage through puberty, along with her father's accepting apprentices who desire the daughter, accounts for her introduction to Hamley Hall and Mr. Gibson's second marriage—without which none of the major events in the novel would go forward. Every incident of moment in the novel thus comes back to the presence of Molly's body and the gradual changes it registers over time. In this way Gaskell confirms her society's equation of the female body with female identity, yet she also distances Molly from this alignment.

Perhaps only when one reads the novel slowly, savoring its moments instead of rushing to discover its conclusion, do Gaskell's techniques for representing slow and steady change come into view. One of the devices she uses for showing Molly's growing sexual maturity, for example, is to have her discover her new semblance in a mirror at intervals throughout the novel. The device, which participates in the conventional notion that women are defined by their appearance, may seem especially suited to interpretive strategies drawn from feminist approaches to psychoanalysis or cinema. But Gaskell's handling of the device also suggests that femininity and physical appearance are not identical essences but are categories linked through culture. Molly is generally surprised by what she sees in the mirror, as if the knowledge it reveals came from without rather than within. Meanwhile, the mirror registers for readers the subtle gradations of maturation in the course of passing months.

As she prepares for her initial dinner at the Hamleys' near the end of part 2, Molly looks in the mirror "with . . . anxiety" for the first time, curious to see how her body might strike others. Gaskell has said nothing of Molly's exterior appearance until now, making the matter a concern to readers only when it is Molly's as well: "She saw a slight, lean figure, promising to be tall; a complexion browner than cream-coloured, although in a year or two it might have that tint; plentiful curly black hair . . . ; long, almond-shaped, soft grey eyes, shaded both above and below by curling black eye-lashes" (*WD,* 66). Readers can recognize the code of erotic promise in the description, but Molly is too young to understand and turns away from the mirror remarking, "I don't think I am pretty"—though she isn't sure (66).

Gaskell has Molly look in the mirror again several months later, in part 5, shortly before her father's wedding. This time, a more mature seventeen, she is starting to grasp the significance of the changes she sees: "She was almost startled when she looked into the glass, and saw the improvement in her appearance. 'I wonder if I'm pretty,' thought she. 'I almost think I am'" (*WD,* 157). Four months later, in part 9, *Cornhill* readers might have expected to see Molly poised before the mirror as she prepares for her first ball. Intent on being correct in appearance and avoiding discomfiting stares, however, Molly bypasses the mirror in favor of watching her beautiful stepsister before it, though she confesses her own wish to be erotically attractive: "I should like to be pretty!" (*WD,* 291). Cynthia, more worldly, refrains from telling Molly what she and readers opine—that Molly has attained a beauty she doesn't yet perceive or comprehend.

Three months later Roger has declared his love to Cynthia, and Molly has begun to admit to herself that she loves Roger. But the Molly of early chapters is still visible when she looks in the mirror with Cynthia by her side. And when she sees the contrast—the marks of her hoydenish vigor ("lips dyed with blackberry juice, her curls tangled, her bonnet pulled awry") contrasting with Cynthia's elegance (*WD,* 395)—she accepts Roger's preference. By the time of part 17, after her extended illness, Molly is fulfilling the erotic promise of those early images in the mirror. Yet even as Gaskell discloses this new beauty, she indicates, as in Molly's first gaze into the mirror, that what Molly sees comes as surprise rather than as recognition: "[At Cumnor Towers] Parkes came and dressed her in some of the new clothes prepared for the Kirkpatrick visit, and did her hair in some new and pretty way, so that when Molly looked at herself in the cheval-glass, she scarcely knew the elegant reflection to be that of herself" (*WD, 648*). "Elegant": the word is the same used earlier to describe Cynthia's superior erotic attractions. Gaskell thus conveys the result of a few months' difference in Molly's life and inducts Molly into the cult of feminine beauty even as she suggests that this reflection of the body cannot ultimately define Molly, whose inward sense of herself is foreign to what she sees in the mirror. As with Gaskell's title and the role models posed for Molly, the text inscribes the presence of bodies but at the same time affirms that the body does not wholly determine identity.

This serial novel, then, over time reveals slowly, steadily Molly's gradual growth physically and intellectually. The interruptions of serial publication are productive spaces that help represent the passage of time and slow the rate of reading to direct perception toward minute changes and gestures that register phases of development. Gaskell's use of the serial format, as well as her complex outlook on women's social position, makes *Wives and Daughters* a rich commentary on the female body, a novel that many deem her masterpiece.

The serial's interruptions, however, can also inscribe changes in the lives of authors as well as characters. Authors' psychological states or life rhythms could inhabit the serial's interruptions, as when Dickens's grief after the death of Mary Hogarth left him unable to provide the scheduled installments of *Pickwick Papers* and *Oliver Twist*,[18] or when Gaskell interrupted *Cranford* for nine months to draft *Ruth* (see chapter 3). But the serial is perhaps uniquely positioned to inscribe the historical presence of authors' bodies that produced the language readers consumed, as in the case not only of Dickens's *Edwin Drood* and Thackeray's *Denis Duval,* which broke off during publication when their authors died, but also Gaskell's *Wives and Daughters,* which broke off midchapter in the eighteenth part because of her sudden heart attack. The heart that does not beat and the textual space that has no words mutually represent each other.

The impact on Gaskell's contemporaries is evident in the obituary notice written by David Masson in the December 1865 issue of *Macmillan's Magazine:*

There are thousands of readers of every age, who will feel it a personal disappointment that they are never to know whether Molly Gibson married Roger Hamley, or how poor Cynthia worked out her fate at last. Such a disappointment is surely one of the highest testimonies to a writer's genius. I heard, not long ago, of an old lady, whose life had not been a very happy one, and who was content enough to die when the time came. In her last illness, when her strength was failing, though her mind remained clear and vigorous, she took much delight in reading a serial story then appearing in print. I think it was Mr. Collins's "No Name." Speaking one day, to the friend who told me the anecdote, of her passing life, she said, simply, "I am afraid, after all, I shall die without ever knowing what becomes of Magdalen Vanstone." It is an odd thing, surely, to think how many readers, who begin to read any novel in numbers, must die before the word "finis" is written at the close. And, when a writer dies, leaving his tale half written, those who followed its fortunes eagerly feel as if something of their own had died with the writer's death.

(MM,
155–56)

Today readers presumably desire completion of the story more than they want a reminder that Gaskell's historical, physical body figured in producing her serial. Yet the incompleteness is in some ways fitting.[19] Molly is left forever virginal, her fate unconsummated and open to multiple possibilities. The open-ended text, with its representation of Gaskell's death and inscrutability about Molly's future, thus reflects features of the novel as a whole, which represents the feminine body without fixing its significance and identity. The ending of *Wives and Daughters* is yet another virgin space that succeeds in representing the female body.

Greenwood asserted that after its abrupt termination all that was left of Gaskell's work was a broken insignia of death like broken pillars in the graveyard, rather than a "triumphal column" inscribing glorious victory that would have stood had she lived to finish this last work. We see in his choice of trope an implicit registering of Gaskell's triumph after all, for "column" is also the descriptor of text in printed volumes. In every respect—in narrative beginnings, in places among competing voices and within Greenwood's periodical—Gaskell left her distinctive achievements standing in the *Cornhill* and in the larger body of work available to readers in her own era and the present.

II

Narrative Authority:
Mary Barton and
Sylvia's Lovers

ELIZABETH GASKELL'S FIRST long work of fiction, *Mary Barton: A Tale of Manchester Life* (published in two volumes by Chapman and Hall in October 1848), is a social problem novel following in the tradition of Harriet Martineau's *A Manchester Strike* (1832), Frances Trollope's *Michael Armstrong, the Factory Boy* (1840), Elizabeth Stone's *The Young Milliner* (1843), Charlotte Elizabeth Tonna's *The Wrongs of Woman* (1843–44), Benjamin Disraeli's *Coningsby* (1844), and Charles Dickens's *The Chimes* (1845).[1] Such works were inspired by the decades of rapid change in nineteenth-century life, and Victorian readers were rallied to specific political causes like the ten hours movement and child labor laws by these dramatic portrayals of suffering individuals.

Gaskell's social problem novel, however, exhibits fundamental doubts about authority, even the authority of storytelling.[2] The initial source of this tone is the narrator, who begins in uncertainty and only gradually moves toward a more confident stance at the work's conclusion.[3] Peter Brooks, studying the nineteenth-century novel in general, says that narrative voice can be seen as an expression of desire: "Narratives portray the motors of desire that drive and consume their plots, and they also lay bare the nature of narration as a form of human desire: the need to tell as a primary human drive that seeks to seduce and to subjugate the listener, to implicate him in the trust of a desire that never can quite speak its name—never can quite come to the point—but insists on speaking over and over again its movement toward that name."[4] Gaskell's first novel reflects a complex desire, both attracted to and repelled by the new industrial city that is its subject: *A Tale of Manchester Life.*

Mary Barton has also seemed to many to be divided into two stories, one about John Barton and another about his daughter Mary. Even the narrator's sex was questionable, as Stone notes: "When Gaskell's first novel was published anonymously, there was some controversy about the gender of the author."[5] Exploring the psychology of male (John Barton) and female desire (Mary Barton) in an emerging urban landscape, then, Gaskell's novel struggles to establish its own authority amid competing voices calling for reform in Victorian society.

In this chapter we trace the development of Gaskell's authoritative voice in her first novel and then examine its properties more closely in a later work, *Sylvia's Lovers*. Whereas Gaskell's style in *Wives and Daughters* borrowed from other voices of the *Cornhill* but became distinctive among them, the narrator of her early industrial novel, like its heroine, remained for the most part trapped within existing forms. Her later work, however, grounded its narrative on the more elemental rhythms of nature, especially those of the sea.

The epigraph from Carlyle raises the question of a writer's authority on *Mary Barton*'s first page, revealing the need to counter a common negative assertion about authors and sounding a key word for the entire text: *know*. "'How *knows* thou,' may the distressed Novel-wright exclaim, 'that I, here where I sit, am the Foolishest of existing mortals; that this my Long-ear of a fictitious Biography shall not find one and the other, into whose still longer ears it may be the means, under Providence, of instilling somewhat?' We answer, 'None *know*, none can certainly *know*; therefore, write on, worthy Brother, even as thou canst, even as it is given thee'" (*MB*, 35; emphasis added). Even though it was written at the urging of her publisher after the novel was complete,[6] Elizabeth Gaskell's preface to *Mary Barton* also challenged her own authority: "I know nothing of Political Economy, or the theories of trade" (38).

In her letters, Gaskell acknowledged a distinctive tone for this first novel, referring to its "tenor" (*LMG*, 54) and explaining that its subject had "impressed" itself on her as a feeling or frame of mind (*LMG*, 74, 120). She confessed to Mary Ewart an underlying doubt about her ability to present the world with absolute accuracy: "I am almost frightened at my own action in writing it. . . .I can only say I wanted to represent the subject in the light in which some of the workmen certainly consider it to be *true*, not that I dare to say it is the abstract absolute truth" (*LMG*,

67). Thus her goal is "the subject" in a certain "light," not a finite, measurable, knowable entity.

Despite these misgivings, the novel's narrator does advance from the apologetic tone of epigraph, preface, and early chapters to a position of more confidence in the second volume.[7] The novel's narrator gains strength as the tale's heroine, Mary Barton, moves from passive participant in the crisis of her community to being someone who first wants to know what has happened, then learns the truth, and finally takes action to affect future events. Mary's development, however, must be supported by the material documents of social order, as if alone she has no substance. This need for proper authorization carries over to the narrator, whose storytelling is frequently tentative, and it shows the struggle in Gaskell's own initial effort to take on the established forms of Victorian fiction in order to validate her vision.[8]

Although most critical studies of this novel focus on its social criticism centered in the story of John Barton (Gaskell's working title was always "John Barton"), Mary's development in the novel has also been frequently noted.[9] The emergence of a stronger personality for this woman departs from that of a typical Victorian heroine. This change is grounded, as Jordan observes, in Mary's development as a detective who can hold in her hands the material clues of history.[10] Without concrete evidence in her possession, however, Mary's identity is endangered. Unlike Molly Gibson in *Wives and Daughters,* who can add the qualities of others to a core of self, Mary appears to have no fundamental substance to build on; instead, she needs to clothe herself in external forms in order to act in her world. This heroine's dependence on documentation finally means that the authority of the novel's narrator and that of its author also remain problematic.

Mary's work at the beginning of the novel for Miss Simmonds, "milliner and dressmaker" (*MB,* 63), gives material form to the upper classes while achieving little public identity for herself (especially since she is not even paid for her first two years). Like the workers who seek a "charter" recognizing their place in society, Mary's efforts will need documentation. Managers like Carson Sr., with the strength of capital recognized by society, can create the very documents that give them power in this new industrial age. The "out-patient's order" for workers to be treated at hospital (109), for instance, is actually manipulated by

Carson to disenfranchise the ill Davenport and sweep his complaint out of sight. Carson's son, similarly, draws an ugly caricature of the workers (235), annotated by Falstaff's description of soldiers as "food for powder," in order to define their public identity. In retaliation, the workers endow John Barton with a special role when they tear into pieces "the identical letter on which the caricature had been drawn . . . and *one was marked*," drawing lots for the assassin (241). Later the "placards" advertising the reward for capture of the murderer (265) represent the moneyed class's countermove, the documentation of Barton's doom.

Money can serve as one kind of documentation in the emerging era of the middle class, but as in Mary's work for Miss Simmonds, early Victorian women have little access to it. A gentleman's money—the "fifty pound" Esther's officer friend leaves her—shapes women's lives even more damagingly than wages, which Esther had pocketed "easily enough at the factory" (*MB,* 210). And then she could not earn money on her own with the store she opened in Chester. Margaret is paid by the well-to-do for her singing (190), but her patrons provide the texts they wish to hear and control the venue for her talent. To gain standing in society, then, Gaskell's heroine Mary must discover what skills she possesses that can be represented on paper and that will further her own ends.[11] Her possession of such papers marks her creator's progress with the manuscript that contains the character.

Mary's effort to build a public identity and validate it with documents takes its first significant step with the valentine from Jem, on which she copies for her father Samuel Bamford's poem lamenting the worker's life (*MB,* 154).[12] This piece of paper first validates Mary in the traditional role as marriageable object; but with Bamford's words added ("God help the poor, who, on this wintry morn, / Come forth from alleys dim and courts obscure"), it also suggests her less conventional identification with the politically active working class.

Unknown to her, of course, her father uses the same paper as "wadding" for the gun that kills the mill owner Carson (*MB,* 289),[13] and this text becomes a site for the definition of a new figure in Victorian society. As John Barton altered the "little piece of stiff writing-paper," compressing it "into a round shape," he initiated the violent act that would erase Mary's traditional value to society because the daughter necessarily shares the father's fate: "Feeling as if in some measure an accessory, she hid it [the wadding] unexamined in her hand" (290). Who would marry a murderer's daughter?

The paper will further undermine Mary's value in the marriage market when its link to Jem is uncovered. She worries that it is not "blank as it appeared to be" (*MB,* 289) but seems to point to Jem as the murderer. The text "looked very like the writing which she had once known well—the writing of Jem Wilson, who, when she lived at her brother-in-law's, and he was a near neighbour, had often been employed by her to write her letters to people, to whom she was ashamed of sending her own misspelt scrawl. She remembered the wonderful flourishes she had so much admired in those days, when she sat by dictating, and Jem, in all the pride of newly-acquired penmanship, used to dazzle her by extraordinary graces and twirls" (290). This man who once, in several senses, spoke for her (transcribed her words and sought her hand) would further define her place (as an outcast) if he were the author of the letter as bullet: she "saw written on it Mary Barton's name, and not only that, but the street in which she lived! True, a letter or two was torn off, but, nevertheless, there was the name clear to be recognized" (290). While she quickly deduces that Jem's handwriting is a false clue, other circumstances in the case point to him as murderer and thus to her own loss of stature in this society.

Gaskell's text stresses the paper's materiality when Mary recovers the larger piece it was torn from, allowing the document to represent Mary as daughter to one man and lover of another: "Yes, it fitted; jagged end to jagged end, letter to letter; and even the part which Esther had considered blank had its tallying mark with the larger piece, its tails of *y*s and *g*s" (*MB,* 300). The shared substance of the two pieces linked to the material of a bullet makes Mary feel the undeniable physical tie to her father: "And then, as if that were not damning evidence enough, she felt again, and found some little bullets or shot (I don't know which you would call them) in that same pocket [of her father's], along with a small paper parcel of gunpowder" (300). Although the hand that fired the gun was her father's, Mary feels direct involvement in the events that resulted in Carson's death.

The paper also represents the potentially shared material life Mary might otherwise have anticipated if married, since it had been "a val-entine sent to her by Jem Wilson, in those days when she did not trea-sure and hoard up every thing he had touched, as she would do now" (*MB*, 299). When Mary burns this paper, "powdering the very ashes with her fingers, and dispersing the fragments of fluttering black films among the cinders of the grate" (302), she accepts the loss of the two identities recognized by her society, daughter and potential wife and mother, just as the "warrant empowering [the policeman] to seize the body of Jem Wilson, committed on suspicion" (274) robs Jem of his identity as re-spected citizen and substitutes a new, doomed one.

The heroine's loss of a conventional self in *Mary Barton,* however, leads her to assert a new identity—an emerging Victorian type, the de-tective who must, to use that key word from the novel, *know*.[14] Her initial documentation as detective is the lawyer's card, "Mr. Bridgenorth, 41, Renshaw Street, Liverpool" (*MB*, 322), given her by Job (on the back of which she writes a significant clue, the name of Will's ship, the *John Cropper*) and the money Margaret lends her, "some of the mint I've got laid by in the old tea-pot" (*MB*, 320). Although she has no business card with her own name printed on it, and this is at best a tenuous contract with expense account, Mary can at least begin her investigation. The problematic nature of her unconventional female identity, however, is revealed again by the documents through which she tries to confirm her role. And her battle with material traces her author's searching for au-thority in writing.

Society moves swiftly to fix Mary's role according to its own cate-gories. She receives a summons, "a bit of parchment" (*MB*, 313), man-dating her testimony against Jem, making her complicit in what happens to her lover's body, now held in prison. Another "ominous slip of parch-ment" (325), the summons Jem's mother receives, even more insidiously takes away female identity. The woman who gave birth to Jem Wilson must provide evidence that would result in that body's death, a cancella-tion of the primary role society had offered her. At the same time, news-papers like the *Guardian* (344) and the *Courier* (426) record the public perception of all these events.

The document Mary hopes to find in order to save those dear to her is Jem's *alibi* (*MB*, 305), which must take the form of a document in court records. The "certificate" (332) Mary asks of a doctor, confirming that

Mrs. Wilson is unable to travel—and thus testify—would also further her cause. Jem's letter from prison to Job Legh is not the "dreaded . . . confession of guilt" (382) that would seal his doom; in fact it includes a protestation of innocence. Wrapped "carefully up in a bit of newspaper" (383) by Job, however, it cannot document Jem's innocence within the larger social system that surrounds him.

By her heroic trip to Liverpool and her even more courageous journey across the water with "two rough, hard-looking men" (*MB*, 354), Mary succeeds in reaching the *John Cropper;* but Will's words, taken down as testimony, rather than her own will be the ones that free Jem. On that frantic ride, Mary even loses her marginal documentation, the lawyer Bridgenorth's "card" (361), since her own voice is too weak to carry across the water and the boatmen must call out for her.

As critics have noted,[15] Mary, like many Victorian women, is speechless at critical moments. Hearing of Carson's murder, "Mary's lips could not utter a negative" (*MB*, 271). Learning that Jem is the main suspect, she provides "no answer; but such a blanched face, such wild, distended eyes, such trembling limbs, instinctively seeking support!" (281). Seeing the wadding paper evidence, "she spoke no word" (296). And learning that Will's ship has sailed, "Mary's voice seemed choked up in her throat" (346). She can speak eloquently as a love object at the trial (389–99), taking the one role she is allowed in Victorian society. But she suffers complete physical collapse at other crisis points—after reaching the *John Cropper* (362), at the trial (394), and at her father's repentant death (442). Perhaps even more tragic, Mary, like Jem's mother, is forced to testify at court in ways that belie her own understanding; and her speech generates the court records that can convict Jem.[16]

Alternating with these instances of weaknesses or powerlessness, however, are moments of unusual understanding. Like a detective, Mary seeks to *know* what is happening in her world. For instance, after finding the paper wadding, her first clue, "she wandered about, too restless to take her usual heavy morning's sleep; up and down the streets, greedily listening to every word of the passers by, and loitering near each group of talkers, anxious to scrape together every morsel of information, or conjecture, of suspicion, though without possessing any definite purpose in all this" (*MB*, 291). Frequently her knowledge is conventional, as when she asserts Jem's innocence to the doctor: "Many have no doubt of

his innocence—those who *know* him, sir" (331; emphasis added; see also
336). But at other times, especially once she leaves her home in Manchester, she is called on to come to understandings no typical nineteenth-
century woman was expected to endure. When she fears Jem's ship has
left, her young guide Charley says, "No! I did not say he's sailed; mother
said that, and women *know* nought about such matters" (349; emphasis
added).

At times Mary is aware only that she is approaching a limit to her
own comprehension. When Job wants to take her away from the trial
after her testimony, she cries, "Oh! I don't *know* about any thing but that
I must stay" (*MB*, 392; emphasis added throughout paragraph). But she
and Jem each must come to carry privately the "terrible knowledge"
(417) of her father's guilt. At the trial Mary finds a special power, "she
knew not how or by what," enabling her to keep "the tremendous secret
imprisoned within her" (389). Confident that her guilty father will come
home to Manchester, she tells Jem she must return alone: "And if you
guess, I *know* you well enough to be sure you'll understand why I ask
you never to speak on that again to me, till I begin" (419). This shared
knowledge must remain painfully unacknowledged for many years: "One
thing was certain! it was a miserable thing to have this awful forbidden
ground of discourse; to guess at each other's thoughts, when eyes were
averted, and cheeks blanched, and words stood still, arrested in their
flow by some casual allusion" (419). She later tells Job, who does not
understand John Barton's guilt: "If you *knew* all, you'd pity me" (424).
And when her father dies, Mary "*knew* nothing more for many min-
utes" (442).[17]

The identities of the detective heroine and the narrator blur when
material evidence (what they know) passes from Mary's hands into the
words spoken by the voice of the novel: "I must tell you; I must put into
words the dreadful secret which she believed that bit of paper [the valentine from Jem] had revealed to her" (299). A shared anxiety about the
power of such documents further links these two figures: when Mary
receives a summons, the narrator admits, "Many people have a dread of
those mysterious pieces of parchment. I am one. Mary was another"
(*MB*, 313).[18]

The difficulties many characters have in knowing and in getting

things "into words" derive in part from this novel's unusual setting, the
new industrial city of early Victorian England. That rapidly changing
landscape posed problems for the narrator as well, as W. A. Craik explains: "She realizes that in Manchester she is writing of a place unfamiliar
to most: the millworkers and their families, a new class in 1848, confined
to the Northern English region, are a social class every detail of whose
way of life may be new." [19] In part for this reason, the narrator takes a
rural vantage point in telling this tale: "All was so still, so motionless, so
hard [in Mary's Manchester life]! Very different to this lovely night in the
country in which I am now writing, where the distant horizon is soft and
undulating in the moonlight, and the nearer trees sway gently to and fro
in the night-wind with something of almost human motion; and the rus-
tling air makes music among their branches, as if speaking soothingly to
the weary ones, who lie awake in heaviness of heart" (*MB*, 303). The
difficult topic of this "condition of England" novel also militates against
narrative confidence: "I am not sure if I can express myself in the technical terms of either masters or workmen, but I will try simply to state
the case on which the latter deliberated" (220). In the end, with this
traditional Romantic viewpoint distanced from an unfamiliar subject
matter,[20] the narrator, like Mary, will find that documents are necessary
to lend credibility to this account of events. And in both character and
narrator we see Elizabeth Gaskell seeking the forms in which her story
can be embodied.

In chapter 19 the narrator moves as a material presence from the
Romantic rural setting into the urban world of narrated events: "I left
Mary, on that same Thursday night which left its burden of woe at
Mr. Carson's threshold, haunted with depressing thoughts" (*MB*, 267). A
narrator can derive authority from being on the scene, which may have
prompted Edward Chapman to ask for a preface to this novel; but the
speaker in *Mary Barton* is only occasionally *there* and often once removed:
"I was not there [at the trial] myself; but one who was, told me that her
[Mary's] look, and indeed her whole face, was more like the well-known
engraving from Guido's picture of 'Beatrice Cenci' than any thing else
he could give me an idea of" (389).

Whether distant or close to events, the narrator's pleasure at providing enlightenment spurs the account:

> *I must return to the Wilsons' house . . . there is always a pleasure in*
> *unravelling a mystery, in catching at the gossamer clue which will guide*
> *to certainty. This feeling, I am sure, gives much impetus to the police.*
> *Their senses are ever and always on the qui-vive, and they enjoy the*
> *collecting and collating evidence, and the life of adventure they experi-*
> *ence; a continual unwinding of Jack Sheppard romances, always inter-*
> *esting to the vulgar and uneducated mind, to which the outward signs*
> *and tokens of crime are ever exciting.*

(*MB*, 273)

Gaskell here links the art of storytelling with detective work and the narrator's aim with her heroine's desire.[21] Thus she encourages her readers also to pursue the goal of "knowing" and praises Mary's effort to clear Jem, even though there are dangers in contemplating or narrating "crime."

The narrator's physical presence within the narrative, however, can also create problems. Gaskell's emphasis on physicality in all her works suggests that a visible figure can strengthen narrative authority, as is the case with Mary Smith in *Cranford* (see chapter 3). But this narrator does not take on that role absolutely. Sympathizing with Esther's plight, the sometimes there, sometimes removed narrative persona of *Mary Barton* asks, "To whom shall the outcast prostitute tell her tale!" (*MB*, 207). And referring vaguely to people walking the city streets one Sunday morning, the speaker acknowledges their "animal state of mind and body": "But upon them I will not dwell; as you and I, and almost every one, I think, may send up our individual cry of self-reproach that we have not done all that we could for the stray and wandering ones of our brethren" (328).

The difficulties of a narrator's appearing in the scenes of the novel are also suggested when the heroine's body is represented in print within the world of the novel.[22] Mary's sense of her private self is repeatedly challenged when she takes on a public identity. First she is "named" in rumor as the reason for Carson's murder ("the dirty hussy!" [*MB*, 278]): "They'd got her name quite pat. The man had heard all they said. Mary Barton was her name, whoever she may be" (278). Then this false identity is broadcast more widely by Sally Leadbitter, "a Gazette Extraordinary the next morning at the work-room" (335), who recognizes Mary's public role as potential advertising for Mrs. Simmonds: "Many a one would come and have their gowns made by Miss Simmonds just to catch a glimpse at you, after the trial's over. Really, Mary, you'll turn out quite a heroine" (335). But such misrepresentation as romantic "heroine" makes Mary "sick and weary of her visitor" (336), both because it casts Jem in the false role of murderer and because it neglects her rejection of both suitors. Analogously, the narrator's body inserted into the text becomes subject to misinterpretation.

There is, then, a complex interaction of subject and object in *Mary Barton,* as the narrator reporting on what is happening becomes a participant in those same events.[23] Mary's physical beauty underscores her role as object or spectacle when Margaret responds to Mary's complaint "I wish I could sing." Margaret says, "Many's the time when I could see, that I longed for your beauty, Mary!" (191). Margaret regains her sight only when she marries and thus looks on Will, the approved suitor, within the marriage plot rather than allowing herself to be a spectacle before an unknown public. And Mary so struggles with an atypical feminine public role that she ends the novel offstage in Canada. The narrator of all these events likewise shows an uneasiness at becoming an object.

Elizabeth Gaskell repeatedly felt a similar strain of standing in the public eye as she anticipated readers' response to her first novel. Gaskell's pain, especially on receiving the strong Manchester reaction, helps account for her narrator's struggle to find the authority necessary to tell this story. Uglow reports that Gaskell's worries about reaction were not unfounded: "As soon as it appeared *Mary Barton* sparked off furious arguments, especially, of course, in Manchester." And she notes that the "drama and pathos were heightened when the book was read aloud, as nineteenth-century novels so often were."[24]

A little less than halfway through the work, however, the narrator's tone begins to move from uncertainty toward greater confidence. The strengthened narrative stance of the second volume couples doubt about absolute knowledge with universally acknowledged human limits: "But think of Mary and what she was enduring! Picture to yourself (for I cannot tell you) the armies of thoughts that met and clashed in her brain; and then imagine the effort it cost her to be calm, and quiet, and even, in a faint way, cheerful and smiling at times" (*MB,* 329–30; chap. 24). By this point in the novel, the narrator is confident in asking the reader to first "picture" (as if their shared subject were real), then "imagine" (go beyond what is tangible to recognize undisputable feelings). Similarly, in describing the senior Carson's sleepless night, the narrator says paren-thetically, "I don't know that he exactly used the term vengeance in his thoughts; he spoke of justice, and probably thought of his desired end as such" (381). This is narrative precision rather than doubt.

A later stage of authorial development in *Mary Barton* comes when the narrator reaches limits no writer presumably could surpass, as when Jem encounters the returning shell of Mary's father: "If you think this account of mine confused, of the half-feelings, half-reasons, which passed through Jem's mind, as he stood gazing at the empty space where that crushed form had so lately been seen,—if you are perplexed to disen-tangle the real motives, I do assure you it was from such an involved set of thoughts that Jem drew the resolution to act as if he had not seen that phantom likeness of John Barton; himself, yet not himself" (*MB,* 413–14). The narrator's desire not to confront John Barton's guilt directly is a similar recognition of limits to human experience: "I would rather see death than the ghastly gloom which darkened that countenance" (436). Such insistence on the complexity of human emotion is unlike the fa-miliar narrative trope by which stock responses are invoked, as in roman-tic moments: "What tender passionate language can I use to express the feelings which thrilled through that young man and maiden, as they lis-tened to the syllables made dear and lovely through life by that hour's low-whispered talk" (431). Mary assumes a similar stance at the trial when she admits her love for Jem is "above what tongue can tell" (390). The narrator assumes readers of romantic fiction will already have in store specific responses to such familiar love scenes, whereas the more complex and rare emotions that John Barton feels at having committed murder do not easily take shape in conventional language.

In the end, Mary's testifying becomes taking action against human problems, an impulse Elizabeth Gaskell herself responded to in her char-ity work in 1840s Manchester and in the text of this 1848 novel. Her sometimes visible narrator speaks emotionally at one point, "Oh! I do think that the necessity for exertion, for some kind of action (bodily or mental) in time of distress, is a most infinite blessing, although the first efforts at such seasons are painful. Something to be done implies that there is yet hope of some good thing to be accomplished, or some addi-tional evil that may be avoided; and by degrees the hope absorbs much of the sorrow" (*MB,* 301). Although this passage has been read as a reflection of Gaskell's mourning for her son who died of scarlet fever, its application to Mary's case also reminds us that "the time of distress" would also mean the labor unrest in her own Manchester.

The more important document toward which *Mary Barton*'s many lesser pieces of paper lead, then, is the narrator's own record of events, which must be Gaskell's manuscript, first shown to close friends and associates, then submitted to Edward Chapman for possible publication, and finally put into Victorian readers' hands in the form of two printed volumes in the winter of 1848. The confusion Mary faces in taking a train to Liverpool might suggest the new novelist's recognition that a mighty system will distribute her book to a wide public that will then take her as an object: "Common as railroads are now in all places as a means of transit, and especially in Manchester, Mary had never been on one before; and she felt bewildered by the hurry, the noise of people, and bells, and horns; the whiz and the scream of the arriving trains" (*MB*, 343).

What Gaskell seeks in this novel is the literary form whose authority pervades and surpasses the material context of 1840s Manchester. When the narrator articulates old man Carson's hope that "a perfect understanding, and complete confidence and love, might exist between masters and men . . . [as they come] to acknowledge the Spirit of Christ as the regulating law between both parties" (*MB*, 460), Gaskell's narrator has approached the authority of her culture's highest wisdom. The author developed such a voice more fully over the course of the next dozen years, speaking for her own ideals of Victorian morality in the accomplished texts of *Sylvia's Lovers* and *Wives and Daughters*. In 1848, however, she was still searching for the appropriate stance and tone to do the work of bringing opposing classes together. Her standing is not unlike that of the tragic Esther, who knows some of the darkest truths of her society but cannot present herself fully to those who need her.[25]

Esther has the voice but not the body of Mary's mother at the crucial meeting with her niece. Mary opens her door to a ghost:

> *They were the accents of her mother's voice; the very south-country*
> *pronunciation, that Mary so well remembered. . . . So, without*
> *fear, without hesitation, she rose and unbarred the door. There,*   (*MB*, 287)
> *against the moonlight, stood a form, so closely resembling her*
> *dead mother, that Mary never doubted the identity, but*

exclaiming (as if she were a terrified child, secure of safety when near the
protecting care of its parent)—
     "Oh! mother! mother! You are come at last!"
     She threw herself, or rather fell into the trembling arms, of her
long lost, unrecognized Aunt Esther.

But this is a person, a body, that is not to be touched: "You must never
kiss me. You!" (298). The disembodied voice of belated wisdom has no
material home.

To tell the stories she wished to narrate, to do the work she felt a moral
imperative to undertake, Elizabeth Gaskell created a narrative persona we
can see fully developed in a related novel from her maturity, *Sylvia's Lovers*
(published in three volumes by Smith, Elder in February 1863). In this
work the narrative voice is so strong that, despite its immateriality, it
needs no external documentation. Whereas her first major novel sought
in the work of predecessors (other social problem novels) and in the
documents of her culture (letters, court papers, newspapers) a material
form in which to appear before the public, her later fiction found substance in deeper and more enduring matter.
     At the midpoint of *Sylvia's Lovers,* the hated press-gang rings the
Monkshaven fire bell as a ruse to lure village men into a trap: "All were
startled in their household content and warmth by the sound of the fire-
bell busily swinging, and pealing out for help" (*SL*, 255). This event is
emblematic of the novelist's raising a warning cry to readers "in their
household content and warmth." The Victorian reading public generally
recognized what was occurring when they encountered the earnest fiction of their day: "Every one knew what it meant. Some dwelling, or
maybe a boiling-house was on fire, and neighbourly assistance was sum-
moned with all speed" (256). But in *Sylvia's Lovers* the fire bell is a false
alarm, and the novel continues this lifelong concern of Gaskell's, more
central than any individual social issue: the question of authority. Who
has the right to speak to society? Where should such a person stand in
addressing the larger community? And most important, what form must
a speaker's words assume in order to assert their validity for author and
audience? Only if these questions are answered can an author undertake

the kind of work Elizabeth Gaskell desired to do in addressing Victorian England.

The fire bell rung by a press-gang, "leading men into a snare through their kindliest feelings" (*SL*, 256), represents an unauthorized voice, calling with a familiar message but perverted by a hidden intent. Responding to that voice, the villagers "pressed onwards into the market-place, sure of obtaining the information desired there, where the fire-bell kept calling out with its furious metal tongue" (256). When the men arrive at the center of the village, however, ready to help the victims of calamity, they find emptiness, a silent "blank" (259). Authority has been emptied of moral purpose. Later the villagers themselves will "ring t' fire-bell then t' some purpose" (261), as Daniel Robson argues when he suggests they burn the Randyvowse, the tavern that has housed the press-gang. But that ringing too lacks authority, for it denies a call to national unity and duty (resisting the French and preventing violent revolution at home) that many endorsed. The bell's sound on both occasions exhibits a hollowness, the absence of absolute moral purpose. The voice that narrates this event, however, the narrator of *Sylvia's Lovers,* has a powerful authority painstakingly developed over the fifteen years of Gaskell's career after her first full-length novel.

Like Mary Barton, other Gaskell heroines—Molly Gibson in *Wives and Daughters,* Margaret Hale in *North and South,* the title character in "Cousin Phillis"—will be good readers (see chapters 1 and 4 and the epilogue). And the context of documents that surrounds them will reinforce their authority within their social circles. But the protagonist in *Sylvia's Lovers,* one of Gaskell's most finished works, is conspicuously uninterested in printed material, as a number of critics have noted.[26] When Philip Hepburn, in order to be with her, offers Sylvia Robson lessons in reading and writing, she tells him, "I'll try and learn. Only, I'm just stupid; and it mun be such a trouble to you" (*SL*, 113). In her dogged resistance to formal learning Sylvia represents her class, as the narrator reports: "Most people fifty or sixty years ago . . . understood without going through reasoning or analytic processes, and if this was the case among the more educated people, of course, it was still more so in the class to which Sylvia belonged" (318). Even later in her life, as the wife of a prosperous businessman, Sylvia will still long for the illiterate life of the

Haytersbank farm rather than more refined activities associated with church and town.

The 14 April 1863 *Manchester Examiner and Times* acknowledged the challenge of setting a novel in a rural scene of the previous century: "No educated person appears upon the stage; we are thrown altogether amongst the untutored inmates of a moor farm—a draper's shop—a press-gang—or a market-place in Monkshaven" (*CH,* 452). And the 3 April 1863 *Daily News* specifically saw Gaskell's central character from this environment as distinctive: "Sylvia, the heroine of the tale, is presented to us as a beautiful human animal, without a thought beyond the shippon and its cows, or the farm and its produce, ignorant of the merest elements of education, and depending solely upon such sympathy as her unsophisticated nature can awaken for the interest we are expected to take in her fortunes" (*CH,* 445). Although the *Daily News* did not think Gaskell rose to the challenge of making Sylvia interesting, the *Manchester Examiner and Times* gave her more credit: "Perhaps Mrs. Gaskell designs to show her power in all this; if so, she has achieved her aim" (*CH,* 452). The 28 March 1863 *Examiner* agreed: The novel "deals, among simple and unfashionable people, with the truest poetry of life, in thought, feeling, and action" (*CH,* 441).

In *Sylvia's Lovers* a greater distance separates the illiterate central character from the knowledgeable persona who tells her story than was the case with *Mary Barton*. Still, the narrator of the second novel exhibits an authority that is connected to the unlettered nature of her protagonist. Returning to Brooks's paradigm, we can argue that desire in Mrs. Gaskell's work is now more sharply focused and realized by a particular form, a plot including both ambitious hero and subversive female:

> The ambitious hero thus stands as a figure of the reader's efforts to construct meanings in ever-larger wholes, to totalize his experience of human existence in time, to grasp past, present, and future in a significant shape. This description, of course, most obviously concerns male plots of ambition. The female plot is not unrelated, but it takes a more complex stance toward ambition, the formation of an inner drive toward the assertion of selfhood in resistance to the overt and violating male plots of ambition, a counter-dynamic which . . . is only superficially passive, and in fact a reinterpretation of the vectors of plot.[27]

We will now explore the subversive role of illiterate Sylvia in Gaskell's late novel, for she resists the domestication Nancy Armstrong has seen as recorded in and made up by middle-class fiction in the eighteenth and nineteenth centuries.[28] We also look closely at the ambitious heroes Philip Hepburn and Charley Kinraid, as well as the narrator whose voice structures this three-volume work. The narrative authority in this novel derives not from its links to social structures, as was the case with *Mary Barton,* but from its connections to natural shapes, especially that of the sea. In chapter 4 we will see the natural rhythms of female life as similarly linked to the structure of Gaskell's *North and South.* Unlike the fire bell rung by the treacherous press-gang in *Sylvia's Lovers,* then, Elizabeth Gaskell's voice in her mature fiction is a natural call to Victorian citizens to consider great questions of life and death.

The sea's presence is the background for all human events in *Sylvia's Lovers.* Sylvia's first confrontation with life's major crises occurs in front of an "enduring" nature: "She had gone to church with the thought of the cloak-that-was-to-be uppermost in her mind, and she had come down the long church stair with life and death suddenly become real to her mind, the enduring sea and hills forming a contrasting background to the vanishing away of man" (*SL,* 75). Not a great reader, Sylvia is constantly drawing out her thoughts within hearing of the sea rather than in the context of printed wisdom. In her youth the waves shape experience: "The long monotonous roll of the distant waves, as the tide bore them in, the multitudinous rush at last, and then the retreating rattle and trickle, as the baffled waters fell back over the shingle that skirted the sands, and divided them from the cliffs; her father's measured tread, and slow, even movement; Lassie's pattering—all lulled Sylvia into a reverie, of which she could not have given herself any definite account" (87–88). The seashore is also where the adult Sylvia later takes her daughter Bella: "Here it [her baby] was all her own; no father to share in it, no nursemaid to dispute the wisdom of anything she did with it. She sang to it, tossed it; it crowed and it laughed back again, till both were weary; and then she would sit down on a broken piece of rock, and fall to gazing on the advancing waves catching the sunlight on their crests, advancing, receding, for ever and for ever, as they had done all her life long" (359–60). Although the waves can be "cruel" (360) in such events as the supposed drowning of Kinraid or the near drowning of Bella, they are also the source of renewed life: "Sylvia heard the sound of the passionate rush and rebound of many waters" (369) just before she came upon the scene in which the crew of a Newcastle smack, including Kinraid, was rescued by villagers.[29]

The town of Monkshaven, which also influences Sylvia's life, is itself shaped by the sea. It is built on water, with New Town and Old Town separated by "the stream running away towards the ocean" (*SL,* 484).[30] The town's "amphibious appearance" (2) is noted at the novel's beginning, and the surrounding landscape of "purple crags" and "wooded 'bottoms'" (3) even resembles the crests and troughs of waves. The seasonal nature of the whaling industry structures the lives both of Monkshaven men at sea and of residents in town, the all-male world of the ship as well as the female environment of home (49). And finally, the temporal pattern of life for both men at sea and women in the house alternates between two basic states: "It [spring] was the time of the great half-yearly traffic of the place [town]; another impetus was given to business when the whalers returned in the autumn, and the men were flush of money, and full of delight at once more seeing their homes and their friends" (191).

In her narrative structure Elizabeth Gaskell echoes the alternating structure of peak and valley characterizing the sea and life based on the sea, earning authority for the voice that speaks in the novel by shaping it to this natural rhythm. Her story of Monkshaven life resembles "the long flights of stone steps—worn by the feet of many generations—which led up to the parish church, placed on a height above the town" (*SL,* 63). That is, each step up is like a wave rushing forward or another sentence in a story; each stop is the trough before the next wave, the gap between the present and the next sentence. The stairway to the church is made up of many short flights of steps (chapters), each ending "in a small flat space, on which a wooden seat was placed" (64), resting places like the spaces between chapters. In the churchyard at the summit of these steps "lay the dead of many generations," a resting place or heaven for those finished with life's journey, the end and final meaning of their stories. The words spoken in prayer in the church inspire "solemn thoughts" among the listening sailors, "not conscious thoughts, perhaps—rather a distinct if dim conviction that buying and selling, eating and marrying, even life and death, were not all the realities in existence" (64). Furthermore, the long "church stair, as it was called, [visible] from nearly every part of the town" (65), is a beacon shaping lives like the church at its top: "Homeward-bound sailors caught sight of the tower of St. Nicholas, the first land object of all. They who went forth upon the great deep might carry solemn thoughts with them of the words they had heard there" (63–64). Thus the church offers the wisdom of experience to those struggling to climb to it. And in patterning her own narrative, Gaskell copies the fundamental structure of the church stair, the rhythmic step and pause of the upward journey, the ebb and flow of the sea.[31]

The alternation of wave and trough is especially copied in the shifting moods and affections of the novel's illiterate protagonist. With her distinctive personality, Sylvia appeals to many different people in her world: "It seemed to be Sylvia's fate to captivate more people than she cared to like back again" (*SL,* 347). Sylvia attracts not just her lovers, Philip Hepburn and Charley Kinraid, but the faithful family servant Kester, the brothers John and Jeremiah Foster, and even Hester Rose, whose affection for Sylvia overcomes a jealous love for Philip. Because this heroine resists learning and formal study, however, we must conclude that her appeal rests in her emotional life, not her intellectual life, in what the narrator calls "the strange mystery of Sylvia's heart" (488).[32] And as with *Mary Barton,* the protagonist's unusual strength, deriving from her ties to the sea, is ultimately a key to the narrator's authority and to the author's style.

Much as in the earlier work, *Sylvia's Lovers* raises the issue of authority at its very beginning. The novel's epigraph is Tennyson's plea from *In Memoriam* for a reassuring "voice" from "behind the veil." As in Tennyson's poem of loss, in Gaskell's novel men are lost at sea;[33] and the protagonist suffers especially at the broken contact with her lover, Charley Kinraid. "Oh! Charley! come to me—come to me!" (*SL,* 353) she calls after giving birth to another man's child. Indeed, the illusory presence of Sylvia's lover is problematic from the very beginning of the novel, raising for the protagonist a fundamental human challenge, facing the difference between death and life. Kinraid's alternating being—present and then absent, alive and then thought dead—is a reflection of the narrative's effort to represent an illusory reality in natural structures.

When first referred to in the novel, Kinraid is dead, or nearly so. Donkin, the traveling tailor, reports to the Robson family that "Kinraid (that's he who lies a-dying)" had resisted the press-gang, which left "Kinraid for dead, as wasn't dead, and Darley for dead, as was dead" (*SL,* 54–55). In being impressed later by the royal navy, Kinraid vacillates between life and death in the minds of others: Sylvia's other suitor, Philip Hepburn, wonders, "Was then his rival dead? had he left this bright world? lost his life—his love?" (217). Yet another time, Kinraid is "dead" (430) when, to avoid slaughter by the French in battle, he "thought that his best course was to assume the semblance of death" (430). In loving Kinraid, then, Sylvia faces the universal human problems of absence, loss, and finally death.

The transition from life to death, inescapable in the human condition, is consistently explored in the novel's recurring motif of presence and absence.[34] And this motif is another element in a narrative reflecting the natural rhythms of existence, of eternal forms like that of the sea. The whaling profession Charley follows, lifeblood of the Monkshaven community, includes the pain of absence, as an eloquent narrator explains: "For six long summer months those sailors had been as if dead from all news of those they loved; shut up in terrible, dreary Arctic seas from the hungry sight of sweethearts and friends, wives and mothers. . . . Whose bones had been left to blacken on the gray and terrible icebergs? Who lay still until the sea should give up its dead? Who were those who should come back to Monkshaven never, no, never more?" (*SL,* 19). Even the tales Kinraid and Daniel tell about their trade emphasize the sudden movement from one state to another (100–102).[35]

The threat of impressment these men face in the time of the novel's events further stresses separation and absence, a note sounded on the novel's opening pages: "Men were kidnapped, literally disappeared, and nothing was ever heard of them again" (*SL,* 6). The initial attack on returning whalers inspires a familiar text from Monkshaven's vicar: "In the midst of life we are in death" (67). And the maimed hand of Sylvia's father serves as a prominent material sign of this threat (38) within the home, since he had cut off several fingers rather than let himself be taken.

From the funeral of Darley, killed in that same initial attack, to Philip's death, also involving water, Sylvia is challenged to accept the hard facts of personal loss. In the first event, "she had come down the long church stair with life and death suddenly become real to her mind, the enduring sea and hills forming a contrasting background to the vanishing

away of man" (*SL*, 75). Near the end of the novel the narrator acknowledges, "Every one who loved her, or whom she had loved, had vanished
out of her life; every one but her child, who lay in her arms, warm and
soft" (418). This "vanishing" occurs over and over again in her most passionate relationship with Charley Kinraid.

Even before he leaves her to travel over the seas, Charley seems liable
to vanish. The young Sylvia is upset that Charley, whom she had just met,
"had gone away out of her sight into the thick mist of unseen life from
which he had emerged—gone away without a word, and she might
never see him again" (*SL*, 113). As a rumored lover of other women also,
Kinraid is a character whose presence is difficult to determine and who
repeatedly is tied to the fact of death: "He kept company with my poor
sister as is dead for better nor two year, and then left off coming to see
her and went wi' another girl, and it just broke her heart" (84), says the
dead woman's brother William, but his story is never completely confirmed in the novel.

In his courtship of Sylvia, Kinraid's appearance is sometimes magical, as if his physical self were only a desired illusion. After Sylvia had
spilled her tea at the Corney's, "while she was thus fluttered and crimson,
she saw through her tearful eyes Kinraid on his knees before her, wiping
her gown with his silk pocket handkerchief, and heard him speaking
through all the buzz of commiserating voices" (*SL*, 141). Owing a kiss as
forfeit, Sylvia perhaps pays, but the novel does not picture the scene:
"One instant Charley Kinraid was missing from the circle of which he
was the life and soul; and then back he came with an air of satisfaction on
his face" (146). And his declaration of love seems to come from someone
Sylvia had dreamed up: "It was strange she should be so much startled,
for the person who entered [her house] had been in her thoughts all during those long pauses" in her work (193). Is Kinraid there or not there?
Sylvia is seldom sure. But the narrator who presents her doubt possesses
confidence. The sources of that confidence lie in the novel's representations of absence and presence.

The heroine's struggle with a vanishing lover is doubled in the loss
of her father. Even before he meets his end, Daniel's presence had been
problematic. The man who gave up part of his hand to prevent the loss
of his autonomy hides his entire body under the bed to avoid capture
(*SL*, 278). The feared punishment of transportation (300) would remove

him so many thousands of miles from home that to all practical purposes he would have vanished: Sylvia feels "the dread of losing him to that fearful country [of Botany Bay] which was almost like the grave to her, so all but impassable was the gulf" (301). And death by hanging would be, as Philip knows, absolute: "The separation impending might be that of the dark, mysterious grave—[he knew] that the gulf between the father and the child might indeed be that which no living, breathing, warm human creature can ever cross" (301). So powerful is that event that Gaskell allows it to occur between chapters (314), a fact noted by Geraldine Jewsbury in the 28 February 1863 *Athenaeum:* "She shrinks from this part of her narrative; it is hastily hurdled over" (*CH,* 434).

If Sylvia faces repeated threats of loss with her father and her lover, she herself becomes a problematic presence to her second suitor, Philip Hepburn. The subject of absence, paradoxically then, is ever present in the novel. With Kinraid missing, Sylvia endures Philip's company but is barely there herself (*SL,* 270). When they marry, after her father's death and the assumed death of Kinraid, Philip is no more confident of her presence (342–43). And with his betrayal of Kinraid revealed to Sylvia, Philip must endure the physical separation always hinted at in her emotionally distanced relationship to him. Her absence from him is represented by the darkness of the poor silhouette "done in the first month of their marriage, by some wandering artist, if so he could be called . . . the only thing he took away from his home" (387–88). After his military career and pensioning at St. Sepulchre, Philip thinks of his former friends and family, only to be told, "Ten to one they're dead, or removed, or something or the other by this time" (467).

In one more turn of the novel's fine irony, Philip eventually becomes a second absent suitor for the novel's heroine, her child's father noted for "non-appearance" (*SL,* 396). When Sylvia understands that Philip witnessed Charley's impressment, "she saw him no more than she saw the inanimate table" (383). Philip "did not know whether she was conscious of his presence; in fact, he knew nothing but that he and she were sundered for ever" (383). His letter to Hester links absence with death: "You must all look on me as one dead; as I am to you, and maybe shall soon be in reality" (405). Ironically, of course, with Kinraid later married to another, Sylvia eventually comes to lament Philip's absence:

"I began for to wish I hadn't said all them words i' my passion . . . and my mind has come out clear. Philip's dead, and it were his spirit as come to t' other's [Charley's] help in his time o' need" (475).

The surprise disappearances of loved bodies is made even more un-settling in the novel by the fact that many characters can appear just as mysteriously as they vanish. When Daniel is about to be taken away by constables, Philip appears to Sylvia "at the top of the brow, running rapidly towards the farm" (*SL,* 277). Kester says of Philip's later disappearance at a time when Kinraid is known to have returned to Monkshaven, "It seems strange how as one man turns up, another just disappears" (399). Coulson adds of Kinraid, who was thought lost at sea, "them that's dead is alive; and as for poor Philip, though he was alive, he looked fitter to be dead" (399). Philip appears out of nowhere to rescue the wounded Kinraid in battle (431), but he disappears just as swiftly under the alias Stephen Freeman.

Such ominous comings and goings are softened only slightly in that Bella appears in the novel as a welcome surprise: "By-and-by, the time came when she [Sylvia] was a prisoner in the house; a prisoner in her room lying in bed with a little baby by her side—her child, Philip's child" (*SL,* 350). But unlike the situation in *Ruth* (discussed in chapter 3), the narrator's announcement of new life comes without previous hints, more because of Victorian convention than from a thematic insistence that life is ever renewing.[36] Although becoming a mother inspires Sylvia to live, the child becomes one more character liable to sudden vanishing: Kester reports of her fall into the sea, "Some one said as they passed t' man a-sittin' on a bit on a rock up above—a dunnot know, a only know as a heared a great fearful screech i' t' air" (492). Although Bella's presence before Jeremiah Foster (408)—and his being charmed by her—ensures her own and her mother's future comfort, she disappears at the end of the novel by traveling to America and is lost in the past (503).

The appearance of an adult Sylvia, the physical woman who can have children replacing the innocent child, is similarly sudden in the nar-rative: "For she was at that age when a girl changes rapidly, and generally for the better. Sylvia shot up into a tall young woman; her eyes deepened in colour, her face increased in expression, and a sort of consciousness of unusual good looks gave her a slight tinge of coquettish shyness with the few strangers whom she ever saw" (*SL*, 114). This new Sylvia will appear almost as a magical (and erotic) event for Philip when he sits in the Robson's kitchen:

(126)

> *And at length his yearning watch was rewarded; first, the little pointed toe came daintily in sight, then the trim ankle in the tight blue stocking, the wool of which was spun and the web of which was knitted by her mother's careful hands; then the full brown stuff petticoat, the arm holding the petticoat back in decent folds, so as not to encumber the descending feet; the slender neck and shoulders hidden under the folded square of fresh white muslin; the crowning beauty of the soft innocent face radiant in colour, and with the light brown curls clustering around.*

This woman, like Molly in *Wives and Daughters,* is clearly a material being; but like so many others in the novel, she can be replaced by "vacancy": "About seven o'clock Sylvia persuaded her [mother] to come upstairs. Sylvia, too, bade Philip good-night, and his look followed the last wave of her dress as she disappeared up the stairs; then leaning his chin on his hand, he gazed at vacancy" (299).

Still, the overriding concern of the novel remains the alternating presence and absence of the specksioneer. In the difficult time after Bella's birth, Sylvia declares to Philip, "Oh, Philip, I've been asleep, and yet I think I was awake! And I saw Charley Kinraid as plain as iver I see thee now, and he wasn't drowned at all. I'm sure he's alive somewheere; he were so clear and life-like" (*SL*, 354). In fact, in one ironic sequence Sylvia sees Kinraid before he returns to claim her. He is on board a "Newcastle smack" (371) in danger of crashing onto the shore in a heavy wind; and she, with no idea that he is one of the sailors in trouble, joins other villagers in the rescue. She is told by one woman, "A could see their faces [earlier], they were so near. They were as pale as dead men, an' one was prayin' down on his knees. There was a King's officer aboard, for I saw t' gowd about him" (371). Once again Kinraid is there but not there, alive but linked to death. And finally he appears before Sylvia as the man she had promised to wait for, a man she now believed to be dead: "She had not gone a yard—no, not half a yard [without recognizing him]—when her heart leaped up and fell again dead within her, as if she had been shot" (377). Finding she has married Philip in his absence, Charley is "gone!" (383) almost immediately; but she can never again believe completely in his absence: "She could not get over the impression that Kinraid must be lingering near" (406).

Sylvia's passionate desire helps account for her conviction that Charley exists; but even less sensitive characters are also tortured by threatened or desired appearances. The meticulous businessman Philip, now married to Sylvia, struggles to complete the vanishing of his rival: he convinces himself intellectually that "Kinraid was in all probability dead—killed by either the chances of war or tempestuous sea; that, even if not, he was as good as dead to her; so that the word 'dead' might be used in all honest certainty, as in one of its meanings Kinraid was dead for sure" (*SL,* 329). His desire to banish his nemesis involves a betrayal of the literal meaning of words, and yet Kinraid reappears out of nowhere for Philip. In a recurring dream of his rival's return, Philip "was generally sitting up in bed when he found himself conscious, his heart beating wildly, with a conviction of Kinraid's living presence somewhere near him in the darkness" (343; see also 361). As far away as Acre, Turkey, Kinraid's presence haunts Philip even as he saves his life (431).

Philip's effort to twist words into a desired meaning is reflected in the recurring situation in *Sylvia's Lovers* wherein words have an unintended effect; for, as in all of Gaskell's work, words and material are intimately linked. Language consistently has consequences in the physical realm, and the characters' use of words, especially in connection with the motif of absence, is another clue to the functioning of the narrator.

Sylvia declares to Philip, for instance, that she holds Simpson responsible for her father's death: "My flesh and blood wasn't made for forgiving and forgetting" (*SL,* 333); but those words, almost flesh and blood themselves, "came up into his memory at a future time, with full measure of miserable significance" (334), and they keep him from her when Kinraid has married another woman and she would have her husband back (see also 356). Similarly, Jeremiah Foster promises to chide Philip for any future mistreatment of Sylvia; and those "words came up again in after days, as words idly spoken sometimes do" (349). But Philip too has spoken words that harm more than he intended. Sylvia suffers at his accusation that she thinks of another while married to him: "She used to shudder as if cold steel had been plunged into her warm, living body as she remembered these words; cruel words, harmlessly provoked" (360).

We can see in this reaction a consciousness of the power of language, power often greater than those who use it can predict, echoes of Elizabeth Gaskell's own recognition that her work will have effects she cannot anticipate. Uglow writes that in the composition of *Sylvia's Lover* Gaskell was blocked at the end of the second of three projected volumes, needing the encouragement and pressure of her publisher to complete the novel.[37] Still, in the completed work there is none of the hesitation or equivocation that characterized the earlier *Mary Barton,* especially in its first volume. Alice Rose's instructions to William Coulson, who is writing her will, are a model of Gaskell's confidence in composition. She calls "the grand flourish at the top of the paper which he had learnt at school, and which was there called a spread-eagle" an unnecessary "vanity, . . . and 't may make t' will not stand" (*SL,* 80). When he has to revise one passage, she insists: "put a line under it to show those are my special words" (81–82).

Words, of course, can have less than their desired effect as well as more. Alice Rose cannot keep Philip from the world of business by lecturing him (*SL,* 162); and Bell Robson fails to instruct her daughter adequately through the story of Nancy Hartley, who pined away when a wandering lad left her behind (188). Reviewing such ineffective stories and Sylvia's own unskilled use of language, Schor has concluded: "It is out of Sylvia's illiteracy (and the cultural disempowerment that represents) that the novel's critique of established plots (and culturally scripted disappearance of female power) will arise."[38] Despite the heroine's lack of stories to express or conceptualize her experience and desire in *Sylvia's Lovers,* however, Gaskell still proposes unwritten strengths in her central character. And similar strengths support the novel's narrative authority.

Gaskell's instructive voice in this novel is all the more remarkable in its effectiveness because it is generally disembodied. That is, no on-the-scene witness reports events to listeners, as happens in *Mary Barton;* but a voice nevertheless comes through with a distinctive authority. There are three primary sources for this narrative strength: history (a Victorian perspective on the time of the French Revolution), feeling (respect for "the strange mystery of Sylvia's heart"), and nature (especially the sea) as an unchanging framework for human life. And all are expressed in structural features of *Sylvia's Lovers.*

Even as characters come and go in the eyes of others, then, the novel's narrator remains a constant presence, a voice that embodies the beings of this tale. In scenes where Sylvia thinks of "the lover whom she believed to be dead" (*SL*, 265), for instance, a narrative of absences is compelling:

> *If she could set her eyes on his bright, handsome face, that face which was fading from her memory, overtasked in the too frequent efforts to recall it; if she could but see him once again, coming over the waters beneath which he lay with supernatural motion, await-ing her at the stile, with the evening sun shining ruddy into his bonny eyes, even though, after that one instant of vivid and vis-ible life, he faded into mist, if she could but see him now, sitting in the faintly flickering fire-light in the old, happy, careless way, on a corner of the dresser, his legs dangling, his busy fingers play-ing with some of her woman's work;—she wrung her hands tight together as she implored some, any Power, to let her see him just once again—just once—for one minute of passionate delight.*

(265–66)

The "Power" that soon grants Sylvia this very wish is but one exten-sion of her desire in this scene, something closely akin to the narrative power that composed these very words. Out of "evening sun," "mist," and "flickering fire-light," that is, a being is created "with supernatural motion," "legs dangling, his busy fingers playing." It is a narrative magic that recurs throughout *Sylvia's Lovers*, this fire bell appropriately rung by a Victorian citizen of great standing.[39]

Victorian readers did vary in their reactions to the central charac-ter of *Sylvia's Lovers*. The 28 March 1863 *Examiner* praised the novel's "shrewd character painting" (*CH*, 441) in general; and the 1 April 1863 *Westminster Review* was moved by the "pathetic story of Sylvia's love for the gallant sailor stolen from her by the press-gang, and not, as she is falsely told, by death" (*CH*, 444). But the 14 April 1863 *Manchester Ex-aminer and Times* confessed "Sylvia is more a shadow than a substance, and leaves but a dim impression" (*CH*, 452; see also the 4 April 1863 *Saturday Review*). Reviewers were divided on her use of dialect, as well as on the roles of Philip and Charley. But most, like Geraldine Jewsbury in the 28 February 1863 *Athenaeum*, admired Elizabeth Gaskell's skill as a nov-

elist: "For true artistic workmanship we think 'Sylvia's Lovers' superior
to any of Mrs. Gaskell's former works" (*CH*, 432). And at the heart of
"artistic workmanship" is the novel's authoritative narrator.

The narrative's opening description of Monkshaven works like the
beginning of *The Life of Charlotte Brontë* (discussed in chapter 5) to establish an unquestioned foundation for subsequent events: "I can best make
you understand the appearance of the place [the Fosters' shop in Monk-
shaven] by bidding you think of the long openings in a butcher's shop,
and then to fill them up in your imagination with panes about eight
inches by six, in a heavy wooden frame" (*SL*, 22). In addition to using a
recognizable physical landscape to lend credibility to events, the narrator
reminds readers of the privilege of hindsight, which, pointing to the familiar terrain of the past, also grants authority:

(68)

> *In looking back to the last century, it appears curious to see how little*
> *our ancestors had the power of putting two things together, and perceiv-*
> *ing either the discord or harmony thus produced. Is it because we are*
> *farther off from those times, and have, consequently, a greater range of*
> *vision? Will our descendants have a wonder about us, such as we have*
> *about the inconsistency of our forefathers, or a surprise at our blindness*
> *that we do not perceive that, holding such and such opinions, our course*
> *of action must be so and so, or that the logical consequence of particular*
> *opinions must be convictions which at present we hold in abhorrence?*

Even with a gentle tweaking of complacency ("It is well for us that
we live at the present time, when everybody is logical and consistent"
[68]), the narrative assures readers that the past is known territory and the
voice reporting on it knowledgeable.[40] With such historical authority, a
whaling village's place "in the history of England" (1) can be presented,
even the giant figure of Napoleon described (429), or biblical settings
visited (448).[41]

Many Victorian readers accepted the notion that they could agree
on the shape of the past and its lessons. The 4 April 1863 *Saturday Review*
applauded the fact "that such a system [as press-gangs] should have so
completely passed away as to make its former existence almost incredible
to this generation" (*CH*, 448). The 1 March 1863 *Observer* was similarly
confident of historical knowledge: "Fortunately, we have so far improved
since those days that we can read of such doings now [press-gang raids] as

if they applied to Mexico or Tahiti" (*CH,* 440). Considerable research on Gaskell's part contributed to this element of narrative authority,[42] but personal experience is probably more responsible for the confidence in exploring human feelings, another source of narrative authority in *Sylvia's Lovers.*

The power of Gaskell's unlettered heroine especially emerges through brief scenes of great emotional intensity; and her characterization is at the heart of the narrative authority in *Sylvia's Lovers,* the tone of the fire bell she rings. Sylvia's spontaneous response to the woman of questionable character, "Newcastle Bess," is an early, quick sign of Sylvia's capacity for strong sympathetic feeling: "When folk are glad I can't help being glad too, and I just put out my hand, and she put out hers . . . if you'd been down seeing all t' folk looking and looking their eyes out, as if they feared they should die afore she [the ship] came in and brought home the lads they loved, you'd ha' shaken hands wi' that lass too, and no great harm done" (*SL,* 27). Her "hysterical burst of tears" (30) brought on by a woman's dismay at her husband's being taken by the press-gang prepares for the moment when "tears rained down her face, and her distress became so evident that it attracted the attention of many" (70) at the funeral of Darley, a man Sylvia did not know. Such deft early scenes prepare readers for the powerful feelings she has later in the novel, as when a villager's testimony incriminates her father ("'Couldn't he ha' bitten his tongue out?' asked Sylvia" [332]), and her disappointed relationships with Philip and Charley. Because the novel's main subject is "the strange mystery of Sylvia's heart" (488), these passages provide a chief foundation for the narrative's overall authority.[43]

Geraldine Jewsbury in the 28 February 1863 *Athenaeum* was among those who found Gaskell's portrait of Sylvia convincing: "As charming and pretty a damsel as ever tormented the heart of a lover; but she has a dash of fierce, persistent resentment in her character that effectually redeems her from perfection" (*CH,* 433). The 28 February 1863 *Reader* praised Gaskell's ability to represent the lower classes in general: "Few educated people really know the poor, and still fewer can translate that knowledge into fiction. When we say, therefore, that the novel here noticed is one of the very best of this kind, we award it no slight praise" (*CH,* 437). This paper went on to say that Sylvia "is drawn with so much force and solidity, that the extreme flatness of his [Philip's] portrait feels

like a false note" (438). While not all reviewers felt "the unconscious
fascination which Sylvia could exercise over others" (340), most agreed
with the 29 July 1863 *Guardian* that the "incidents of the tale revolve
around the fair person of Sylvia" (*CH*, 454).[44]

This novel's narrator possesses the authority to issue judgments as
well as to explore emotions, though choosing not to do so concerning all
events. When Sylvia finds her friend Molly insensitive to the solemnity
of Darley's funeral, the narrator says, "Molly had come all the way to
Monkshaven Church in her service, and deserved forbearance accordingly" (*SL*, 65). Such pronouncements grow out of firm religious con-
victions:

(176)

> [Philip] *was like too many of us, he did not place his future life in the
> hands of God, and only ask for grace to do His will in whatever circum-
> stances might arise; but he yearned in that terrible way after a blessing
> which, when granted under such circumstances, too often turns out to be
> equivalent to a curse. And that spirit brings with it the material and
> earthly idea that all events that favour our wishes are answers to our
> prayer; and so they are in one sense, but they need prayer in a deeper
> and higher spirit to keep us from the temptation to evil which such
> events invariably bring with them.*

The narrative voice here resembles that of a novelist Gaskell is sometimes compared to: George Eliot in *Adam Bede* (1859),[45] and it is stronger
than it had been in *Mary Barton*.

Not only historical hindsight and moral certainty grant authority to
this novel, however; the rhythms of nature, especially the sea, are tied to
the narrative structure of *Sylvia's Lovers*. Certainly the phrase "the waves
kept lapping on the shelving shore" (*SL*, 494) sounds as a chorus in
Philip's moving death scene near the novel's conclusion. J. M. Rignall
says, "The unchanging rhythm of the sea is finally the only enduring
connexion between the past and the present, but one that remains inscru-
table, revealing nothing but the mutability and transience of mankind."[46]
Still, the sea has traditionally figured symbolically, and Gaskell's text
draws on its representative power to suggest the opposites of absence and
presence. The sea is full, defined by its amplitude, yet not capable of being
plumbed. It fills its shores and yet in its entirety, always and forever out
of sight, remains incapable of being encompassed. Like Gaskell's narrative

voice, it not only is rhythmic but also has power over life and death. It is a site of mirages and mirrors (given its surface) as well as depths and monumental material force. It gives life and takes it; it is, for sailors especially, womb and burial ground.

The sea's eternal rhythm is echoed in the destinies of the novel's many paired characters.[47] Their alternating good and bad fortune, strong and weak feeling, presence and absence recall the fundamental nature of the sea, and of life shaped by the sea. The two young women Molly and Sylvia, for instance, open the novel and follow related paths toward love and marriage. Charley and Philip, of course, are the novel's chief rivals in love; but Hester and Sylvia also vie at different times for a place in Philip's heart. Philip and William share control of a business first run by the brothers John and Jeremiah Foster and figure as romantic possibilities for Hester Rose (*SL*, 204). The novel, then, even contains paired pairs like William and Philip and Philip and Charley, who offer themselves to Sylvia, and Hester and Sylvia, who together correspond to Sylvia and Molly.

The pairing of characters and the alternating nature of their fortunes is echoed in Monkshaven's geography: a wealthy middle class (New Town) and landed aristocracy (Old Town) are separated by a central bridge (*SL*, 8). This is a temporary order in the larger historical frame, as men like Philip and William "climb the steep heights leading to the freshly-built rows of the new town of Monkshaven, feeling as if they were rising into aristocratic regions where no shop profaned the streets" (166). The Fosters' shop is itself divided into two sides, one for grocery, the other for drapery (22); and the brothers often alternate roles to achieve desired results (169). Monkshaven has two kinds of traded goods, legal and smuggled (22), while Sylvia's choices for the future are initially represented by red and gray cloaks. But the paired shapes of town, store, material, and characters are responding to an underlying natural order, as is clear when Coulson and Hepburn pause on the town's dividing bridge. "It would not do to linger here in the very center of the valley up which passed the current of atmosphere coming straight with the rushing tide from the icy northern seas" (166).

Perhaps most clearly constructing the narrative pattern of *Sylvia's Lovers* are the alternating feelings of the novel's couples. As the 4 April 1863 *Saturday Review* claimed, "Mrs. Gaskell has finely marked the ebb and flow of passion" (*CH*, 449). Hester's feelings toward Sylvia, for instance, change from jealousy to love even as she contemplates their paired relationship: "By slow degrees Hester was learning to love the woman, whose position as Philip's wife she would have envied so keenly had she not been so truly good and pious" (*SL,* 346). Characters can even reverse their opinions of themselves by contemplating switched positions: Philip, for instance, "went over and over again the torturing details, the looks of contempt and anger, the words of loathing indignation [from Sylvia], till he almost brought himself, out of his extreme sympathy with Sylvia, to believe that he was indeed the wretch she had considered him to be" (465).

But even more central to the novel's structure are Sylvia's alternations of feeling toward her lovers: "When she had argued herself into certainty on one side [Kinraid might like her], she suddenly wheeled about, and was just of the opposite opinion" (*SL,* 106). At a time when she is finally beginning to appreciate Philip's devotion to her, she concludes that "her husband's silence was unsympathizing, and shut up the feelings that were just beginning to expand towards him" (346). When she learns of Kinraid's marriage, she concludes that "Philip would not have acted so. . . .For the first time in her life she seemed to recognize the real nature of Philip's love" (437). The story of Philip's battlefield bravery then inspires alternating emotions from Sylvia: "Many a time she sank to sleep with the picture of the event narrated by Mrs. Kinraid as present to her mind as her imagination or experience could make it: first one figure prominent, then another" (452).[48]

Alternating locations, activities, material, and feelings are all linked to the novel's profound exploration of presence and absence, the question of the quick and the dead with which Sylvia struggles from the moment of Darley's funeral. When Kinraid and her father, two of the men whose loss will cause her such pain, enter the house one winter evening, Sylvia's world goes from death to life: "To Sylvia the sudden change into brightness and bustle occasioned by the entrance of her father and the specksioneer was like that which you may effect any winter's night, when you come into a room where a great lump of coal lies hot and slumbering on the fire; just break it up with a judicious blow from the poker, and the room, late so dark, and dusk, and lone, is full of life, and light, and warmth" (*SL,* 97). Of course, life and death are not so easily manipulated as the fire in a lump of coal, but the concern with presence and absence, living and dead, is central to Sylvia's peasant culture:

> *among the uneducated—the partially educated—nay, even the*
> *weakly educated—the feeling exists which prompted the futile*
> *experiment of the well-known ostrich. They imagine that, by*
> *closing their own eyes to apprehended evil, they avert it. The ex-*
> *pression of fear is supposed to accelerate the coming of its cause.*
> *Yet, on the other hand, they shrink from acknowledging the long* (276–77)
> *continuance of any blessing, in the idea that when unusual hap-*
> *piness is spoken about, it disappears . . . they shrink from em-*
> *bodying apprehensions for the future in words, as if it then took*
> *shape and drew near.*

Taking this culture as her subject, and its representative Sylvia as her heroine, Elizabeth Gaskell faced a challenge of representing absence.

The text of *Sylvia's Lovers* shows the confidence of the mature artist, especially when we compare her achievement here with the less successful effort in *Mary Barton*. What she accomplished is represented in Philip's deathbed confrontation with the images of his own life: "All the temptations that had beset him rose clearly before him; the scenes themselves stood up in their solid materialism—he could have touched the places" (*SL*, 498–99). The "solid materialism" of this vision, rising out of the perpetual presence of the sea ("the ceaseless waves lapping against the shelving shore" [497]), matches the literary achievement of Elizabeth Gaskell in *Sylvia's Lovers*. Her words embody the elemental shape of the physical world even as her narrator remains an unseen but ubiquitous presence. The same strengths characterize her other major works: *Ruth, North and South, The Life of Charlotte Brontë,* and *Wives and Daughters*.

Despite a struggle to write the final volume of *Sylvia's Lovers*, Gaskell had reached the point in her career where her "natural" vision could take advantage of established practices in Victorian publishing. We now turn to the period in her life when she was endeavoring to shape her tales into those volumes, weekly installments, and monthly parts of nineteenth-century literature. That story of Mrs. Gaskell's work, then, continues with the controversial novel *Ruth*, the successor to *Mary Barton*, and with "Lizzie Leigh," an important bridge between the two.

III

Left Documents and
Illegitimate Children:
"Lizzie Leigh,"
Cranford, and *Ruth*

AFTER SHE TOOK that first important step in finding a full authorial voice with *Mary Barton*—a process reaching powerful maturity in *Sylvia's Lovers*—Elizabeth Gaskell discovered in the next major phase of her career that she was striving to tell stories, especially stories about the Victorian England in which "Mrs. Gaskell" was so much at home. Her efforts to break from convention left works of art she herself recognized as flawed, a permanent record of continuing struggle.

Written records, of course, were commonplace in Victorian England. One of the profound effects of industrialization was that the actions taken by individuals generated documentary evidence and eventually a collective history. Elaine Scarry writes of how artifacts—tools, weapons, even books—can be considered extensions of the body. "Language," she explains, also "is an artifact, and when it is written down, the verbal artifact becomes a material artifact." The written records of Victorians become, then, in a materialist view of language, extensions of their authors' bodies.[1]

The shape of the tool or weapon or book that someone uses to extend a body is often a product of the models available from the past. We make our needles, spears, and tablets based on what has worked well for our predecessors. Similarly, throughout her career Elizabeth Gaskell tried a number of inherited forms for the stories she told—the ghost story, the multiplot work, the industrial novel. She also embodied her tales in different publication formats—weekly magazine parts; one-, two-, and three-volume issue; monthly installments.

In her work immediately following the publication of *Mary Barton,* Gaskell's characters often leave records behind them in the form of money and letters, physical objects that attest to the presence and actions of individuals. Lizzie Leigh, though lost to society, wraps money in newspaper and her own notes and deposits them for her child, little bundles that testify to her own fragile existence. Abandoned by her lover Bellingham, Ruth clings to a note from his mother and fifty pounds, all that remains to validate her relationship with a man who will be the father of her child. And Mary Smith, the narrator of *Cranford,* writes a letter to Peter, the lost brother of Matty and Deborah Jenkyns, though she assumes it will disappear from the face of the earth. But this "little piece of paper" (*CR,* 128), like so many other Victorian documents, will not disappear; instead this record of action taken restores a family and confirms Mary as a functioning member of Cranford's unique society.

Such documents in her fiction are reminders of the price of authorship Elizabeth Gaskell felt so keenly, for what she wrote did not vanish but had repercussions throughout the social order. She admitted to Eliza Fox after the controversial publication of *Ruth:* "Now *should* you have burnt the 1st vol. of Ruth as so *very* bad? even if you had been a very anxious father of a family? Yet *two* men have; and a third has forbidden his wife to read it; they sit next to us in Chapel and you can't think how 'improper' I feel under their eyes" (*LMG,* 223; [early February?] 1853). In some ways, then, Gaskell's works themselves resemble her primary subject at this time of her career, the illegitimate offspring of fallen women. Left documents and abandoned children are undeniable products of the human power of generation, inspiring both joy and guilt. Written records and offspring can also be considered extensions of the woman's body. Attempting to reduce the shame suffered by women in a patriarchal society, Gaskell clothed her subject of illegitimacy in several forms: the magazine story, the three-volume library edition, and the unplanned series of tales spread out over a variety of publication formats. Characters in her fiction generating documents in their world are representations of their creator's continuing search for the best material form of her own self-expression, embodiments of her vision in powerful cultural artifacts.

As Gaskell failed to find the perfect form in which to embody her vision, so some of the left documents in her novels were only partially successful in accomplishing their aims. Fictional mothers who wrote to protect or help their illegitimate children were ambivalent about the records they created. If we consider for a moment—as we do in this chapter—that, like Lizzie Leigh and Ruth, *Cranford's* narrator Mary Smith may be another "fallen woman" in Drumble (an identity she escapes by traveling to Cranford) insofar as her desires exceed conventional roles available to her, then Gaskell's sense of the limitations of language at mid-century are even more dramatically underscored. Mary is drawn to the odd little village of Amazons because it is a place where unusual stories can be entertained. And the author is drawn away from traditional magazine stories and triple-decker novels where the fallen woman is a problematic subject toward a more free-form and congenial literary mode in which that same outcast figure becomes a reluctant agent for renewal. The unusual form of *Cranford,* that is, created new spaces in Victorian literature where Elizabeth Gaskell could do her work.

Gaskell's emphasis on the physical presence of the fallen woman and her child suggests that recognition and respect for the human body are underlying principles of her writing. This refusal to deny what society rejects is reinforced by an emphasis throughout her work on the sanctity of male as well as female bodies. The story of the Jenkyns brother in *Cranford* shows how left documents and illegitimate children are intricately linked in Mrs. Gaskell's work.

Peter appears as a small part of *Cranford's* background, as is appropriate for a novel focusing on a preindustrial village abandoned by men who have gone to the modern city to seek their fortune. Felicia Bonaparte finds Peter's story "magic . . . enormously satisfying" to the author;[2] but this subplot of Gaskell's novel also illustrates her insistence on respecting the physical form of humanity. The Jenkyns heir is lost to the family because he has challenged gender roles and because his physical autonomy has been violated. Although not quite the illegitimate child of a fallen woman, this exiled man adds to Gaskell's exploration of left documents and social outcasts.

Peter was introduced in the world of the novel as a rebel in the middle of the third part (*Household Words,* 13 March 1852): "'Poor Peter,' [Miss Matty] said; 'he was always in scrapes. . . . He could never resist a joke'" (*CR,* 49). The young Peter consistently tweaks authority, twice dressing up as a lady, once to ask jokingly about the sermon his father had published in a periodical. On the second occasion, in which Peter feigns holding a baby in his arms (52), his irreverent antics lead to his father's flogging him (53), an event that drives Peter from home and from England. Now thought of as an outcast or even a criminal, Peter is further distanced from his family when he disappears after "some great war in India" (59). Peter's absent body represents, then, a failure of masculine parenthood in preindustrial, village England. The text Peter's father attempted to write on his son's body was a crippling one, both for the two men and for the mother, who dies less than a "twelvemonth after Peter went away" (58). Peter escapes that old story of absolute patriarchal authority, but only by separating himself from the culture it represents, preserving an innocence that helps explain his later comfortable presence in a village of "old maids."

Gaskell offers the story of Peter's life through a variety of texts representing his outcast body. At the time Matty Jenkyns's father was preaching "a whole set of sermons" regarding the dangers of Napoleon's invading England, he was also taking "up his pen, and [rubbing] up his Latin, once more, to correspond with his boy," Peter. His son's series of responses to those paternal inscriptions, also in Latin, constitute, according to the novel, "what are called show-letters" (*CR,* 48), an approved construction of his identity, though they also contain signs of a private self (49). Another series of letters by Peter, his captain, and both parents represents the sad story of his departure from England, to fight the French and to flee his father's disapproval. Read aloud years later to the novel's narrator, Mary Smith, these letters become a narrative perilously close to destruction when Miss Matty begins to burn family papers, lamenting that "no one will care for them when I am gone" (44). Peter's threatened body—first flogged, then taken prisoner—survived, as had the private documents chronicling his life; but Peter had at this point no public way to present himself in England, no forum to display the record of his actions. The motif of the exiled or imprisoned male body whose problematic story has no appropriate form recurs throughout Gaskell's fiction.[3] This figure is an analogue to the fallen woman, perhaps the central subject of her thinking in 1850−53.

The key event in her exploration of the fallen woman was the composition and publication of *Ruth* (published in three volumes by Chapman and Hall in January 1853). Written during the same months as *Cranford*'s serialization in *Household Words* (13 December 1851 to 21 May

1853), *Ruth* involved the overlapping of one literary work with another. And since *Ruth* expanded and developed the theme of the earlier "Lizzie Leigh" (*Household Words,* 30 March to 13 April 1850), the three-volume work can be viewed as an outgrowth or development of Gaskell's three-part magazine story.[4]

This mixing of forms was like the confusion of architecture that opens *Ruth,* where a facade of eighteenth-century "shops" in a Midlands town has been added to "mansions" (*R,* 2) of earlier times. The structure of a middle-class mode, periodical literature, surrounds the older three-volume model traditionally preferred by the wealthy landowning class. Reading these works in this chronology of 1850–53, then, was much like entering the building where Ruth works at the beginning of the novel: "People were occasionally surprised, after passing through a common-place-looking shop, to find themselves at the foot of a grand carved oaken staircase, lighted by a window of stained glass, storied all over with armorial bearings" (3). No old story could be left behind for a new one until its complete shape had been acknowledged. And this old story has ancestors firmly embedded in the ideology of pre-Victorian culture. The evolution of Gaskell's stories through these forms subtly altered nineteenth-century opinion about such central tenets of thought as class and gender roles. As Benson says in *Ruth* concerning society and "the fallen woman," "Is it not time to change some of our ways of thinking and acting?" (351), a call for action cited by *Bentley's Miscellany* (3 February 1853), which claimed the novel "better than any sermon" (*CH,* 241).[5] But since all her stories consisted of language in printed form, they also show Gaskell's entrapment in the established discourses and familiar publication modes of her time. Although sometimes branded as dangerous to society (like an illegitimate child), her books became part of the larger record of history.

Although "Lizzie Leigh" is not widely read today, its stature at mid-century is revealed, as Easson notes, in that it was "given pride of place in the magazine's [*Household Words*] first issue, immediately after Dickens's 'A Preliminary Word'" (*CH,* 5). This story of a mother's effort to recover her "fallen" daughter contains essential ingredients of the later *Ruth* and *Cranford,* especially the theme of failure in the existing codes' representation of human behavior. At the same time, however, all these works insist that such codes must be used until alternatives emerge. The study of a faulty but necessary discourse underscores Gaskell's desire to retreat from fundamental material in Victorian society.

"Lizzie Leigh" begins Gaskell's flight from conventional ideology with the figure of the story's title character. Unmarried, pregnant Lizzie Leigh is reduced to the lowest form of human existence in Victorian society, a "shadow" (LL, 23) or someone only alive enough to be "not dead" (7) in the bleak landscape of Manchester (a region itself so grim as to be represented by a blank in the text: "Many a one dies in ——" [12]). To begin the search for this blank in the social order, Mrs. Leigh must renounce the principles of her husband, "the interpreter, who stood between God and her" (1): he had "declared that henceforth they would have no daughter; that she should be as one dead, and her name never more be named at market or at meal time, in blessing or in prayer" (6). In rejecting his judgment after his death, Mrs. Leigh rises to stand "as if the interpreter of God's will" (22), a figure, like Mrs. Gaskell, attempting to reshape the thinking of her society. As is clear at the story's beginning, traditions have lost their force in this family: "It was merely the form of tea that had been gone through" (2).

Even more difficult to escape than the broad principles of a patriarchal system is the importance of one of their central material manifestations—money.[6] After her husband's death, Mrs. Leigh cannot change the life lived by her two sons and herself because "they had never possessed capital enough to improve" their lot (LL, 3), though they owned Upclose Farm. Similarly, Susan Palmer's father is reduced to being "an old man, who, without being absolutely drunk, could not guide himself rightly" (8), because his business had "failed for more money than any greengrocer he had heard of" (10). In other words, money is necessary for functioning in this society. (It is ironic, of course, that the Palmers live on *Crown* Street.)

That money is the base by which social connections are confirmed is underscored in Lizzie's last means of connection to her daughter. Having to hide even her own body in the shadows, the "fallen woman" leaves "little packets" with "two half-crowns" (LL, 18) in them for the care of her child. But so close to absolute invisibility is Lizzie that Susan Palmer cannot take this money: "I never touch it, but I've often thought the poor mother feels near to God when she brings this money" (18). Leigh's money, earned in a way Susan cannot acknowledge, might be kept as a sign of sin and never used to help a child. Fundamental elements of the social order remain in the fallen woman's life, then, but she can no longer use them even in a moral cause.

Her mother, knowing that her daughter cannot be reached within the system, must herself escape conventional behavior in order to reclaim Lizzie. Her decision to let the farm seems to the lawyer Samuel Orme an irrational response to the loss of her husband (LL, 4), but she simply wants to leave behind the rules laid down by her husband and others (especially men) in order to search for her lost daughter. And the new self she constructs becomes visible in chance meetings with only a very few "kindhearted passer[s]-by" (8) in the streets, who turn to ask if they can help her. One such sharp-eyed person is, of course, Susan Palmer, who is said by a neighbor to be "just one a stranger would stop in the street to ask help from if he needed it" (14). Joanne Thompson calls the meeting of these two "the turning point of the story";[7] it is also a model for Mrs. Gaskell's relationship with her readers, who must almost instinctively share values unrecognized in ordinary exchange, values that do not yet have material form (like money) for their expression.

Although the mother's compassion was clearly recognizable to Victorian readers, the restrictions on it may not have been so obvious. Mrs. Leigh can change the clothes she wears, for instance, putting on her Sunday dress in order not to offend Susan Palmer (LL, 13); but there are no officially sanctioned clothes she can put on to rescue Lizzie or her child. Similarly, her granddaughter's distinctive frocks provide evidence of the child's relationship to Mrs. Leigh (17); but, "made out of its mother's gowns" (16), they also proclaim her illegitimate status. The material itself, that is, constitutes her identity and dooms this child.

If money and clothes represent substances of social order, so too does language. And as characters search for words to remedy their plight, so Gaskell explores forms of fiction to seek solutions to Victorian problems.

Words can change people in "Lizzie Leigh," as Will admits to Susan Palmer: "I love thee so, that thy words cut me" (LL, 29). The power of language in altering behavior was also a strong theme in Gaskell's "The Heart of John Middleton," which appeared in *Household Words* in the same year. The chief action of this story—the change of heart of a man of rage—occurs because of words: a girl's request for help, Bible lessons, prayer, preaching, a child's presenting the message of her mother, and storytelling. But language cannot always be controlled: Mrs. Leigh says that "one severe look" from Will "turns me sick, and then I say just the wrong thing, I'm so fluttered" (LL, 19). In asking Susan Palmer about the child's history, "the poor woman's words failed her" (15) again. And even the strong Susan Palmer "could not find the power to speak" to her grandmother of the child's accidental death (26). The story's narrator alludes to the difficulty of describing unconventional behavior, while acknowledging a duty to try: "I need not tell you how the mother spent the weary hours. And yet I will tell you something" (8).

Words, of course, are necessary to confirm identity: Lizzie writes "Call her Anne" (LL, 17) on the "slip of paper . . . that had been pinned to the bundle" in which she leaves her daughter. And much later she fears she will not know her own daughter in heaven because she has never heard her speak: "If I might but have heard her little voice!" (30). But the words Lizzie uses have been given fixed meanings by a social discourse already in place: the final gift she leaves Susan Palmer is a "little parcel, wrapped in a scrap of newspaper, and evidently containing money" (26–27). The newspaper, that is, embodying conventional morality, contains Lizzie's money and defines it as useless, condemned.

Elizabeth Gaskell, of course, wrapped Lizzie and her child in different words—the three-part magazine story published in the inaugural issues of a journal edited by the most famous author of the era. To the degree that her narrative was successful, new words and concepts came together within her audience, allowing a different judgment of Lizzie Leigh, her child, and her mother. Gaskell apparently felt she had offered something of value to the world; she wrote on 26 April 1850 about the magazine's official response to her work: "Do you know they sent me 20£ for Lizzie Leigh? I stared, and wondered if I was swindling them but I suppose I am not" (*LMG*, 113).[8]

Gaskell's message about the need for different judgments of "fallen women," however, was muted by two factors. First, Lizzie and her forgiving mother can live on only if hidden from the rest of society: they retreat to "a cottage so secluded that, until you drop into the very hollow where it is placed, you do not see it" (LL, 31). A similar situation holds in Gaskell's 1850 Christmas story "The Moorland Cottage" (Chapman and Hall), where a family's house is "as secluded in their green hollow as the households in the German forest-tales" (MC, 3). Happiness for them is connected to their cottage's being "like the place the Sleeping Beauty lived in; people sometimes seem to go round it and round it, and never find it" (19). Second, Lizzie's illegitimate daughter must be sacrificed to the moral code: the mother's final action in the story is to "weep bitterly" (LL, 32) for her dead child. To see Lizzie's story differently, a different journal would have been necessary—one not aimed, as Dickens's was, to be "Familiar to their Mouths as Household Words." Gaskell's second full-length novel, *Ruth*, seeks a form in which this story can achieve a different ending, a realm in which both mother and child can survive.

Like Lizzie Leigh, the central figure of *Ruth*, Gaskell's second major novel, is repeatedly placed within the established textures of English society—clothes, money, and language—that construct her status as female, working class, and fallen. Amanda Anderson has pointed out that "Gaskell acknowledges but also shelters her heroine [Ruth] from the forces of social inscription that constituted *Mary Barton*'s Esther." [9] Thus the problematic documents through which Ruth's story is told are signs of Gaskell's continuing effort to construct an alternative identity for "the fallen woman."

Ruth begins the novel defined by her place in the social order. The occasion at which her seducer Bellingham is first seen is appropriately an "annual hunt-ball" (R, 7), and there he adorns the pretty dressmaker as an object of his desire by giving her "a camellia" (16).[10] And he sustains the definition of their relationship by framing it in past constructions: he asks her to find out about "an old hunting-piece painted on a panel over one of the chimney-pieces; the figures were portraits of my ancestors" (30).

More confining than clothes for Ruth, however, is money. Despite "a sort of silent understanding" (R, 23) initially between her and Bellingham at the river accident, he soon attempts to entangle her in a money relationship: " 'If you'll allow me, I'll leave you my purse,' continued he giving it to Ruth, who was only too glad to have this power entrusted to her of procuring one or two requisites which she had perceived to be wanted. But she saw some gold between the net-work; she did not like the charge of such riches" (24). The extra "gold" represents service she might perform for him beyond what is necessary to help the child. He clearly knows that this is excess: "If I remember rightly, there are three sovereigns and some loose change; I shall, perhaps, see you again in a few days, when, if there be any money left in the purse, you can restore it to me" (25).

Ruth later attempts to correct their relationship by returning the money and documenting her expenses on behalf of the child: "But I have got one or two things through another person. I have put them down on this slip of paper; and here is your purse, sir" (*R,* 29). But his strategy is to extend her debt to him and expand the web of financial ties by which he can control her. After she has tea with him at an inn following the visit to her old home, and after she has been seen and denounced by Mrs. Mason, "Ruth remembered the cup of tea that she had drank; it must be paid for, and she had no money with her" (60). And the "jingling of money" (61) she hears when he talks with the landlord reminds her of his power in their relationship.[11] Bellingham knows that money is the tradi-tional agent for his family's class in dealing with others: when his mother wishes him to drop Ruth completely, he knows she, "always liberal where money was concerned, would 'do the thing handsomely'" (91).

The kind of manipulation practiced by the nobility here is also be-ing adopted by some of the rising middle class. Bradshaw also uses money and goods to control his relationship with Ruth, initially offering her presents (muslin) and later wanting to pay her for serving as governess to his daughters.[12] Ruth challenges such principles of exchange: "What right had he to send [a gift] to me?" (*R,* 156). And Benson articulates her rea-soning: "It is a delight to have gifts made to you by those whom you esteem and love . . . but you feel it to be different when there is no regard for the giver to idealize the gift—when it simply takes its stand among your property as so much money value" (157). For Bradshaw to accept Ruth's or Benson's ideas about exchange would be to lose power and status, something he must endure when his son later violates this system. Bradshaw's physical collapse after his son's near fatal accident in the Dover coach is partly due to genuine parental love (414); but he also declines in part because his son Richard has broken middle-class rules of financial exchange in his speculation and later embezzlement. Bradshaw's decision to use bribery in electioneering (260–61) is another model of improper service for a fee that Ruth struggles to escape.

Ruth's relationship with Benson, on the other hand, rests on sym-pathetic feeling rather than money; and like the meetings in the street

between Mrs. Leigh and Susan Palmer, it represents the new vision of connection Elizabeth Gaskell is exploring. When she first despaired utterly
at her abandonment by Bellingham, Benson's physical pain recalled her
to herself: "Ruth, speeding on in her despair, heard the sharp utterance
[of 'acute pain'] and stopped suddenly short. It did what no remonstrance
could have done; it called her out of herself" (*R,* 97). This man, literally
fallen, utters a sound of pain that the "fallen" woman can understand and
respond to; and Ruth expects no money for the help she offers. The material basis of their relationship, though Platonic, lies in physical suffering.

Although Benson later shares his material goods with Ruth, he requires no action from her in return. His philosophy makes no sense to
the rigid Bradshaw. When it is discovered that Richard has taken Benson's
insurance money, Bradshaw assumes an inevitable prosecution: "He has
forged your name—he has defrauded you of money—of your all, I think
you said" (*R,* 404). But Benson's response underscores the separation
between money and value: "It was all my money; it was not my all"
(405). And when "high wages had failed to tempt any to what, in their
panic, they considered as certain death" (424) in nursing during the ty-
phus epidemic, Gaskell asserts that other principles of relationship are
more powerful and more necessary than the financial ones alongside
which they coexist.

One of Ruth's first thoughts after her past is revealed to Eccleston
is that she must find some new way to live without being caught in established money-for-service equations: "But I shall earn no money"
(*R,* 358). Money is, of course, necessary to physical survival, but Ruth
always attempts an unusual precision and honesty in her financial ex-
changes: "Whatever remuneration was offered to her [for her nursing],
she took it simply and without comment: for she felt that it was not hers
to refuse; that it was, in fact, owing to the Bensons for her and her child's
subsistence" (391).

Money is not the only potentially harmful medium surrounding
Ruth, however; language too contains dangers for her. Perhaps the most
important of those dangers hides in euphemistic expressions she does not
understand: "She was too young when her mother died to have received
any cautions or words of advice respecting *the* subject of a woman's life—
if, indeed, wise parents ever directly speak of what, in its depth and
power, cannot be put into words—which is a brooding spirit with no

definite form or shape that men should know it, but which is there, and present before we have recognized and realized its existence" (*R, 44*). Old Thomas, the family friend, would warn her, but "he did not know how. When she came up, all he could think of to say was a text; indeed, the language of the Bible was the language in which he thought, whenever his ideas went beyond practical everyday life into expressions of emotion or feeling" (50–51). His quotation from Peter "gave no definite idea" to Ruth.[13]

This ignorance of even the peril that lies before her leaves Ruth without identity or name. After Bellingham abandons her, Benson finds himself "sole friend and guardian of a poor sick girl, whose very name he did not know" (*R, 110*). Similarly, Mrs. Pearson cannot put into words the history of the Ruth Hilton she has heard about: "Why, ma'am, what could become of her? Not that I know exactly—only one knows they can but go from bad to worse, poor creatures" (321). Rather than speak the conventional words that describe such a "degraded woman" (321), Benson's sister Faith must "whistle" (128); and to erase Ruth's past, Sally alters the young woman's appearance by cutting her "chestnut tresses" (146).[14] Even later, when the time comes for her to inform her son, Ruth's unwillingness to use the coded language defining her leaves Leonard able to speak only vaguely of the new identity brought on his mother and himself: "Mother—will *they* [the Bensons] speak to me about—it?" (346).

The motherless Ruth finds in Sally, the Benson's servant, a model for escaping the traps that money and coded language represent. Not only does Sally suggest through her own life history that women can live independent of men, or at least of husbands (see her monologue in chapter 16), but she also demonstrates, if comically, that women should free themselves from the conventional power of money. She tells Benson and his sister Faith that only she will decide when the wages they pay her should be raised: "As long as I'm content, I think it's no business of yours to be meddling wi' me and my money matters" (*R, 193*). And she demands of John Jackson's nephew, "prentice to a lawyer in Liverpool" (194), that he write out a will for her on parchment because, idiosyncratically, she considers that costly material to have greater authority than mere paper. She insists on her own one-for-one equivalency between word and coin ("I'll gie ye sixpence for every good law-word you put in it" [195]) so that she can feel she controls her own legal status. Such independent action is an inspiration even for the generally cowed Mrs. Bradshaw when she later offers Benson "some money my father settled on me . . . I don't know how much, but I think it's more than two thousand pounds" (407) to forestall her son's prosecution.

Gaskell's comic portrayal, however, detracted from Sally's effectiveness as moral philosopher. Henry Fothergill Chorley in the *Athenaeum* (15 January 1853) liked Sally, "be she ever so old, every so ugly, ever such a dragon in her resolution of 'distancing' the other sex" (*CH,* 206). In the *Leader* (22 January 1853) George Henry Lewes called her the "gem of the book" (*CH,* 218), and *The Sunday Times* four days later used a similar phrase, "a perfect gem" (*CH,* 250). *Sharpe's London Magazine* (22 January 1853) referred to Sally as "a character drawn with a strong and skilful hand, the most original and true to her rugged nature of any in the book" (*CH,* 209). But none of these critics looked closely at application of Sally's ideas in the real world. John Forster in the *Examiner* (22 January 1853) called Sally "a great favourite with the author, who makes her the excuse for pouring out a large store of that quaint humour in which she excells" (*CH,* 223). That is, the comic mode allowed Gaskell's readers to dismiss a key element of her criticism of Victorian life.

Sally's insistence on independence from the dominant mode of exchange, however, as well as her faith in a material record of this principle, is an important guide for Ruth's survival. Bellingham's conventional explanation of her life is clearly inadequate: "Poor Ruth! and, for the first time for several years, he wondered what had become of her; though, of course, there was but one thing that could have happened" (*R,* 278). That she has no social structure like the established system of exchange to call on for support makes her later rejection of her child's father powerful.[15] Ruth declares, "If there were no other reason to prevent our marriage but the one fact that it would bring Leonard into contact with you, that would be enough" (303). Sally similarly rejects Bellingham's offer of "a sovereign" for "some remembrance" of Ruth: "And who are you, that think to pay for my kindness to her by money?" (452). And Benson explains firmly that Leonard "shall never touch a penny of [Bellingham's] money" (454).

Ruth's desire to establish a new and appropriate relationship through new kinds of social documents begins with her fall and concludes just before her death. After first despairing at the note Bellingham's mother leaves for her at the inn in Wales, she has a wild hope: "'Oh, perhaps,' she thought, 'I have been too hasty. There may be some words of explanation from him on the other side of the page, to which, in my blind anguish, I never turned'" (R, 94). The other side is, of course, blank, since Bellingham cannot even conceive of the words that tie her to him. The mother's meaningless document is left behind as shamefully as the son leaves Ruth, who is carrying his own illegitimate child. Ruth must bravely compose her new relation to society as she imagines an "explanation" of the Bellinghams' actions. The letters she receives much later— one from the secretary to the infirmary and one from Mr. Davis, who will become a father to Leonard—are public "testimony" (433) of her redemption in society.

Ruth's life of social service is grounded in the unique household of her friend Benson, where "numerous small economies" (R, 133) make money less important than other forces. As Faith and Ruth become older women, and because Mr. Benson never plays the typical masculine role, this house might belong in Cranford, Gaskell's unusual village where the inhabitants write their own rules. Convention at the Bensons' coincides with better human impulses, which is not the case at Bradshaw's house. Jemima conforms to her father's and to Farquhar's principles, but "rule and line may measure out the figure of a man; it is the soul that gives it life; and there was no soul, no inner meaning, breathing out in Jemima's actions" (248). The Bensons, however, have more closely linked word and deed; and their presence in the novel underscores a shift in Gaskell's thinking. In "Lizzie Leigh" change was not possible without money, and material means were a crucial component of identity. In *Ruth,* however, money is seen as a material factor sometimes susceptible to subordination.

Ruth's success in functioning for a time outside the conventional rules of society is dramatized in Benson's inability to compose "an appropriate funeral sermon" (R, 455) about her life: "Oh, that he could do her justice! but words seemed hard and inflexible, and refused to fit themselves to his ideas. . . . He had never taken such pains with any sermon, and he was only half satisfied with it after all" (456). There are no documents through which to render Ruth's experience. When the time comes to deliver his thoughts, Benson "looked, and, as he gazed, a mist came before him, and he could not see his sermon, nor his hearers, but only Ruth, as she had been—stricken low, and crouching from sight, in the upland field by Llan-dhu—like a woeful, hunted creature. And now her life was over! her struggle ended! Sermon and all was forgotten" (457). Deciding finally to simply read words of prophecy, "the seventh chapter of Revelations, beginning at the ninth verse" (457), Benson acknowledges that words embodying Ruth's unique identity are not yet available to nineteenth-century England. In this sense, perhaps, Ruth does finally escape the social code that had condemned her.[16]

The words most nearly embodying Ruth's distinctive life, of course, like Lizzie Leigh's, belong to Elizabeth Gaskell and constitute the novel *Ruth*. But to offer them in their three-volume form to her readers, this Victorian author had to struggle much as Benson did. As he could not find words for his sermon, Gaskell labored because there was no place to stand and say what she intended about her troubling subject. Hilary Schor explains that in this novel Gaskell aimed to rewrite the Romantic story of the abandoned woman but could not completely escape the tradition: "Her figuration of the fable, intended to carry out her project of deconstructing the mythology of the Romantic story, cannot successfully break from the terms she means to criticize." But Jenny Uglow reminds us of how dramatic the effect of the novel's publication was in Victorian society: "All over the country *Ruth* was debated in drawing-rooms, clubs, churches, chapels—even Oxford colleges."[17]

Reaction to *Ruth* sometimes contained an awareness that the author was stretching the genre's traditional conventions.[18] *Sharpe's London Magazine* (15 January 1853), taking the moralistic tone Gaskell feared, found an absolute incongruity between subject and form: "The subject is not one for a novel—not one to treat of by our firesides, where the young should not be aroused to feel an interest in vice, however garnished, but in the triumph of virtue—not a subject that can be talked of before youths and maidens, much less dilated and dwelt upon by the morbid fascination of such a three-volume novel as *Ruth*" (*CH*, 211). But George Henry Lewes in the *Leader* (22 January 1853) argued that the innovation of form was beneficial: she "has wisely done what very few authors see the wisdom of doing—opened a new mine, instead of working the old one" (*CH*, 215). And the *Morning Post* (29 January 1853) perhaps acknowledged Gaskell's ability to explore new structures when it wrote that she demonstrated "the power of genius in elevating and enabling the most familiar topics" (*CH*, 230).

For her readers a major fault in *Ruth* was the "sin" of lying about Ruth's past by the "man of God," Benson, as was made clear by Émile Montégut in *Revue des Deux Mondes* (1 June 1853) : "When the novel of *Ruth* had been out in England for some months, all the magazines that reviewed it enlarged at length on this innocent lie [Benson's calling Ruth a widow]; some condemned it, others excused it" (*CH*, 309). The contradiction between Ruth's innocent nature and her overwhelming guilt has also puzzled readers from Gaskell's day to our own. William Rathbone Greg in the *National Review* (January 1859) articulated this confusion: "If she intended to describe a saint (as she has done), she should not have held conventional and mysterious language about her as a grievous sinner" (*CH*, 329).

Gaskell's letters speak frequently of the pain of anticipated criticism for her attempts to reformulate the language and ideas of her audience: "I hate publishing because of the talk people make, which I always feel as a great impertinence, *if they address their remarks to me* in any way" (*LMG*, 209). She writes of *Ruth* specifically in October 1852. "I dislike its being published so much, I shd not wonder if I put it off another year" (*LMG*, 204). The last of its three volumes, culminating in the death of Ruth (a conclusion disliked by Charlotte Brontë and Elizabeth Barrett Browning, among others), was especially hard to write:

> *I have not much hope of her* [Ruth] *now this year, now I've been frightened off my nest again.*   (*LMG*, 205; [October?] 1852)

> *It is not* written *yet—although Agnes Sandars was told at a Leamington library that it was coming down next day. I have never asked for any copies for myself. But, as I say again, when or if ever I shall finish it I don't know.*   (*LMG*, 209; 15 November 1852)

Gaskell may have been resisting the conventional ending built into the three-volume form. Christian von Bunsen in a 3 February 1853 letter identified a strict religious logic to the three-part structure of Mudie's Circulating Library texts: "Ruth must needs perish, but atoned and glorified. That is required by man's sense of the Eternal Laws of the

World's-order. To any one who understands this, the last volume will be as valuable and as indispensable as the two former ones" (*CH*, 243). Henry Crabb Robinson seemed similarly convinced of an inevitable outcome for such a story linked to volume structure; he was, according to Easson, unwilling to read the concluding part, though he wrote on 12 February 1853, "I am assured that the end is not unworthy of the beginning & middle" (*CH*, 245).[19]

Struggling with the conflict between her own vision and readers' expectations, Gaskell resented the distractions that took her away from finishing the difficult last volume: "Mr. Chapman . . . informed me that Mr. Forster had given him the MS. of Ruth and that the first 2 vols *were printed;* all complete news to me! But I set to on the trumpet sound thereof, and was writing away vigorously at Ruth when the Wedgwoods, Etc. came: and I was sorry, *very* sorry to give it up my heart being so full of it, in a way which I can't bring back. That's *that*" (*LMG*, 205; [October? 1852]). As Jenny Uglow notes, other projects seemed during this time more appealing: "By November [1851] she had almost finished the first volume [of *Ruth*], but after her visit to Knutsford in October a new subject had begun to fill her mind. *Ruth* was put aside while she wrote a very different kind of story, prompted by her memories of that small Cheshire town. At the beginning of December she sent Charles Dickens the opening episode of *Cranford*."[20]

Despite her anxiety about *Ruth*'s impact, she did not waver in the value of such work:

(*LMG*, 220; 27 January 1853)

> *"An unfit subject for fiction" is* the *thing to say about it; I knew all this before; but I determined notwithstanding to speak my mind out about it; only how I shrink with more pain than I can tell you from what people are saying, though I wd do every jot of it over again tomorrow.*

She also writes:

(*LMG*, 221, 226; 7 March [1853])

> *I have spoken out my mind in the best way I can, and I have no doubt that what was meant so earnestly* must *do some good, though perhaps not all the good, or not the* very *good I meant. . . . I think I have put the small edge of the wedge in, if only I have made people talk & discuss the subject a little more than they did.*

And in the next month she says:

> *But from the very warmth with which people have discussed the*
> *tale I take heart of grace; it has made them talk and think a little*   (*LMG,* 227;
> *on a subject which is so painful that it requires all one's bravery*   7 April
> *not to hide one's head like an ostrich and try by doing so to forget*   [1853])
> *that the evil exists.*

As with "Lizzie Leigh," in *Ruth* Elizabeth Gaskell left behind a flawed document, a product of her imagination rejected (like an illegitimate child) by many in her society.

If fallen characters in "Lizzie Leigh" and *Ruth* could escape conventional morality only through death, in *Cranford* Elizabeth Gaskell more nearly achieved a realm in which Victorian principles could be reconsidered.[21] Gaskell's efforts in the fall of 1853 to reconstitute the fallen woman in *Ruth* spill over into *Cranford,* as the intriguing character of Mary Smith, the narrator, is touched by the author's continuing struggle with issues of legitimacy.

In the spontaneous growth and development of this work in *Household Words* Gaskell and her audience found a congenial form. Her irregular production of tales about a village recalling her native Knutsford included a narrator who now and then takes the train from nearby Drumble to visit old friends. Gaskell's linking of subject with publication schedule reinforced her original audience's involvement with the tale. On 8 January 1853, for instance, Mary explained that she had been gone from Cranford longer than usual ("the greater part of that year" [*CR,* 80]); her readers had been similarly parted from this ongoing story for an uncharacteristically extended period, since 3 April 1852. This gap in the publication schedule reflected, then, the time in Gaskell's own life when she finally steeled herself to complete the third and final volume of *Ruth.* And Yarrow reminds us that, despite its recursive narrative reaching back over many decades, "the end of the novel is contemporaneous with its publication."[22]

Just as Gaskell herself was drawn to *Cranford* from the troubled composition of *Ruth,* so Mary Smith, a resident of the larger industrial town of Drumble, finds herself increasingly interested in the odd little village of old maids. Central to the charm of both community and novel is the freedom allowed individuals. In a place where one resident "acknowledged that she always confused carnivorous and graminivorous together, just as she did horizontal and perpendicular" (*CR,* 112), eccentricity is valued. Captain Brown, one of the few males to earn a place in Cranford, is "thought very eccentric" (10), as is Matty Jenkyns's onetime suitor, Thomas Holbrook (34). In fact the narrator claims "each [of the residents] has her own individuality, not to say eccentricity, pretty strongly developed" (1).[23]

A freedom from conventional rules not enjoyed by Lizzie Leigh or Ruth Hilton determines the clothes, money, and language of this out-of-the-way community. Dress in Cranford, for instance, "is very independent of fashion" (*CR,* 2), says the narrator, and proudly asks, "Do you ever see cows dressed in gray flannel in London?" (5). Although "expenditure in dress in Cranford was principally in that one article referred to"—the cap (73)—bonnets are sometimes worn two at a time and are always selected idiosyncratically.[24]

Even money, that especially difficult medium for Lizzie Leigh's daughter and for Ruth, is made to reflect Cranford's unique values, often at variance with those of the Victorian middle class: "We none of us spoke of money, because that subject savoured of commerce and trade, and though some might be poor, we were all aristocratic" (*CR,* 3). Residents often adopt peculiar systems of valuation, like Miss Matty's "way of make-weight" (148) in selling candy to children when she sets up her tea shop. Of course money does matter, as is shown in the Jenkyns sisters' meticulous keeping of accounts (72) and the schemes to support Miss Matty after the bank failure (138). But actions like Miss Matty's redemption of a worthless Town and County Bank note for the poor farmer Mr. Dobson (123) underscore these ladies' unwillingness to let the outside world define their relationships. As the narrator concludes, many of the financial transactions in Cranford bear "a different value in another account-book that I have heard of" (139), that is, in heaven. Indeed, Mary Smith's father has trouble explaining their dealings, just as Benson did writing his sermon for Ruth's funeral: "Confound it! I could make a good lesson out of it if I were a parson; but as it is, I can't get a tail to my sentences—only I'm sure you feel what I want to say" (141).

Even more striking than its construction of dress and money is *Cranford's* restructuring of language and traditional forms that embody ideology, such as letters, diaries, books, newspapers, and magazines. In

Cranford Gaskell uses her characters' distinctive documents to hint at new ways of embodying such difficult topics as the fallen woman's story.

Talk in the village goes by special rules. There is a distinct "phraseology of Cranford" (*CR,* 3); "short sentences of small talk" are the rule during social visits (3); and "many a rolling three-piled sentence" (15) dominates Miss Jenkyns's speech. Cranford's unique language also has special material forms, as has been noted by numerous readers: [25] the social calling cards left at each others' houses; the cards they play Preference with; the "great black and red placard" (128) advertising Signor Brunoni's show; the copied "receipts" describing conjuror's tricks carried by Miss Pole to Signor Brunoni's show (85), where each element—a finger, the ball, the wrist—is designated by a letter of the alphabet; the diaries "in two columns" that Deborah and Matty's father made them keep, one column for what they thought would happen each day, the other for what had occurred (107); Thomas Holbrook's library containing "true and beautiful words [that] were the best expression he could find for what he was thinking or feeling" (32) and perhaps even his "six-and-twenty cows, named after the different letters of the alphabet" (32); Miss Matty's discreetly placed license to sell tea (144).[26]

Although a statement in its printed form may have one precise meaning in Drumble or elsewhere, it is often reformulated for use in Cranford. Newspapers, for instance, the ubiquitous chronicler of Victorian middle-class life, are used by the Jenkyns sisters to prevent a new carpet from fading in the sun. Rather than dictating behavior to readers, these papers are made to respond to the natural order of the sun's movement as it shines through windows to different spots on the floor on its daily journey across the sky. Mary and Miss Matty are "busy, too, one whole morning . . . in following [Miss Jenkyns's] directions, and in cutting out and stitching together pieces of newspaper, so as to form little paths to every chair, set for the expected visitors, lest their shoes might dirty or defile the purity of the carpet" (*CR,* 14). Instead of shaping human actions, then, these papers are rearranged to follow the patterns of social and family life. Mary Smith proudly concludes, "Do you make paper paths for every guest to walk upon in London?" (14). As one interpretation of Mary's own story may in the end suggest, these paper paths also represent a way for the fallen woman to rechart her life.

The placing or leaving of important documents to achieve certain results occurs, then, in *Cranford* as well as in "Lizzie Leigh" and *Ruth*. One specific set of such records in the story inspired by Knutsford connects the subject of the fallen woman with Gaskell's own effort to find the best material form for her vision. Letters in this novel sometimes resemble illegitimate children sent out into the world like Mrs. Gaskell's fictions.

Cranford's correspondence frequently acknowledges connections to the larger world. A letter from Mary Smith's father about the dangers of Town and County Bank (*CR,* 119) comes, for instance, at the same time Miss Matty is invited to a meeting of the bank's shareholders. Letters frequently bring Mary from Drumble to the village, since she has "several correspondents who kept me *au fait* to the proceedings of the dear little town" (12). And a letter from "a cousin of" Matty's "who had been twenty or thirty years in India" precedes his arrival in Cranford (27).

Letters also connect the family members of Cranford. One of the father's sermons, for instance, inspires a letter from his wife "on occasion of the publication of the same Sermon" (*CR,* 45). (Such private expressions, by the way, sometimes find embodiment in more permanent forms, like the "Ode" addressed to the rector's wife that "appeared in the 'Gentleman's Magazine'" [45].) The letters kept and reviewed by Miss Matty and Mary Smith constitute a cumulative record of family events. Matty's burning "yellow bundles of love-letters, sixty or seventy years old" (42) seems a destruction of living history, as is also the case when Peter, in Burma, receives his own letters "returned from England with the ominous word 'Dead' marked upon them" (152).

Letters certainly chronicle the greatest family tragedy, the loss of Peter; but within that body of writing readers must pay attention to the instances where feeling breaks through form. Peter's "show–letters" written from school to his father (*CR,* 48), for instance, reveal both a public and a private identity: "Now and then, the animal nature broke out in such a little sentence as this, written in a trembling hurry, after the letter had been inspected: 'Mother, dear, do send me a cake, and put plenty of citron in'" (49). The form can even represent a sham, as when Peter makes copies of "all those twelve Bonaparte sermons" written by his father for "a lady" (51), who is actually Peter himself dressed up in one of his practical jokes. These documents mock the material of the father's life. Later letters between him and his parents after he leaves

England, however, reveal their true feelings; and these important records are kept by Matty. She tells Mary, "Stay! those letters will be somewhere here" (56).

Larger print documents like books sometimes function as letters. When Holbrook takes his fateful journey to Paris, he leaves Matty a book, a record of his affection: "The book he gave her lies with her Bible on the little table by her bedside" (*CR,* 39). This document inspiring Matty is similar to the "handsomest bound and best edition of Dr. Johnson's works" that the younger Jenkyns sister later gives Mary in her and Deborah's names (153). And both left documents resemble a "picture . . . of the Virgin and the little Savior" (109) given by an Indian mother to Mrs. Brunoni/Brown for inspiration as she flees that harsh country, which has taken all her children but Phoebe.

Successful written documents, then, connect characters along meaningful lines, sometimes breaking with conventional Victorian middle-class forms. The print given Mrs. Brown is of Mary, a woman who conceived a child out of wedlock; and Christ represents the illegitimate child whose body is valued in Gaskell's work, though often cast out of proper Victorian society. The odd, brief story of the conjuror's wife in India anchors within the narrative of *Cranford* the theme of illegitimacy occupying Elizabeth Gaskell so intensely at this time of her life; and it produces the letter left by a woman (Mary Smith), perhaps fallen, to recover an exiled, if not illegitimate, child (Peter Jenkyns).

In telling Mary about her struggle, Mrs. Brown inadvertently reveals the presence in India of one Aga Jenkyns, the condemned and exiled son. In carrying forward the plot of the prodigal son, this portion of Gaskell's text is a link to the stories of Lizzie Leigh and Ruth,[27] as well as a key statement about Elizabeth Gaskell's own art.

In fact, the earlier story of Peter's flight from home itself contains some of the central elements of the fallen woman's story, though Gaskell blurs traditional gender lines in telling it.[28] Peter's original offense was to challenge his father's strict notion of masculine and feminine roles. Peter is described twice "dressing himself up as a lady" (*CR,* 51). The second time he walks back and forth in his father's garden disguised as his sister, Deborah, but holding a pillow shaped, as Matty explains, "into—into— a little baby, with white long clothes" (52). Peter constructs, that is, the fallen woman, an image so shameful Matty tells Mary years later, "You are sure you locked the door, my dear, for I should not like any one to hear" (52).

Peter's violation of decorum infuriates his father, who "tore his clothes off his back—bonnet, shawl, gown, and all—and threw the pillow among the people over the railings; and then he was very, very angry indeed; and before all the people he lifted up his cane, and flogged Peter!" (*CR*, 52–53). In the graphic image of the flung pillow, Gaskell deftly suggests the harm visited upon the illegitimate child by proper Victorian society.[29] Peter, both fallen woman and disgraced son, then, does what Ruth tried to do: drop out of the system. He goes overseas, eventually to India and beyond. He exists only in a gap of Victorian life, as Matty says: "When I sit by myself, and all the house is still, I think I hear his step coming up the street, and my heart begins to flutter and beat; but the sound always goes past—and Peter never comes" (59).

The narrator Mary Smith's motives for writing to the Aga Jenkyns Mrs. Brown referred to seem obvious enough: she wants to restore Miss Matty's brother to her, should he have survived after all; and Peter's return would remedy his sister's financial situation after the fall of Town and County Bank. But Mary seems interested in Peter's story for other reasons as well, hinting at troubling events in her own past. In looking at a letter to Peter returned unopened, Mary feels a special kinship with the mother, someone who lost a child, a child who, though not illegitimate, endures exile from his society: "The writer of the letter [Peter's mother]—the last—the only person who had ever seen what was written in it, was dead long ago—and I, a stranger, not born at the time when this occurrence took place, was the one to open it" (*CR*, 56). There are, in fact, elements in Mary's life and personality that link her to this woman and to the figure of the fallen woman.[30]

Like Ruth, Mary seeks to escape the rigid formulas of Victorian morality. Both want to get to the basis of life, the matter that matters beneath clothes, language, and money. Although she values letters, Mary also recognizes that "correspondence . . . bears much the same relation to personal intercourse that the books of dried plants I sometimes see ('Hortus Siccus,' I think they call the thing,) do to the living and fresh flowers in the lanes and meadows" (*CR*, 23). Drumble does not seem to offer her "living and fresh flowers" or "personal intercourse." She seeks vital connections within the human community, and Cranford's ladies appeal to her because their odd conventions enable love. Her last words about that place are, "We all love Miss Matty, and I somehow think we are all of us better when she is near us" (160).

The same principle of seeking the meaning within or beneath form is revealed when Mary explains how most people have habits of saving (for her it is string; for Miss Matty, candles): "An old gentleman of my acquaintance, who took the intelligence of the failure of a Joint-Stock Bank, in which some of his money was invested, with stoical mildness, worried his family all through a long summer's day, because one of them had torn (instead of cutting) out the written leaves of his now useless bankbook; of course, the corresponding pages at the other end came out as well; and this little unnecessary waste of paper (his private economy) chafed him more than all the loss of his money" (*CR*, 40). Mary is drawn to this anecdote because, like her friends in Cranford, she understands the distance of money from absolute value, as well as the need to save what can be personally useful.[31]

Mary is also a person who fears public scrutiny, perhaps because she has suffered misinterpretation by those who endorse absolute moral standards. Generally reluctant to talk about herself in describing the life of Cranford, she apologizes when she must explain an absence from the village (her father in Drumble wants her home): "I must say a word or two here about myself" (*CR*, 117). During the great Cranford panic, when people are all admitting their worst private fears, she confesses that "my pet apprehension was eyes—eyes looking at me, and watching me, glittering out from some dull flat wooden surface; and that if I dared to go up to my looking-glass when I was panic-stricken, I should certainly turn it round, with its back towards me, for fear of seeing eyes behind me looking out of the darkness" (98). This fear might be linked to what she admits, somewhat tongue-in-cheek, is a habit of indiscretion: "In my own home, whenever people had nothing else to do, they blamed me for want of discretion. Indiscretion was my bugbear fault. Everybody has a bugbear fault; a sort of standing characteristic—a *pièce de résistance* for their friends to cut at; and in general they cut and come again. I was tired of being called indiscreet and incautious; and I determined for once to prove myself a model of prudence and wisdom" (111). Mary seeks to prove herself "prudent" in writing to Aga Jenkyns, who is also guilty of indiscretion as a youth and even later: "With the odd vehemence which characterised him in age as it had done in youth, he had sold his land [in Asia] and all his possessions to the first purchaser, and come home to the poor old sister, who was more glad and rich than any princess when she looked at him" (152).[32]

Indiscretion and resistance to public judgment, of course, do not prove Mary a fallen woman, sneaking away from shame in Drumble to a little village where she can reclaim a lost innocence. Eileen Gillooly convincingly sees Mary's eyes in the mirror as evidence of "an other" repressed by Victorian patriarchy and the older women of Cranford who treat her as a child. Thus she is driven by aggression, "provoked by the conflict between self-denial and desire, between the internalized cultural demand to submit oneself to the role of daughter and a psychological resistance to that demand."[33] But Mary's feelings of guilt at writing also constitute one more strand linking her to Peter's suffering mother, as well as to Lizzie Leigh and Ruth Hilton.

The sudden collapse of Miss Matty's finances causes Mary to "compose a letter to the Aga Jenkyns" (*CR*, 127), an act she had contemplated earlier; but she does so now "treacherously," as if betraying some code or taking an action for which she has been denied authority. And she feels guilty having written: "I began to be very much ashamed of remembering my letter to the Aga Jenkyns, and very glad I had never named my writing to any one. I only hoped the letter was lost" (146).

Fallen women have no rights, of course: Lizzie Leigh may leave money for her child, but it will not be used; and Ruth finds the back of the note written by Mrs. Bellingham blank where she had hoped it would validate her relationship with that woman's son. So Mary's authorship of a document asserting the value of family seems to exceed the rights extended to her by others, taking her into unfamiliar ("queer") territory:

(*CR*, 128)   *At last I got the address, spelt by sound; and very queer it looked! I dropped it in the post on my way home; and then for a minute I stood looking at the wooden pane, with a gaping slit, which divided me from the letter, but a moment ago in my hand. It was gone from me like life—never to be recalled. It would get tossed about on the sea, and stained with sea-waves perhaps; and be carried among palm-trees, and*

*scented with all tropical fragrance;— the little piece of paper, but an
hour ago so familiar and commonplace, had set out on its race to the
strange wild countries beyond the Ganges!*

Even more emphatically denied to the fallen woman than money and
status is the right to produce the offspring she necessarily must bear.
More valuable than any document, the body of that illegitimate child is
often doomed to separation from parents ("never to be recalled"),
thrown into a difficult world ("tossed about on the sea"), tainted from
birth onward ("stained with sea-waves"), perhaps most likely to survive
when farthest from home ("strange wild countries beyond the
Ganges").[34]

Yet this left document produces exactly the desired result, not just
for Matty and Peter, but also for Mary. When Peter magically appears in
Cranford, he acknowledges the author of the letter that, in a sense, created him: "Is your name Mary Smith?" (*CR*, 150), he asks. In responding
"Yes!" Mary escapes the shame she felt in writing. While she asserts that
"her doubts as to his identity were set at rest" (150), this exchange validates her own stature as well.

Elizabeth Gaskell released her works to the public with a mixture of
delight and shame shared by the fallen women of her own imagination.
She wrote, for instance, on 7 April 1853: "My books are so far better than
I am that I often feel ashamed of having written them and as if I were a
hypocrite" (*LMG*, 228). However, *Cranford* caused her less guilt than
other things she had written and would write: "I am so pleased you [John
Ruskin] like it. It is the only one of my own books that I can read again;
—but whenever I am ailing or ill, I take 'Cranford' and—I was going to
say, *enjoy* it! (but that would not be pretty!) laugh over it afresh!" (747;
[late February?] 1865). The unplanned composition of the novel seems
to have resulted in an open form that has pleased all its readers.[35]

Her narrator admitted that her stay in that little village was always
being extended: "I thought that probably my connection with Cranford
would cease after Miss Jenkyns's death" (*CR*, 23). Similarly, Gaskell had
not intended a full-length novel when she started this work: "The beginning of 'Cranford' was *one* paper in 'Household Words'; and I never
meant to write more, so killed Capt Brown very much against my will"
(*LMG*, 747–48 [late February?] 1865). The appeal of this unique village,

however, where a guilty woman's writing might still restore a family, drew her on to complete eight more installments.[36] And the work's unique form was appreciated: Henry Fothergill Chorley in the *Athenaeum* (25 June 1853) observed: "Possibly, it was commenced by accident, rather than on any settled plan; but if this was the case, the author early became alive to the happy thought pervading it;—since she has wrought it out just enough and not too much—so as to produce a picture of manners, motives and feelings which is perfect" (*CH,* 194). The *Examiner* (23 July 1853) recognized that Gaskell's tale had no obvious antecedent: "Not a single person in it is thought worth a page of the regular drawing and colouring which is the novelist's stock in trade" (*CH,* 196). Some years later John Ruskin would write to Gaskell (21 February 1865) about the work's open-ended form: "I can't think why you left it off! You might have killed Miss Matty, as you're fond of killing nice people [like Captain Brown], and then gone on with Jessie's children, or made yourself an old lady—in time—it would have been lovely" (*CH,* 199).

    Cranford embodied the subjects haunting Elizabeth Gaskell in the most just framework she could imagine at this time in her career. Like the buildings of the "assize-town in one of the eastern counties" (*R,* 1) where Ruth first worked as a dressmaker, however, Gaskell's narrative involved the overlay of new structures on older ones: "Lizzie Leigh" retold in *Ruth* continued in *Cranford.* Thus, as liberating as the form of this spontaneous series of tales in a weekly magazine was for author and readers, its base remained traditional narrative structures in established publication formats.

    Troubled women gained more control of the documents shaping their identities in these three works, from Lizzie's useless money, through Ruth's idealized back of Mrs. Bellingham's note, to Mary's unauthorized query for Peter Jenkyns. Just as this "queer" letter worked the miracle of Peter's return, so Gaskell's novel represents effective cultural work taking Victorian readers away from familiar frameworks of middle-class life. But Gaskell's characters and her audience could never completely escape the material artifacts of Victorian life except in death. Clothes, money, and documents were too much extensions of the patriarchal structures to completely recast the experience of fallen women.

    Charlotte Brontë, who lived at a greater distance herself from all such frameworks, asked her friend on 22 May 1852: "Do you—who have so many friends, so large a circle of acquaintance—find it easy, when you sit down to write—to isolate yourself from all those ties and their sweet associations—as to be quite *your own woman?*" (*CH,* 193). As Elizabeth Gaskell tried to leave behind outworn literary modes to create a new form for fiction, she arrived at the distinctive and enduring story of *Cranford,* a narrative she could very nearly "enjoy" throughout her life. In the serialization of her next major work, however, she came to understand more fully how the existing publication structures frustrated her self-expression.

IV

Textual/Sexual Pleasure
and Serial Publication:
North and South

Two traditional accounts of composition and response—a Dickens success story and an (apparent) Gaskell failure—have been cited for decades to illustrate the properties of serial fiction. The skyrocketing sales of Charles Dickens's *Pickwick Papers* after the fifth monthly number in July 1836 (from four hundred copies to forty thousand) have traditionally represented the achievement of genius, as the author's narrative captured the first genuine mass audience for literature. The pattern of this development, from slow start to later explosion, has dominated our understanding of this particular text and of literary history in the nineteenth century.

Elizabeth Gaskell later serialized *North and South* in Dickens's weekly *Household Words* (2 September 1854 to 27 January 1855). In Dickens's view this work slowed sales of the journal and necessitated frequent editorial change. According to most scholars, Gaskell failed to understand the demands of parts publication and was repeatedly unable to provide the proper climactic ending for each weekly installment, often running over her allotted space with a rambling narrative in manuscript. Angus Easson, for instance, has written: "Though [Dickens] handled Gaskell diplomatically, her apparent lack of response [to calls for condensation], plus declining sales during publication, cannot have helped Dickens's temper." [1]

However, from the beginning Elizabeth Gaskell disagreed with Dickens about what constituted proper and effective structure for individual installments. Just as her style in opening the installments of *Wives and Daughters* differed from those of other writers in the *Cornhill* like

Thackeray, Trollope, and Collins (see chapter 1), so her conception of the nature of a single part and the relationship of successive parts departed from a standard that Dickens had established. The ensuing battle between author and editor about magazine policy involved different narrative aims and rival assumptions about readers' pleasure.

Whereas Dickens wanted each part to be self-contained—with a clear climax and resolution—Gaskell wanted a more leisurely pace for the development of plot and the entanglement of her audience. Indeed, what she was attempting in the whole of *North and South* casts the conventional paradigm of the serial's appeal in a different light. And the sustained attraction of any long novel issued in parts—what kept readers coming back to *Pickwick* through the remaining fourteen months of its publication after the explosive July installment, for instance—is a major topic that has been insufficiently explored by literary scholars.

The sources for prolonged reading pleasure found in Gaskell's fiction suggest a dynamics not traditionally linked to the serial form. Norman Feltes in *Modes of Production of Victorian Novels* has reinterpreted the "moment of Pickwick" from a Marxist perspective, finding significant elements of its success in the nature of changing publication modes and audience desire, not simply in the author's genius. We suggest here that interpretations of Dickens's achievement and Gaskell's "failure" have been shaped by issues of gender. Traditional, masculinist concepts of plot have even determined critical understanding of serial form itself, neglecting other important aspects of literary experience found in Elizabeth Gaskell's work.

North and South was not the first serial fiction Gaskell published under Dickens's editorship. "Lizzie Leigh," as we explained in chapter 3, was serialized in three parts in *Household Words,* opening the inaugural number of the magazine on 30 March 1850. Each part of "Lizzie Leigh" was certainly self-contained. The story's subtitle is "In Four Chapters," and the first and second parts "contained" one chapter each. The end of the first part, moreover, ended on a distinct note of suspense. Anne Leigh, whose husband James dies at the beginning of the part, rents out the farm and moves to Manchester with her two sons to look for their "fallen" sister Lizzie; Will, the eldest, has fallen in love with Susan Palmer and feels inhibited in his courtship by his mother's quest to reclaim Lizzie. The part ends with him poised to encounter his mother: "When Tom had left the room he prepared to speak" (LL, 11). But if the part ends on a note of suspense, it looks forward not to an event or action, but to a conversation, a relationship, between a mother and her son.

It is easy to see why this part construction might satisfy both the editor Dickens and the author Gaskell. The ending of the second part is not skewed toward suspense, since the ending of this part coincides with the end of a revelatory conversation between Mrs. Leigh and Susan Palmer, during which Mrs. Leigh learns that Susan's "niece" is Lizzie's child. Yet because Mrs. Leigh has yet to encounter her daughter, the part also looks forward to a final part, and a final meeting, suggested by the story's title. In this short serial, then, Gaskell maintained a balance between "connectedness" and suspense, self-containment and anticipation, as forms of narrative pleasure; and Dickens was pleased enough to solicit more work from her for his periodical.

As Margaret Homans observes, "Lizzie Leigh" was the first story Gaskell ever wrote, though publication was delayed for over a decade. When it appeared without attribution in *Household Words,* many inferred that the story was Dickens's own, given its prominent place in the first number. And the story was first published in the United States under Dickens's name. Partly as a result of arbitrary circumstance, then, this story suggests that Gaskell's fiction could fulfill conventional expectations about serial form well enough to be taken for work by the age's acknowledged master of the installment format.[2]

The successful serialization of *Cranford* in *Household Words* owed much to its special character as a series of related tales and to the fact that, as Winifred Gérin writes, Gaskell was able to write for once "under no professional or personal pressures."[3] Dickens's major concern was to secure additional parts for *Household Words.* Were it not for the novel's rich, quiet humor and engaging characters, the editor's delight with it might be surprising, for this work is an unusually clear instance of plot emerging in patterns contrary to traditional concepts.

The first four installments presented assorted vignettes of life in Cranford but neglected a sustained "rising action"; rather than a forward-driving plot, the four parts appearing from 13 December 1851 to 3 April 1852 invited renewed and deepening acquaintance with a community. There followed a nine-month hiatus in *Cranford's* publication;[4] when it resumed in the 8 and 15 January 1853 issues of *Household Words,* the fifth

part quickened with an advancing plot and concluded on a note of suspense as the still-unnamed narrator wondered if Aga Jenkyns could be
Matty Jenkyns's lost brother Peter. Thereafter *Cranford* became in large
part Matty's story, with a clearly advancing plot, until the work concluded in the 21 May 1853 issue. Yet even here, as readers later discovered, *Cranford* had not reached a definitive climax that cut off the text
from author and audience, for a separate sketch titled "The Cage at
Cranford" appeared in the November 1863 *All the Year Round*. In 1853
and 1854, meanwhile, *Cranford* pleased Gaskell, Dickens, and the readers
of *Household Words*. Some parts of *Cranford* manifested the suspense and
rising action traditionally associated with Dickens's own parts structure;
but in other respects the novel's larger plot, serial issue, and structure
suggest a different model.

  In fact, the serial novel's intrinsic form more closely approximates
female than male models of pleasure, even though it has been best known
as a medium for male authors. Susan Winnett argues that male sexual
experience has provided the pattern for contemporary critical models of
pleasure in reading. Many narrative plots do rise in tension, peak, and
return to equilibrium. Winnett notes, however, that such a definition of
plot structure encourages the interpretation of "a particular action in the
light of what it *will have meant* at a future moment that it is simultaneously
determining and resisting."[5] Furthermore, other, generally unexplored
aspects of plot involve excitement that does not end in quiescence, arous-
als that look forward as beginnings and are not dependent on later endings or resolutions. Winnett explains that, in contrast to male sexuality, experiences of tumescence and detumescence associated with female
sexuality—pregnancy and breast feeding—are ultimately oriented not
toward reestablishing the state of quiescence that preceded arousal but
toward inaugurating and sustaining new beginnings and connections.
Moreover, the rhythm of female tumescence-detumescence is not subject to willed intentions but is partly controlled by forces and an individual (the nursing child) outside the mother. Winnett concludes that
new models of plot and pleasure need to be constructed: "I want to explore the different narrative logic—and the very different possibilities of
pleasure—that emerge when issues such as incipience, repetition, and
closure are reconceived in terms of *an* experience (not *the* experience) of
a female body."[6]

Rather than inviting sustained arousal of attention until the narrative climax is reached, spending the driving energy of narrative, and sundering readers from textual experience, the installment novel offers itself as a site of pleasure that is taken up and discharged only to be taken up again (some days or weeks later), and again, and again. Moreover, the engagement and discharge of pleasure in each installment is always oriented toward the future, toward new beginnings and sustained connections with the text, since an installment ends but the narrative continues ("to be continued") until the novel's serial run concludes. Finally, this rhythm of textual pleasure is not entirely controlled by serial readers; no matter how much they might want to sustain interest and pleasure in the text, they must wait until the next installment appears.

Elizabeth Gaskell considered the appeal of retrospectives—the view from a known point of closure—in "The Poor Clare" (1856), a story also published in Dickens's *Household Words* near the time of *North and South* and one for which she chose a masculine narrator. This three-chapter story is told, on 12 December 1747, at the end of a long life "bound up with extraordinary incidents" (PC, 271). The narrator suggests that, for him, events often have greatest value when seen in retrospect: "I suppose most old men are, like me, more given to looking back upon their own career with a kind of fond interest and affectionate remembrance, than to watching the events—though these may have far more interest for the multitude—immediately passing before their eyes. If this should be the case with the generality of old people, how much more so with me!" (271). Although this story may well have been inspired by Gaskell's friendship with Charlotte Brontë and her visits to the bleak landscape around Haworth, it is also a study of disturbed states of mind, especially obsession with the past. And its structure shows Gaskell's experimentation with conventional narrative form.

In "The Poor Clare" an interest in putting the past in order relative to the present is passed on to the narrator by the "London uncle" who becomes his benefactor: "All the books [in his library] treated of things that were past; none of them planned or looked forward into the future" (PC, 286). And the legal trade that the nephew learns from his uncle is similarly backward looking: "Many cases of disputed property, dependent on a love of genealogy, were brought to him, as to a great authority on such points" (285). Although the specific trials the apprentice faces (his beloved is haunted by an evil double) clearly affect his health, the mental attitude necessary to the profession he has adopted also leads to instability:

> *I have seen a child on a common blown along by a high wind,*
> *without power of standing still and resisting the tempestuous force.*
> *I was somewhat in the same predicament as regarded my men-*
> *tal state. Something resistless seemed to urge my thoughts on,*
> *through every possible course by which there was a chance of at-*
> *taining to my object [solving the case assigned him by his uncle].*   (293)
> *I did not see the sweeping moors when I walked out: when I held*
> *a book in my hand, and read the words, their sense did not pene-*
> *trate to my brain. If I slept, I went on with the same ideas, al-*
> *ways flowing in the same direction.*

For months he fears falling into the "old channel of thought" (294) created by genealogical research. And the apparent cure for his condition is to live in the present and for the future: "I had an illness, which, although I was racked with pain, was a positive relief to me, as it compelled me to live in the present suffering, and not in the visionary researches I had been continually making before" (293).

A different but not contradictory perspective—looking into the future toward a specific, fixed end—is represented by Bridget Fitzgerald in her cursing of Squire Gisborne: "You shall live to see the creature you love best, and who alone loves you—aye, a human creature, but as innocent and fond as my poor, dead darling—you shall see this creature, for whom death would be too happy, become a terror and a loathing to all, for this blood's sake" (PC, 283). To the superstitious eighteenth-century minds of the story's characters, this effective curse arranges events along a determined path into the future as much as a genealogist's research codifies the past. And the woman assumed by many to be a witch, whose "former self must be buried,—yea, buried quick, if need be" (323), according to her confessor, is a counterpart to the narrator. Ironically, of course, this curse dooms not just Gisborne but Bridget's own granddaughter; and the narrator's mirror obsession nearly costs him happiness with Lucy as, rather than build a life with her, he awaits the answer to questions of family history.

Another figure concerned with shaping events in time is the Catholic Father Bernard, "chaplain to the Sherburnes at Stoney Hurst" (PC,

321) and later returned to "duties in Antwerp" (322). A man who receives the penitent's confession of past actions and prescribes for the future, he can offer the unusual case of Bridget Fitzgerald only retreat from humankind, sisterhood among the "Poor Clares" of Antwerp. Bridget's service to the poor, even to her enemy Gisborne, allows her to claim "She is freed from the curse!" (333) in the last sentence of the story, but the cost is her own death. This conclusion reverberates back through the story to suggest that the double had been conquered and that Lucy and the narrator had in the end been able to marry. (He writes on first seeing her, "I am not sure if [her face] was beautiful, though in after-life I grew to think it so" [294].) But the priest's ministrations brought little relief to Bridget's sufferings in this life. Similarly, when the narrator declares, "I had no doubt but that we should prove Lucy to be by right possessed of large estates in Ireland" (308) he misses the point that assigning her a specific place in a historical scheme will not eliminate her double.

The narrator's primary story concerns this young woman he calls "poor Lucy": "I myself only came to the knowledge of her family history after I knew her; but to make the tale clear to any one else, I must arrange events in the order in which they occurred—not that in which I became acquainted with them" (PC, 271). This principle is not adhered to completely, however. Whereas the story's first chapter chronicles the separation of Bridget Fitzgerald from her daughter Mary, the middle chapter recounts the narrator's life and his search for "any descendants of the younger branch of a family to whom some valuable estates had descended in the female line" (286) and his falling in love with Lucy. The third and final chapter connects the two story lines by filling in the middle years of Mary's marriage and Lucy's flight from the double. It concludes with Bridget's penitence as a Poor Clare and the final cancellation of the curse.

The story's structure, then, buries the traditional romantic conclusion—the union of narrator with Lucy—and highlights instead Bridget's release from her suffering. Itself set a century before publication in the 1856 extra Christmas issue of *Household Words,* "The Poor Clare" allowed Gaskell's readers the privilege of historical hindsight, which discounted both witchcraft and such Catholic practices as the exorcism involved in Lucy's rescue. But the circular structure of the tale—its end casts us back into the middle—undermines the belief that history itself can be known and thus controlled. The narrator's apparently happy

married life with Lucy is lost in his own narrative, though he seems satisfied to have solved the key questions of genealogy.

In "The Poor Clare," then, Elizabeth Gaskell unsettles several conventional narrative strategies. Her masculine narrator asserts that stories
should be told from the point of conclusion and all events shown to lead
to that final point. Yet the form he chooses to embody his life's own
narrative exhibits a circular rather than a linear structure. And the moral
of the tale seems to be that life's events do not easily fit into strict chrono-
logical and causal sequences, since all such efforts to impose order—his
uncle's, Bridget's, Father Bernard's, and his own—are shown to be questionable at best.

Gaskell's more famous novel, *North and South,* also conformed to a
linear structure established by its installment mode of publication; yet her
story often seemed to resist a steady forward movement. The serial form
itself has traditionally been viewed as artistically inferior because it frac-
tures or impedes unified plots driving toward endings that confer meaning on entire novels, as well as being an expression of capitalist practices
that appropriate storytelling and intimate audience relations to mask ra-
tionalized production of text and the creation of additional demand for
the product.[7] We suggest that the serial form can be reconceptualized if
it is seen in relation to feminine issues, especially the material and cultural
conditions of Victorian women readers, and to feminist theoretical paradigms. And we revisit the question of the installment issue of *North and
South* under Dickens's editorship to see if Gaskell's unwillingness to shape
her story to the space allotted in *Household Words* derived at least in part
from the dictates of her own vision of artistic work.

Although financial control of serial publication generally rested with
Victorian men, the prevalence of women as readers and writers of fiction
played a significant role in the serial's popularity in Gaskell's time.[8] In this
sense the Victorian serial can be said to have "had it all," since it did not
subvert dominant economic structures or aesthetic paradigms but nonetheless offered pleasure to women readers. This could be so for serials
written by male and female writers alike, but it will be instructive to look
at the principal unit of the serial—the part—to see how major writers'
conceptions of part structure differed along gender lines.

Although women were a major presence among novelists in the first
third of the century, and though some prominent women (such as Harriet

Martineau in her *Autobiography*) emphatically rejected serialization as a suitable medium for fiction, women's entry into the literary market as mass readers and popular writers and the emergence of serial fiction as a dominant publication mode in the nineteenth century can be seen as related phenomena.[9] So great was the association of novels with female authorship that, as Gaye Tuchman and Nina Fortin discovered in examining the Macmillan publishing archives, "in the 1860s and 1870s men submitting fiction were more likely to assume a female name than women were to use either a male or neuter name." [10] And male serial authors regularly inscribed the expectation of female readership even when subject matter might seem to dictate male readership. Thus Edward Howard paused in the midst of his largely nautical *Life of a Sub-editor,* serialized in *Metropolitan Magazine* from 1834 to 1836, to explain the finer points of naval rigging: "My lady readers must understand that the truck is that round thing at the top of all the masts, that looks so like a button." [11] Women readers and writers dominated the fiction market when serial publication flourished, then, and cultural conditions as well as models of female pleasure on the lines Winnett suggests could have fostered women's pleasure in the serial form.

Victorian and twentieth-century commentators have often noted the sense of intimacy and connection that serial publication created between audience and text or audience and author. This result of serial publication, besides helping to perpetuate Victorian domestic ideology, could have worked to extend female readers' associations of pleasure with renewed and sustained relationships as they met and came to know characters in part after part over as much as two years. Elizabeth Gaskell's letter to an aspiring woman novelist with young children is usually cited to illustrate women's enforced subordination of personal achievement to domestic responsibility. Yet her remarks also suggest that she perceived her relation to fictional characters much as she did her relation to her family: "When I had *little* children I do not think I could have written stories, because I should have become too much absorbed in my *fictitious* people to attend to my *real* ones" (*LMG,* 694–95; September 25 [1862?]). For female readers the extended time of serial publication could have deepened their own sense of relationship to fictional characters and their fortunes. And at least one serial female novelist has recorded that her own close relationship to the audience affected her production of text. Mary

Elizabeth Braddon revamped the ending of her adaptation of Flaubert's *Madame Bovary* (itself a serialized novel in its original publication) because while writing she found herself "so apt to be influenced by little scraps of newspaper criticism, & by what people say to me."[12]

The intimacy between text and audience encouraged by serial publication could have suited women readers. Recently Mary Field Belenky and others have argued that women respond best to what the authors term "connected knowing," learning in which women develop a relationship to what they study and integrate material with their lived experience to construct personally empowering knowledge. Belenky and her coauthors do not suggest that men are excluded or fail to profit from this kind of learning process, only that women resist being forced into other learning modes (e.g., those requiring them to consider material as separate and autonomous, subject to impersonal procedures). Serial publication fostered a similarly "connected" relation of readers to fiction, since, as we argue elsewhere, "readers and reviewers engaged in provisional assumptions and interpretations about the literary world, which then shaped the evolving understanding of works as they continued to unfold part by part. And a work's extended duration meant that serials could become entwined with readers' own sense of lived experience and passing time."[13] Because authoritative pronouncements were not available on a work of fiction in process, moreover, serial fiction offered women—even within the confines of dominant male social structures—a space in which to explore and discover their own reactions to a literary work.

The material format of the serial was also adapted to the material conditions of middle-class female readers. Although the issuing of fiction in parts has sometimes been related to increasing pressures on time and leisure in the male-dominated commercial world of Victorian society, female lives were also defined by their vulnerability to interruption. In *Cassandra*, Florence Nightingale has given perhaps the most famous statement of this condition:

> *Women are never supposed to have any occupation of sufficient importance not to be interrupted, except "suckling their fools"; and women themselves have accepted this, have written books to support it, and have trained themselves so as to consider whatever they do as not of such value to the world or to others, but that they can throw it up at the*

first "claim of social life." They have accustomed themselves to consider intellectual occupation as a merely selfish amusement, which it is their "duty" to give up for every trifler more selfish than themselves.[14]

If this condition held for the single, upper-middle-class Nightingale, then married women and mothers of small children, even with the help of servants, could hardly have immersed themselves all day long in a novel.

Conduct books nonetheless encouraged women to maintain reading programs. Isabella Beeton urged that the "mistress of the house" save time late in the morning for, among other things, "the pleasures of literature." Regarding domestic evenings, Beeton stated, "It has often been remarked . . . that nothing is more delightful to the feminine members of a family, than the reading aloud of some good standard work or amusing publication."[15] Most accounts of serial fiction (especially the work of Dickens) being read aloud have featured a paterfamilias giving voice to characters and events. We should consider, however, what difference it makes to our understanding of Victorian fiction and culture if we envision a woman reading aloud instead—especially since reading aloud was a frequent duty for female household members.

The periodicity of the serial narrative could also have functioned to align such literary work with women while not excluding or marginalizing male readers. The scheduled release of literary parts consorted not only with mechanized production but also with ideologies of women founded in biological periodicity, or menses. As Edward H. Clarke, a nineteenth-century American physician at Harvard, remarked, "Periodicity characterizes the female organization, and develops feminine force. Persistence characterizes the male organization, and develops masculine force."[16] Dr. Clarke's pronouncement is notorious because he went on to argue that women's periodicity, rather than persistence, meant that women were unsuited either for intensive study associated with higher education or for sustained professional work outside the home. Both Elaine and English Showalter and Elizabeth Helsinger, Robin Sheets, and William Veeder record contemporary refutations of this strand of Clarke's argument. Yet the works they cite also assert the periodicity of feminine physiology (though noting that such biological functions did not preclude persistence of intellectual or physical energies). When Dr. Henry Maudsley joined the debate, he used "periodical functions" as a euphemism for menses—a resonant phrase since "periodical" is a familiar term in Victorian studies. Curiously, Martineau asserted that she experienced a "fluctuation . . . as regular as the tides" in the composition of each monthly number of her political economy series.[17]

The serial novel, which incorporated periodicity (as well as persistence), may have been an ideal mass-market strategy not only because it was attuned to capitalism but also because it presented structures attuned to female experience in an age when women were major consumers of literature. Of course novels appeared in weekly, biweekly, and bimonthly installments as well as in monthly parts, but the cyclic periodicity that typifies serial fiction differs significantly from the model of the whole volume and should remind us that periodicity suppressed in critical discourse has an analogue in the biological periodicity that was an important part of every Victorian woman's life—an experience outside the confines of accepted social or literary discourse in the Victorian age.[18]

Serial fiction did not serve, and most likely could not have served, as a medium for what today is called *écriture féminine,* but the form did, in certain instances, allow women authors to inscribe the female body in the silent spaces between numbers that answered to the silencing of female experience in the larger culture. In *Daniel Deronda* George Eliot (who practiced some form of birth control while living in extralegal union with George Lewes)[19] raised the possibility of unwanted pregnancy for Gwendolen after Grandcourt's death in the novel's book 7, published in August 1876. Serial readers had to wait a full month, until book 8 was published in September, to learn this crucial element of Gwendolen's fate. For women readers this month-long interval could have gestured toward bodily functions signaling pregnancy or menses so familiar as not to require verbal articulation.

Although not as strikingly as in *Daniel Deronda,* Elizabeth Gaskell also made use of the interval between parts to indicate female bodily change and the introduction of physiological cycles. Between the first and second parts of *Wives and Daughters* (published from August 1864 to January 1866 in the monthly *Cornhill Magazine*), Molly Gibson underwent puberty. A young girl of twelve in the first part (August 1864), in the second installment Molly was a postpubescent young woman of seventeen who attracted sexual attention (September 1864). Gaskell used the space between parts to indicate a change that may be said always to occur offstage, but one that is dramatic and certain nonetheless. By calling attention to this physical change in a young girl's body at the same time she omitted to narrate it, Gaskell perhaps exemplified Elaine Showalter's point that a female subculture emerged from a whole array of physical experiences "increasingly secretive and ritualized" that was shared but could not be openly articulated.[20] The inherent periodicity and silent spaces between parts that characterized serial fiction could have enabled women writers and readers to indicate and recognize such female bodily experiences.

Although the serial may not be a form of *écriture féminine,* many of the distinctive features of serial fiction are analogous to or even homologous with models of feminine narrative developed by a number of theorists and critics. As Hélène Cixous remarks in "Sorties," if a woman "is a whole, it is a whole made up of parts that are wholes, not simple, partial objects but varied entirety, moving and boundless change, a cosmos where eros never stops traveling"; similarly, a woman's "writing also can only go on and on, without ever inscribing or distinguishing contours . . . she goes and goes on infinitely." Estelle Jelinek has advanced a comparable argument about the structuring of feminine, as opposed to masculine, autobiographies. Feminine autobiographies, she proposes, tend to be irregular and fragmentary, "organized into self-sustained units rather than connecting chapters," thus mirroring the "pattern of diffusion and diversity" in women's social (and socially constructed) lives.[21]

A serial novel is itself a whole made up of parts that at once function as self-contained units and as building blocks of a larger aesthetic structure. Although the serial eventually ends and takes its place within the literary establishment as an entire, completed work awaiting interpretation and judgment, the long middle of a serial form approximates in significant terms the patterns identified by Cixous and Jelinek. Indeed, as Margaret Beetham remarks of the periodical genre as a whole, " 'Closed' or 'masculine' forms are seen as those which assert the dominant structures of meaning, by closing off alternative options and offering the reader or viewer only one way of making sense of the text and so, by analogy, of the world and the self. By contrast the 'open' form, the form which refuses the closed ending and allows for the possibility of alternative meanings, is associated with the potentially disruptive, the creative, the 'feminine.' " She terms the periodical "a potentially creative form for its readers," though noting as well that the regular issue and format in the periodical implicitly position readers in social groups and at given vantage points.[22]

Many patriarchal terms used to describe the female rather than the male body have been applied to the serial novel as well. As Rachel Du Plessis and others remark, masculine terms are often those used to describe "good writing" ("lean, dry, terse, powerful, strong, spare, linear, focused, explosive") versus the feminine terms often associated with "bad writing" ("soft, moist, blurred, padded, irregular, going around in circles"). The serial has often been censured for padding, digression, and irregularity, all evoked in Henry James's famous term for Victorian novels, "baggy monsters." It is precisely the bag, however, that Ursula Le Guin advances as a preferred, feminist model of narrative in her "Carrier Bag Theory of Fiction." She repudiates the notion that "the proper shape of the narrative is . . . the arrow or spear, starting *here* and going straight *there* and THOK! hitting its mark (which drops dead)." Instead, she proposes that "the natural, proper, fitting shape of the novel might be that of a sack, a bag." In this model of narrative, conflict is only one of many possible elements in shaping plot, not *the* determinant, since the purpose of "narrative conceived as carrier bag/belly/box . . . is neither resolution nor stasis but continuing process." She argues that her own plots are "full of beginnings without ends, of initiations, of losses, of transformations and translations." Le Guin's terms can also be usefully applied to serial fiction, to stories that depend on beginnings that end only provisionally, at the end of a part, before the narrative is further transformed in additional parts.[23]

Yet even if, from a material, cultural, and theoretical vantage point, serial fiction had particular relevance to female readers, the serial form did not subvert or exclude dominant male experience or ideology; an individual installment, viewed as an independent entity, was both an apt commercial product and a single instance of aroused and discharged interest and textual pleasure. And of course the name most closely associated with the serial form was that of a male: Charles Dickens. Indeed, as Gaye Tuchman, writing with Nina Fortin, suggests, the history of nineteenth-century fiction can be viewed as a story of the displacement (by men) of women as authors and the elevating of the aesthetic prestige of the novel. Although she focuses on the customary volume editions rather than serial novels, Tuchman's account of the prevalence and then decline of women novelists in the publishing industry roughly coincides with the heyday and decline of serial fiction.

Citing 1840–79 (when serialization also flourished) as the period when women dominated the submission and acceptance of novels, Tuchman argues that 1880–99 marked the redefinition of the novel, when the number of submissions and acceptances was distributed evenly between men and women, whereas men dominated between 1900 and 1917, also a time when modernist aesthetics caused the serial to decline as a preferred form for "high" literary art. Tuchman's detailed research on Macmillan's publishing archives may indirectly suggest as well, then, that the serial form was a particularly congenial medium for women writers and readers. Indeed, she notes that when the aesthetic paradigm shifted to the shorter, "high art" novel in the 1890s, many women were either unwilling or unable to abandon the long form of the novel that flourished in midcentury (188)—and that is associated with the serial novel as well.[24]

A final element, one prominent in *North and South,* deserves attention in an exploration of sexual and textual pleasure in the serial form: romance and eroticism.[25] Beginning with part 12 of *North and South,* when Margaret throws her arms around John Thornton, a pattern of erotic tension begins to develop and is sustained until the novel's final pages, when it is released in the couple's second embrace that mirrors the first: "He gently disengaged her hands from her face, and laid her arms as they had once before been placed to protect him from the rioters" (*NS,* 529–30). From the moment Margaret first touches him, John becomes intensely aware of her physical presence and returns again and again to the memory of their embrace: "Mr Thornton remained in the dining-room, trying to think of the business he had to do at the police-office, and in reality thinking of Margaret. Everything seemed dim and vague beyond—behind—besides the touch of her arms round his neck—the soft clinging which made the dark colour come and go in his cheek as he thought of it" (244; see also 274). Yet because Margaret spurns with stinging words the marriage proposal he offers the next day, Thornton thereafter combines apparent indifference to her presence with intense erotic awareness: "[Margaret] fancied that, from her being on a low seat at first, and now standing behind her father, he had overlooked her in his haste. As if he did not feel the consciousness of her presence all over, though his eyes had never rested on her!" (276). Margaret eventually realizes she has fallen in love with Thornton, but a number of obstacles prevent their union until the final page: Thornton's mistaking Margaret's brother Frederick for her lover; Margaret's lie to the police to protect Frederick; the hurt Margaret and John inflict on each other by their forthright (if not ingenuous) comments; and more. This strand of the novel is a familiar one: it is the erotic plot that characterizes romance fiction.[26]

The eroticism in romance fiction, as in Gaskell's work, consists of the feminine desire to be desired and the impetus toward, yet prohibition of, desire for a male erotic figure. This structure prolongs and intensifies erotic arousal, making desire, more than its release, the focal point. It is of course a model of desire predicated on cultural norms for middle-class women. If they are encouraged to attract an erotic partner and to form intimate emotional bonds made possible in part by the postponement of sexual activity, they are also prohibited from directly expressing their own desire for a heterosexual partner. Such a structure suggests male control of female sexuality to ensure paternity but also reflects a feminine quest for emotional security and protection from abandonment.

This Victorian pattern has persisted into twentieth-century romance fiction, as Janice Radway makes clear in a study based on interviews with readers of such fiction. According to these readers, Radway explains, the middle of a romance narrative "must create some form of conflict to keep the romantic pair apart until the proper moment . . . many authors settle for misunderstanding or distrust as the cause of the intermediary delay of the couple's happy union." The heroine should be "strong" or "fiery," and possessed of "intelligence, a sense of humor, and independence."[27] The romance hero should be "strong and masculine, but equally capable of unusual tenderness, gentleness, and concern for [the heroine's] pleasure." The plot of the romance must above all be developmental and filled with anticipation, traits Radway links to the form's eroticism: "[Readers] want to identify with the heroine. . . . The point of the experience is the sense of exquisite tension, anticipation, and excitement created within the reader as she imagines the possible resolutions and consequences for a woman of an encounter with a member of the opposite sex. . . . In all their comments about the nature of the romance, the Smithton women placed heavy emphasis on the importance of *development* in the romance's portrayal of love." Radway also says, "It matters little whether that care and attention [from the hero] are detailed in general terms or presented as overtly sexual as long as they are extensively described. However, this focus on his attention to her is in itself erotic, for even the most euphemistic descriptions of the heroine's reception of his regard convey the sensual, corporal pleasure she feels in anticipating, encouraging, and finally accepting those attentions of a hero who is always depicted as magnetic, powerful, and physically pleasing." [28] Although scholars offer varied reasons for romance readers' attraction to this genre, most agree that the eroticism it offers is defined by "Waiting, anticipation, anxiety." [29]

The features of waiting, anticipating, and postponing fulfillment are also salient features of serial fiction. The serial might be said to further prolong the duration of desire; and since this prolongation is identified as a central feature of romance fiction, the prolonged narrative of the serial form may lead to erotic intensification in a feminine economy of desire. In the case of *North and South,* moreover, serial issue could have allowed erotic tension to fade in the intervals between parts only to revive and extend its duration with each succeeding part. [30] Winnett's narrative model is again relevant here, especially her reminder that female arousal can occur at any time during the sexual act and can resurface again and again and again. Margaret remarks in part 19, when she realizes she loves Thornton, "It [her love for him] has come upon me little by little, and I don't know where it began" (*NS,* 401). The frequently expressed impatience with Gaskell's deflection of an industrial novel plot into a romance plot is a shrewd critique from the vantage point of political strategies and concerns, but it may also be useful to assess this narrative structure in terms of feminine sexuality and patterns of pleasure.

We propose, then, that the plot of Elizabeth Gaskell's *North and South* resembled the model of feminine narrative pleasure offered by Winnett and others. When Dickens first reviewed the manuscript of *North and South,* he praised its "character and power" and noted especially "a strong suspended interest in it (the end of which, I don't in the least foresee)." However, Dickens's advice about the work's serialization was presented in absolute terms: "Let me endeavour to shew you as distinctly as I can, the divisions in which it must fall." In an outline, he presented what he thought should be the first six installments; each entry began with the phrase "I would end No. [ ] with . . . ," showing his concern that each part have an effective conclusion. In another letter Dickens also insisted, "I believe you are aware that it will at least be necessary to begin every weekly portion as a new chapter."[31] Although Dickens summarized the content of three of the proposed first six installments, he identified the last event to be narrated in every case. Thus the rhythm of reading, as it was shaped by the sense of each part's beginning in a precise place and coming to a felt conclusion, may have been more important to Dickens as editor than what element of the narrative's subject the author should present every week.

Dickens also stated unequivocally that "if it were divided in any other way—reference being always had to the weekly space available for the purpose in *Household Words*—it would be mortally injured." Dickens, of course, is the magazine's editor; but he seems to assume that on her own Gaskell would be unable to conceive of an appropriate division into parts. Dorothy Collin notes how Dickens assumed that he, rather than Mrs. Gaskell, would take care of the whole question of parts structure. She cites Dickens's letter of 18 February 1854, written before he received any manuscript: "Don't put yourself out at all as to the division of the story into parts. I think you had far better write it in your own way. When we come to get a little of it into type, I have no doubt of being able to make such little suggestions as to breaks of chapters as will carry us over all that easily."[32] Indeed, modern scholarship has generally accepted this interpretation of this phase in the novel's publication history.

Dickens's plan for the novel rearranged some of Gaskell's material; and his efforts almost always were directed at creating self-sufficient units with powerful conclusions.[33] He even offered to take over the matter of parts structure completely, including "sometimes" writing "a word or two of conclusion" for the author. Even as he admits "I hope these remarks will not confuse you," Dickens's letter ends with additional stress on the absolute necessity of turning the parts structure over to him as editor: "I am bound to put before you my perfect conviction that if it did not [follow this pattern], the story would be wasted—would miss its effect as it went on—*and would not recover it when published complete*" (Dickens's emphasis).[34] For Dickens, the entire life of this novel through all its editions would be a product of the rhythm of its first appearance, a rhythm he was intent on controlling.

The plot of *North and South,* however, reveals important distinctions from traditionally conceived (masculinist) plot. As opposed to the story about *Barnaby Rudge*—so clearly plotted with the end in mind that Edgar Allan Poe deduced the entire plot from the early numbers[35]—the opening number of *North and South* hardly contained within itself the germ of its resolution. The first two chapters, in fact, were so carefully crafted that they constitute a brilliant complete short story. It is also difficult to argue that the novel's end point determined or conferred sole meaning on this beginning when there was no hint of the removal to Milton or of John Thornton. And after even the first five parts of the novel had appeared, so astute a reader as Charlotte Brontë thought the novel was to focus on religious doubt.[36] This discontinuity between beginning and end has been one basis for censuring the book, but if we recur to Cixous's or Le Guin's notions of transformations and ongoing process, or Winnett's model in which narrative arousal can occur at unforeseen (and even arbitrary) moments, this larger narrative shape is less disturbing. (From the economic standpoint of *Household Words,* of course, censure of such a dilatory plot remains applicable.)

The shape of an individual part could also, in Gaskell's hands, diverge from Dickens's emphasis on "strong suspended interest" or from the traditional, linear emphasis on event. Interest in the affective lives of characters, more than in events' outcomes, often characterizes individual parts of *North and South.* The twelfth part, for instance, takes the shape of "woman's work" as identified by Margaret Hale in that installment: "If I saved one blow, one cruel, angry action that might otherwise have been committed, I did a woman's work" (*NS,* 247). The part opens when tension during the strike has built to a point of impending explosion, and the thrust of the narrative seems to be toward violence. But the tension building toward a cataclysmic event is instead deflected into the connectedness of a courtship plot.[37] When workers threaten Thornton, Margaret throws her arms about him, and she rather than John is the one wounded (not seriously, as it turns out). This protective action then initiates the forward movement of the courtship plot, and the part ends looking ahead not to another explosive event, but to the developing relationship of Margaret and John. In this installment too, then, Gaskell "saves a blow," prevents an "angry action," and focuses on "woman's work" of nurturing and affection.[38]

The divergence between Dickens's and Gaskell's notions of serial publication, however, is most evident in the major textual variant between the serial version, over which Dickens exercised some authority, and the volume edition, which Gaskell could superintend with less external interference. Given her attention to documents in her previous fiction—the material of court summons, alibi, and valentine in *Mary Barton,* Mrs. Bellingham's cruel note to Ruth, and *Cranford's* many letters, including the one that restores Peter to Matty—it is no wonder that Gaskell sought to control the material form of her novels at this important stage of her career. She understood her fiction as a product of her self, almost as much a part of her as her own children. When she composed her two full-length novels with an eye to their less restricting two- and three-volume appearance, she did not come into conflict with Chapman and Hall and established Victorian publishing practices. And *Cranford's* irregular composition in generally self-contained, two-chapter episodes fit in nicely with her schedule in 1851–53 and provided relief from the struggle to finish *Ruth.* But the chapters of *North and South* had to appear in units of six to eight double-column pages in *Household Words;* and Gaskell resented the fixed way her work would be portioned out to readers.

The serial *North and South* differed from the volume edition primarily in its conclusion, where Gaskell expanded the final four chapters to make eight. Most of this addition involved a return visit paid by the heroine Margaret Hale from England's industrial North to her old home in the country's rural South. The life of her father's old friend, Mr. Bell, is nicely extended (he had died suddenly in the serial text) so that he can accompany her on the trip. But what was kept out of the narrative by Dickens and *Household Words* was not so much event as commentary and reflection. In August, for instance, Dickens was angry to find proofs returned from Mrs. Gaskell "*unaltered*" by the author. The editor had wanted "a great condensation and a considerable compression, where Mr. Hale states his doubts to Margaret."[39] Mrs. Gaskell apparently did not want to reduce this kind of narrative, which presents argument and counterargument rather than advancing the story's action.

The entire novel of *North and South* had progressed through a series of stages in understanding, as different or opposing perspectives clashed:

North against South, Church of England against Methodism, men against women, worker against employer, servant against mistress. Each install-ment, then, constituted a debate from different positions: capital versus labor, wealth versus poverty, age versus youth, old versus new, agriculture versus industry. And the completion of every number generally repre-sented a new moderation of views as characters (and readers) slowly but steadily moved closer to shared values, a technique Gaskell had followed in the earlier *Mary Barton*.[40]

The expanded conclusion of *North and South* was needed, then, less to complete a sequence of action than to provide one more stage in the dialectical evolution toward a new, transforming perspective.[41] Gaskell asked several of her friends if she should revise the serial text for volume publication. To Mrs. Anna Jameson she wrote, "I can not insert small pieces here & there—I feel as if I must throw myself back a certain dis-tance in the story, & re-write it from there; retaining the present inci-dents, but filling up intervals of time &c &c." (*LMG,* 329). Mrs. Jameson responded that "there should be more gradation in effect [in the novel's conclusion], and the rapidity of the incidents at the close destroys the proportions of your story as a work of art."[42]

In the expanded last chapters Margaret sees the limits of her past life against the promises of a new. And the most memorable passages from the new text involved more time devoted to acknowledging con-traries and coming to terms with them. Margaret, for instance, recognizes that even in "timeless" old England, represented by her native village of Helstone, "There was change everywhere; slight, yet pervading all" (*NS,* 481). She admits to continual change within herself as well: "And I too change perpetually—now this, now that—now disappointed and peevish because all is not exactly as I had pictured it, and now suddenly discovering that the reality is far more beautiful than I had imagined it" (489). One of the most frequently cited passages from Gaskell's revision is Margaret's long meditation after Mr. Bell's death that concluded chap-ter 48 in the volume edition.[43] The heroine uses this occasion to moder-ate her estimate of life's opportunities: "On some such night as this she remembered promising to herself to live as brave and noble a life as any heroine she had ever read or heard of in romance. . . .And now she had learnt that not only to will, but also to pray, was a necessary condition in the truly heroic" (502). Such balancing of opposed principles, such extended description of a character's relation to her environment and circumstances, was important enough to Gaskell's novel that it figured prominently in her revisions of the serial text.

In her own account of composition and serialization, Elizabeth Gaskell felt the need to extend both the time of her own work on the novel and the length of the story's natural form. She complained to her friend Anna Jameson of not having "happy leisure hours" for her own work;[44] and she insisted that, if "the story had been poured just warm out of the mind, it would have taken a much larger mould" (*LMG,* 330). She wrote to Jameson late in the process of composition that the "story is huddled & hurried up. . . .But what could I do? Every page was grudged me, just at last, when I did certainly infringe all the bounds & limits they set me as to quantity. Just at the very last I was compelled to desperate compression. But now I am not sure if, when the barrier gives way between/2 such characters as Mr Thornton and Margaret it would not go all smash in a moment" (328–29).

However, Gaskell also seemed to accept Dickens's judgment about the necessities of magazine publication and to admit to her own inability to work within this mode. For instance, at one point she wrote: "I have tried to shorten & compress [the 20 January 1855 installment] . . . but, there were a whole catalogue of events to be got over . . . but, *if you will keep the MS for me, & shorten it as you think best for HW,* I shall be very glad. Shortened I see it must be" (*LMG,* 323). Later letters and comments show that Gaskell resented the magazine's shaping of her novel even if she could not escape it.[45] The ways her own structuring of *North and South* attempted to avoid sharp divisions of plot into chapters or installments suggest that she felt the pleasure of reading a text derived from more than engaging, well-constructed individual parts. She faced similar pressures to compress material in her masterpiece, *Wives and Daughters,* serialized in the monthly *Cornhill.* However, the installment shape of all Gaskell's serial fiction derives from fundamental patterns of narrative that complement and expand traditional, masculinist formulations.

The serial novella that followed *North and South* in Gaskell's career was *My Lady Ludlow,* which also appeared in Dickens's *Household Words* three and a half years after the completion of Margaret Hale's story.

Although this generally nostalgic portrait of an earlier time did not have nearly the impact of *North and South,* its serial form in some ways continues the story of Gaskell's relationship with Dickens as editor.

Uglow reports that the publication in *Household Words* of "Half a Lifetime Ago" in 1855 "plunged [Gaskell] into another taut correspondence with Dickens about space, divisions, and corrections." After "The Poor Clare" (1856) she began sending her material elsewhere: "The Siege of the Black Cottage" (1857), "The Doom of the Griffiths" (1858), and "An Incident at Niagara Falls" (1858), for instance, to the American journal *Harper's*. But a need for ready cash apparently brought her back to Dickens and *Household Words* in 1858. She wanted to finance a trip to the Continent for her daughter, Meta, who was suffering after breaking off an engagement. As Uglow reports, "She got her money for *My Lady Ludlow*. In fact she got it three times over": first £100 from Dickens, then additional payments later for volume editions from Sampson Low and George Smith.[46]

Critical judgment has not been high concerning *My Lady Ludlow* (19 June to 15 September 1858), but Edgar Wright has recently argued that the work's fourteen "episodes, amusing or affecting in themselves, mark stages in a progressive change of attitudes and in the development of Lady Ludlow herself as one of Gaskell's most finely conceived characters." And Uglow writes that "this novella, often criticized for its shapelessness, is far cleverer and more experimental than first appears." Although *My Lady Ludlow* apparently "overran Dickens's word limit," [47] its parts structure features the dramatic conclusions routinely demanded for *Household Words* material.

Climactic, forward-looking installment endings especially dominate the interpolated tale of the de Créquy family, devastated by the French Revolution. *My Lady Ludlow* insists that its historical plot has been shaped into a particular narrative order. Lady Ludlow tells the story to Margaret Dawson, insisting on a familiar structure: "People seldom arrive at my age without having watched the beginning, middle, and end of many lives and many fortunes" (*MLL,* 119). She also acknowledges that she had received the greater part of her account from Pierre, a participant in key events: "In telling you most of this, I have simply repeated Pierre's account which I wrote down at the time" (106). Pierre, she says, "had evidently thought over the whole series of events as a story—as a play, if one may call it so—during the solitary hours in his after-life, wherever they were passed, whether in lonely camp watches, or in the foreign prison where he had to drag out many years" (106). And that "story" had parts, for she points out that after narrating Virginie's escape from his mother's house, "here what he had to say came to a sudden break" (106). (That particular break, by the way, was accentuated in *Household Words* by the week between the 31 July and the 7 August installments.)

The consciously structured narrative of *My Lady Ludlow* pursues an extended contrast between the peaceful, gradual change of nineteenth-century English history and radical revolution in late eighteenth-century France. For the more exciting portion presenting events in 1790s Paris, Gaskell gives away the tragic outcome early in her telling (the two aristocratic lovers are guillotined [*MLL*, 77]). Dickens would probably have let suspense continue through more numbers, as he does a year later in his exploration of the same subject, *A Tale of Two Cities,* which also ran in *Household Words* (30 April to 26 November 1859). Still, most parts of Gaskell's novella add discrete units to the ongoing tale and end on high dramatic notes.

Number 3 (3 July 1858), for instance, concludes with the narrator's reference to Lady Ludlow's learning, through an "unlucky incident . . . which I am going to relate" (*MLL,* 45), that Mr. Horner wants to educate members of the lower class. That incident inspires Lady Ludlow to tell the story of the de Créquy family through the next four installments. Number 4 (10 July), which initiates the history, ends with the surprising arrival in London of Clément and his mother, who have fled the revolution in France (58). The dramatic admission by Madame de Créquy— that, though Clément has returned to France in an effort to rescue his love, "I did not give him my blessing!" (72)—resonates at the end of number 5 (17 July). Number 6 (24 July) concludes with Pierre's witnessing the clandestine meeting of Virginie and Clément in Paris (87), an event foreshadowing the fatal discovery of their status as aristocrats. Pierre watches Virginie sneaking out of Madame Babette's house for the rendezvous with Clément (101) on the final page of number 6 (31 July). And installment 7 (7 August) ends with Clément's death and the suicide of the rival lover Morin (117).

My Lady Ludlow's narrative of intrigue, passion, and betrayal at the time of the French Revolution, then, is pulled forward by a tension of dramatic installment endings, though the body of each part often includes a number of digressions. The main narrative chronicling Lady Ludlow's battle with Mr. Gray about education for the masses also comes in carefully structured parts, generally with dramatic conclusions looking to the future. Again the primary narrator, Margaret Dawson, speaking specifically about the relationship of Bessy to Miss Galindo, acknowledges having imposed order on what she reports: "I will try and arrange [events]; not, however, in the order in which I heard them, but rather as they occurred" (*MLL,* 179).

The order in which events occurred is punctuated by dramatic announcements, often at the ends of parts. The 17 August installment, for instance, concluded: "But something happened to the lad [Harry Gregson] before this purpose [of sending him away] could be accomplished" (*MLL,* 132). That "something" is narrated as the conclusion to the 24 August part: "Harry Gregson has fallen from a tree, and broken his thigh-bone" (146). Word of the tragic death of Lady Ludlow's son, the last of her nine children, comes as the conclusion to the 4 September issue (161). The 11 September part ends with the revelation that Miss Galindo has an unknown young woman, Bessy, coming to live with her. That Bessy is the illegitimate daughter of a man Miss Galindo might have married is narrated in the next number, the novel's penultimate installment, which ends with the surprise announcement that the aristocratic Captain James is courting Miss Brooke, daughter of a Birmingham tradesman and Dissenter (194), something the Old World Lady Ludlow can hardly credit.

In this last serial work of more than a few installments before the time of "Cousin Phillis" (*Cornhill Magazine,* 1863–64) and *Wives and Daughters* (*Cornhill,* 1864–66),[48] then, Elizabeth Gaskell conformed to a considerable degree to the plot structure Dickens sought as editor of the weekly *Household Words.* She had the skill, that is—when circumstances forced her—to adapt her work to the demands created by the literary industry of her time. As we argued in chapter 1 concerning the appearance of *Wives and Daughters* in the *Cornhill,* however, Gaskell's preferred serial form did not rely on dramatic endings and tension-filled plot. In "A Dark Night's Work," a short serial (January 24 to March 21 1863) published near the same time as *Wives and Daughters,* Gaskell also presented her view of time and change as steady but often unremarkable.

In this nine-part novella issued in Dickens's second weekly periodical, *All the Year Round,* the narrator discusses the gradual progress of life in the village of Hamley, especially the relationship of Ellinor Wilkins and her father: "The next two years passed over in much the same way—or a careless spectator might have thought so" (DNW, 28). Then Gaskell uses an extended metaphor to make the point graphically that often an effort must be made to recognize process: "I have heard people say, that if you look at a regiment advancing with steady step over a plain on a review-day, you can hardly tell that they are not merely marking time on one spot of ground unless you compare their position with some other object by which to mark their progress, so even is the repetition of the movement. And thus the sad events of the future life of this father and daughter were hardly perceived in their steady advance, and yet over the monotony and flat uniformity of their days sorrow came marching down upon them like an armed man" (28). Gaskell's conviction that most change occurs relentlessly but nearly invisibly is often represented in the subtle evolution of character and plot in her fiction, both the long three-volume form and the novels published in installments.

In this particular story she exploits the irony that "a dark night's work" appears to change the lives of father and daughter completely: "One minute of passion, and my life blasted!" (DNW, 55), says Wilkins. But Gaskell's narrative had already shown his gradual slide into personal indulgence in the novella's first five chapters (three installments), and we recognize the single event as the continuation of many that had preceded it. In chapter 2 readers learned that early in his marriage Wilkins "required more and more the stimulus of society" (7; 24 January 1863). In the next chapter the narrator says that, with his daughter entering adulthood, Wilkins never "broke out into any immoral conduct, but he gave up time to pleasure" (15). In chapter 4, "Mr Wilkins was sinking from the intellectually to the sensually self-indulgent man" (29; 31 January 1863); and in the chapter narrating Dunster's murder we are told of Wilkins's continuing extravagance, "the lot darkening over the father, and including the daughter in its cloud" (43; 7 February 1863).

That Dickens remained unhappy with Elizabeth Gaskell's style of narration is as clear in his response to "A Dark Night's Work" as it was in the case of *North and South.* Suzanne Lewis reports: "Author and editor could not agree on chapter divisions, and the story was far too long for the space allocated by Dickens." While she concludes that "the story was unsuited to publication in weekly parts,"[49] a case can also be made that Gaskell did not wish to pursue the audience Dickens knew so well in exactly the manner of his successful fiction. She resented, for instance, Dickens's decision to change her story's title. Uglow says she had called it simply "A Night's Work," and his addition of "Dark" pushed the story, as Lewis says, toward melodrama.[50]

Gaskell's conclusion to the military metaphor of time's advance suggests how she hoped readers might become more sensitive to events that lacked the outward drama typical of sensation novels: "Long before Mr Wilkins had recognized its [sorrow's] shape it was approaching him in the distance—as, in fact, it is approaching all of us at this very time; you, reader, I, writer, have each our great sorrow bearing down upon us. It may be yet beyond the dimmest point of our horizon but in the stillness of the night our hearts shrink at the sound of its coming footstep" (DNW, 28). One goal of Mrs. Gaskell's work is surely to make her audience more alert to such footsteps in the future.

Although Gaskell's heroine Ellinor divides her life on a single tragic moment—"the old life of yesterday" (DNW, 57) versus "the long, weary course of small lies, to be done and said, involved in that one mistaken action" (63)—she nevertheless continues to change slowly. In chapter 12 (14 March 1863) the narrator claims she "seemed" to have gone suddenly from childhood to old age: "Her youth had gone in a single night, fifteen years ago, and now she appeared to have become an elderly woman; very still and hopeless in look and movement, but as sweet and gentle in speech and smile as ever she had been in her happiest days" (115). But her identity in "happiest days" had never been erased completely. When she agrees to travel in Italy with the Forbeses, the woman who is "only four-and-thirty" (115) appears differently: the "change of scene . . . was like a renewing of her youth; cut so suddenly short by the shears of fate" (129). Meeting Ellinor after years of separation, her onetime lover Ralph Corbet "wondered if he was as much changed in appearance as she struck him as being on that first look of recognition" (158–59; 21 March 1863); but soon after that first impression, he finds her face "now almost the same to him as of yore" (162). Change in Gaskell's preferred literary forms is continuous but not often conspicuous, punctuated at times by moments of drama, but more often gradual, sustained, and subtle.

Viewed in its totality, then, Mrs. Gaskell's work shows that serial publication by male and female authors in the Victorian age could "have it all" in its ability to integrate female and male structures of experience. Readers could have the pleasure of each installment read as a satisfying unit, with bound whole volumes always the final product of the publication process. Or they could, without threatening the status quo, enjoy a serial text's pleasure by having all the parts over the months of publication, thus making of reading a prospective and ever-renewed experience until the end was reached long after the text began. This was so even when women read fiction by the age's best-known male authors like Dickens. But their pleasure in serial fiction could have been heightened in installments by writers like Elizabeth Gaskell, whose handling of individual parts suggests approaches to plot that lie outside traditional, masculinist norms of textual pleasure and whose distinctive strategies in a given part remind us why serial publication as a whole may have been a pleasure to its female readers.

In the next major work of her career after *North and South,* Elizabeth Gaskell took on a distinctly feminine subject, the life of Charlotte Brontë. We will next consider the specific strategies she adopted in constructing this volume edition aimed at correcting the public apprehension of a friend, a woman, and a writer.

V

Engendered Lives: Gaskell's *Life of Charlotte Brontë*

AT THE CLOSE OF HER two-volume biography of Charlotte Brontë (published by Smith, Elder in 1857) Gaskell confesses inability to come to judgment on her subject: "I cannot measure or judge of such a character as hers. I cannot map out vices, and virtues, and debateable land" (*LCB*, 526). In part this is the stance of an engaged narrator assumed by Gaskell out of affection for the friend she memorializes, as well as exemplifying the sense of "connection" to a subject we discussed in chapter 4. Moreover, as Ann Marie Ross notes, Gaskell's sympathies and authorial voice are presented throughout the biography in dialogue with Brontë's, and this strategy precludes the detached appraisal of a disinterested judge. Yet Gaskell's declaration has puzzled commentators on the *Life of Charlotte Brontë,* since it seems clear that she indeed reached conclusions and presents a powerful argument about Brontë's character.[1]

The declaration, however, gestures toward one of the crucial contexts of the biography: in refusing to reach fixed conclusions, Gaskell is declining to adopt the conventions of obituary. With the *Life of Charlotte Brontë,* both obituary and biography become additional Victorian forms in which Gaskell finds unused spaces and that she alters through her own writing.

Obituaries exist precisely to fix, sort, and assess the characters and achievements of the famous. Obituaries devoted to Brontë immediately after her death, whether in brief accounts of her life or retrospective surveys of her career as a novelist, have long been mentioned as inspiring the request from Brontë's family and friends that Gaskell undertake the biography. Ellen Nussey, Charlotte's closest friend, read the obituary in the

June 1855 *Sharpe's London Magazine,* was outraged at what she considered
its distorted representations of Brontë's domestic life at Haworth, and
prevailed on Brontë's husband and father to authorize a biography and
approach Elizabeth Gaskell about writing it.[2]

Various motives have been attributed to Gaskell's assent to their request; the biography has been seen variously as an act of duty toward or
love for a friend, a desire that a writer be truly understood by her audience, a deliberate effacing of the novelist in favor of the woman whose
exemplary virtue conformed to regimes of domestic ideology, a feminist
protest against those same regimes, and a representation of the woman
writer.[3] We suggest that when the biography is reinserted into its periodical context, especially the obituaries that preceded it and the reviews
that followed it, this work emerges as a more deliberate, engaged intervention in public discourses than is often appreciated.[4] The obituaries
also clarify Gaskell's complicated investment in the rhetorical skill she
devoted to recounting Brontë's life in the two years she devoted to the
project. Even before the biography Gaskell's own repute and stance as
novelist were entwined with Brontë's. Her representation of Brontë is
thus self-defense as well as defense, self-advertising as well as rescue of a
beloved friend and sister novelist. The reviews of Gaskell's biography,
especially those preceding the threat of lawsuits by Lady Scott, demonstrate how brilliantly she succeeded in her strategies.

These reviews, like the obituaries and Gaskell's response to them,
confirm as well the crucial role of gender in Victorian representations of
authorship. After examining the biography and its periodical context, we
will turn briefly to James Froude's biography of Thomas Carlyle, which,
by disclosing the considerable privileges allotted to masculine authorship,
illuminates the constraints under which Brontë labored. Yet Froude's
biography and its periodical context suggest that arguments about difference must be tempered: representations of genius, heroic endurance,
frailty, solitude, and suffering (whether mental or physical) converge in
surprising ways in both biographies and their periodical contexts.

Little has been written about the obituary as literary form, despite
its familiarity to Victorian and twentieth-century audiences. The obituary is clearly tied to the periodical press, depending on mass-circulation
newspapers and magazines and interest in celebrity.[5] As twentieth-century
obituary writer Alden Whitman remarks, the obituary is neither eulogy,

résumé, scholarly essay, nor full-scale portrait. Assessment, however, is crucial—Whitman titles his collection of obituaries *Come to Judgment*. To him, good obituaries convey a "vivid and accurate impression" by representing the "main facts" of a person's life and providing "a lively expression of personality and character."[6] He proffers the metaphor of snapshot for the obituary, a medium that fixes an image presented to and circulated among mass audiences.

Obituaries are inherently the earliest biographical commentaries on the complete lives of literary figures, for which they construct narrative plots. Peter Brooks conceives of plot as "the internal logic of the discourse of mortality" and remarks that "prior events, causes, are so only retrospectively, in a reading back from the end. In this sense, the metaphoric work of eventual totalization determines the meaning and status of the metonymic work of sequence."[7] Building on Brooks (whose model of plot Winnett links to masculine sexuality), we might say that obituaries transform lives into texts, confer a linear plot, then provide plot and character analysis. Obituaries of Brontë were thus minibiographies whose encapsulations of a life provided rival models that Gaskell strove to complicate, enliven, and transcend. The obituaries also established the horizon of expectations against which her published biography had its impact and effect, so that to revisit the obituaries is to clarify the biography's function as rhetorical intervention.

The earliest obituaries of Charlotte Brontë are permeated by considerations of gender, authorship, and domesticity. Harriet Martineau's account in the *Daily Mail,* one in the *Belfast Mercury* providing a spurious Brontë genealogy, and another in *Sharpe's London Magazine* are most frequently cited. But that in the 7 April 1855 *Athenaeum* was also widely read and reprinted. While praising Brontë as one of three "remarkable" sisters in a "literary home," the single paragraph also foregrounded the volatile—and highly gendered—issues of notoriety and oddity: "The author of 'Jane Eyre,' of 'Shirley,' and of 'Villette,' was a personage too much talked of in her day, and of too marked a peculiarity as a novelist, to pass out of remembrance" (*A,* 406). As a number of recent critics have commented, entering the public sphere so that one's name and person became public, exposed to public view, was fraught with danger for bourgeois women writers, since it threatened to equate the professional woman with the demimonde or with the prostitute, who also marketed her person in public.[8] The *Athenaeum* obituary was, it should be added, accurate in its mention of notoriety; one of the many rumors circulating during Brontë's lifetime was that she was related to Lord Nelson, whose Sicilian title was "duke of Brontë."[9] But to devote one of five sentences recounting her life and death to notoriety was to make a "public woman" of her. The obituary also emphasized Brontë's challenge to gender norms by identifying her as a woman warrior: "'Currer Bell' . . . [was] the literary title under which she fought her battle and won her reputation."

The trope of warrior was replayed and greatly augmented by Margaret Oliphant in "Modern Novelists—Great and Small," which devoted several paragraphs to *Jane Eyre* in the May 1855 issue of *Blackwood's Edinburgh Magazine* just one month after Brontë's death. Not specifically an obituary (Brontë's name was never mentioned), it nonetheless fixed the cultural significance of the novel and character with which Brontë was most closely identified and did so in terms important to Gaskell's involvement in Brontë's biography. Jane Eyre is here an incendiary, a self-declared feminist, an aggressive warrior locked in hand-to-hand combat with men—or rather, with men's outworn chivalric notions. If a decade ago, Oliphant asserts, true love in novels meant "reverent, knightly, chivalrous true-love," all that ended with the "invasion of *Jane Eyre*": "Suddenly there stole upon the scene, without either flourish of trumpets or public proclamation, a little fierce incendiary, doomed to turn the world of fancy upside down. . . .something of a genius, something of a vixen—a dangerous little person" who introduced love as fierce battle between man and woman (*B, 557*). The wild rumors over the book's authorship, she continued, had obscured its real significance, which lay in signaling a new feminist generation intent on redefining gender relations:

> *Nobody perceived that it was the new generation nailing its colours to its mast . . . a wild declaration of the "Rights of Woman" in a new aspect. . . .Here is your true revolution. France is but one of the Western Powers; woman is half of the world. Talk of a balance of power which may be adjusted by taking a Crimea, or fighting a dozen battles—here is a battle which must always be going forward—a balance of power only to be decided by single combat, deadly and uncompromising. . . .She is a fair gladiator—she is not an angel. . . .And this new Bellona steps forth in armour, throws down her glove, and defies you—to conquer her if you can.* (B, 557–58)

The essay defended the novel's use of "improper" material by arguing that such candor was possible only where innocence created boldness; yet the result was confirmation that the novel handled scandalous material.

It is hard to imagine commentary further removed from the domestic pieties usually circulated at the death of a parson's wife or daughter. Oliphant's remarks as recounted thus far might be construed as feminist assertion on her own part. But having completed her scrutiny of Brontë, Oliphant assumed a stance of censure in her survey of the school of fiction founded by *Jane Eyre*. And at this point the wide sweep of the wing that propelled Brontë toward the category of "vixen" and ferocious warrior through her close identification in the public mind with her heroine swept Gaskell before it as well:

> *Mrs Gaskell, a sensible and considerate woman, and herself ranking high in her sphere, has just fallen subject to the same delusion.* North and South *is extremely clever, as a story . . . perhaps better and livelier than any of Mrs Gaskell's previous works; yet here are still the wide circles in the water, showing that not far off is the identical spot where* Jane Eyre *and* Lucy Snowe, *in their wild sport, have been casting stones; here is again the desperate, bitter quarrel out of which love is to come; here is love itself, always in a fury, often looking exceedingly like hatred, and by no means distinguished for its good manners, or its graces of speech.*

(B, 559)

Here is one clue to Gaskell's pressing interest in telling the story of Brontë's life as one that never violated propriety or domestic affections. To the degree that Gaskell was herself included by Oliphant in the cadre of novelists identified as revolutionary feminists, she was rewriting the image of herself when she rewrote the story of the author of *Jane Eyre*.[10]

This brings us to the notorious obituary in *Sharpe's London Magazine* in June 1855, "A Few Words about 'Jane Eyre.'" In this title "Jane Eyre" signifies Brontë herself, "A Few Words" the details of Brontë's life "obtained from a private and we believe authentic source, though we do not pledge ourselves to their accuracy" (S, 341). The notice opened by repeating the oddity of Jane Eyre as a heroine and the notoriety surrounding the novel's publication. But when it shifted to biographical details obtained from its "private source," it proceeded in terms strikingly close to the outlines assumed by Gaskell's own biography. The account's starting point is the bleak moorland landscape that defined and shaped Brontë's life and the parsonage surrounded by gravestones. Noting the early death of Brontë's mother—who, the obituary alleges, married Patrick Brontë against the wishes of her family—the account then turned to the father's eccentricity and neglect of his children: "Engrossed by his own pursuits, the father never even dined with his family nor taught them anything, and the children learned to write and read from servants only" (341). There follows the disastrous episode at Cowan's Bridge School and then, at age nineteen, Charlotte's dilemma as a woman in need of income: " 'At nineteen,' continued Charlotte, 'I should have been thankful for a penny a-week. I asked my father; but he said, "What do women want with money?" ' " After brief employment as a governess and further study in Brussels, which inspired *Villette,* she returned home when duty demanded that she minister to sisters failing in health and a father whose eyesight was threatened (341). The concluding anecdote from the private source is the story of Charlotte's revealing her authorship of *Jane Eyre* to her father:

> *She marched into his study with a copy of her work, wrapped up*
> *in a Review of it, which she had received, and the following con-*
> *versation ensued:—*
>> *"Papa, I have been writing a book!"*
>> *"Have you, my dear?" (He went on reading.)*
>> *"But, papa, I want you to look at it."*
>> *"I can't be troubled to read manuscript."*   (S, 342)
>> *"But it is printed."*
>> *"I hope you've not been involving yourself in any such silly*
> *expense!"*
>> *"I think I shall gain some money by it; may I read you*
> *some reviews of it?"*

More details were quoted from a "lady, who afterwards became intimate with Miss Brontë," and the obituary concluded with the brief happiness of Brontë's marriage, which tragically ended just when "time and an increased knowledge of life should have corrected the eccentricity, without lessening the originality, of her genius" (342).

The obituary hardly seems shocking now, despite the function assigned to it in twentieth-century scholarly accounts of inspiring outrage;

and the handling of dialogue is really quite skillful. But then it should be. The entire obituary is a very lightly edited transcription of Gaskell's 25 August 1850 letter to Catherine Winkworth (*LMG*, 123–26) after meeting Brontë in the Lake District at the home of Sir James and Lady Kay Shuttleworth. Lady Shuttleworth misinformed Gaskell about supposed opposition to the marriage of Brontë's parents and described the moorland landscape to her, but much in the letter evidently came from Brontë herself. In other words, the "scandalous" and "shocking" obituary in *Sharpe's London Magazine* that led to Gaskell's being asked to write a biography was itself composed principally of Gaskell's own letter of 1850, one so detailed, "precise," and close to the finished biography that, as Alan Shelston remarks, "it is scarcely an overstatement to suggest that this letter in a way represents the *Life* itself in embryonic form." [11]

Here is a startling perspective both on Gaskell's agreeing so readily to write the biography and on the work she actually did. The close connection of the *Sharpe's* obituary to Gaskell's 1850 letter was first noted in 1963 by Richard Gilbertson, who offered the unlikely argument that Gaskell wrote the *Sharpe's* piece herself; the matter has subsequently been revisited by J. G. Sharps and by Dennis Robinson. [12] But in general Gaskell scholarship has been resistant to this instance of intertextuality, perhaps because the entanglement complicates gendered conceptions of Gaskell herself, whose sweetness and tact are so often noted—for example, by Robinson. [13] It seems unlikely that the *Sharpe's* obituary would have remained unknown to Gaskell, given her interest in other obituaries. She mentioned Harriet Martineau's obituary in a 12 April 1855 letter to Frederick Greenwood (*LMG*, 337) and the *Athenaeum* account in her 4 June 1855 letter to George Smith—which also noted her inability to obtain the *Belfast Mercury* obituary despite attempts to do so (347). To posit a writer who knew that words she originally wrote had distressed the oldest friend of a novelist for whom Gaskell felt deep affection; who kept silent about the obituary's source (so far as her collected letters indicate); and who embarked on the biography Nussey requested but stuck by the outlines of the account that upset Nussey in the first place is to suggest a writer who harbored depths on depths rather than a cheerful housewife bustling about to assuage hurt feelings. The *Sharpe's* obituary, then, is another possible reason for Gaskell's desire to ameliorate any suggestion of taint in Brontë's domestic sphere by filling in the details that an obituary necessarily omitted, to honor her own artistic vision and, above all, to link rather than separate proper womanhood and female authorship.

The strategy by which she might defend Brontë yet honor the writer was evident in Harriet Martineau's obituary in the 6 April 1855 *Daily News*—though in passing Martineau herself linked Brontë to themes of disruptive passion: "Passion occupies too prominent a place in her pictures of life. . . .Her heroines fall in love too readily, too vehemently, and sometimes after a fashion which their female readers may resent" (*CH,* 302). But the emphasis of the obituary does not fall here. Martineau defended the integrity of Brontë as writer, presenting her as a novelist who refused to write merely for money when she could have made a handsome income by doing so, and confirmed that the Lowood School episode was based on biographical material, here linking the life to the fiction. But Martineau denied that Jane Eyre was herself a version of Brontë, emphasizing instead the suffering born of grief and solitude amid which *Shirley* was written and stressing Brontë's perfect domestic propriety, to which her writing career posed no threat: "She seemed a perfect household image—irresistibly recalling Wordsworth's description of that domestic treasure. And she was this. She was as able at the needle as the pen. The household knew the excellence of her cookery before they heard of that of her books" (*CH,* 304).[14] It is perhaps no coincidence, either, that Martineau's own compelling need as a single woman intellectual and atheist to negotiate representations of female authorship led her to a strategy that was in part to be adopted and refined by Gaskell in a full-length biography.

One last item in the periodical press should be noted as helping to construct the discursive formations the biography participated in and responded to. This was Matthew Arnold's poem "Haworth Churchyard, April 1855," published in the May 1855 number of *Fraser's Magazine.* The poem was suppressed for over twenty years when Harriet Martineau, whose apparently impending death Arnold linked to Brontë's recent burial, inconveniently got well. But the poem demonstrates that, even before the biography, the motifs of the road from Keighley, the parsonage set amid graves, the brother blighted by sensual indulgence, and the Byronic genius of Emily were already well established:[15]

Where, behind Keighley, the road
Up to the heart of the moors
Between heath-clad showery hills
Runs, and colliers' carts
Poach the deep ways coming down,
And a rough, grim'd race have their homes—
There, on its slope, is built
The moorland town. But the church
Stands on the crest of the hill,
Lonely and bleak; at its side
The parsonage-house and the graves.
. . . . .

(F, 528, 530)

(How shall I sing her?)—[She] whose soul
Knew no fellow for might,
Passion, vehemence, grief,
Daring, since Byron died,
That world-fam'd Son of Fire; She, who sank
Baffled, unknown, self-consum'd;
Whose too-bold dying song
Shook, like a clarion-blast, my soul.

Of one too I have heard,
A Brother—sleeps he here?—
Of all his gifted race
Not the least-gifted; young,
Unhappy, beautiful; the cause
Of many hopes, of many tears.
. . . . .
But some dark Shadow came
(I know not what) and interpos'd.

Arnold's poem and the obituary in *Sharpe's* indicate that the much-noted opening of the *Life of Charlotte Brontë* in part merely recirculated entrees to Brontë's life already published. But this recycling clarifies as well the contrasting, and brilliant, rhetorical use Gaskell made of landscape in the full-length biography. Gaskell's care to place Brontë in the particular locale of the Yorkshire moors borders on the anthropological, since the

biography shares with the novels *Ruth* and *Sylvia's Lovers* the strategy of
opening a narrative by grounding it in thick descriptions of local culture
and the terrain that shaped it.[16] The immensity, isolation, and bleakness
of the moors, according to Gaskell, produced a rough, passionate, unpol-
ished race given to aggressive impetuosity and harsh words. Necessarily
aware of the charges of coarseness against Brontë, Gaskell reversed the
usual process, identified by Peter Brooks, of metonymic sequence giving
way to metaphoric totalization in plot. In Gaskell's hands the metaphor
of coarseness circulated by obituaries is dissolved back into metonymic
juxtaposition or sequence by displacing coarseness from Brontë and her
fiction onto the landscape and local population amid which Brontë lived.
Gaskell begins by exploding nostalgia for a past that had persisted from
Edward III's days to those of the early nineteenth century: "The idea of
the mistress and her maidens spinning at the great wheels while the master was abroad, ploughing his fields, or seeing after his flocks on the
purple moors, is very poetical to look back upon; but when such life
actually touches on our own days, and we can hear particulars from the
lips of those now living, details of coarseness—of the uncouthness of the
rustic mingled with the sharpness of the tradesman—of irregularity and
fierce lawlessness—come out, that rather mar the vision of pastoral innocence and simplicity" (*LCB,* 62). She recounts tales of riots (73–75),
stolid indifference even by a brother to a youth's near-fatal slitting of an
artery (65), squires who fancied cockfighting (68), and cruel seductions
(92–93) that the little Brontë children moved among. Coarseness is all
around the young Charlotte Brontë, but it is always outside, in others'
experiences or characters that she could later put to good use in fiction
without suffering their taint. If the rhythm of the moors imparts poetic
structure to the biography,[17] their presence is also a rhetorical means of
distancing Brontë from coarseness that threatened to engulf, and sully,
the woman author constructed in public discourses.

Gaskell also used the most disturbing elements of Branwell and
Emily Brontë's lives to displace coarse language and action onto Charlotte's then less famous siblings. Gaskell stinted nothing in unveiling
Branwell's sexual transgression and descent into alcoholism despite his—
alone of the Brontë children—having received the privilege of education
because of his sex. Here was coarseness indeed, and without the miti-
gating excuse of great art produced.[18] Although always acknowledging

Charlotte's passionate love and admiration for Emily, Gaskell also discharged coarseness onto the enigmatic sister.[19] It is Emily, not Charlotte, who has the most "masculine" mind (*LCB,* 230), who claps white-hot iron on her arm after a stray dog bites her, and who beats her bulldog Keeper into submission when he threatens her (268–69). Establishing that Charlotte drew on Emily's character for *Shirley,* Gaskell then seems to judge that feminine character in ways she refrains from applying to Charlotte at the end of the *Life:* "The character of Shirley herself, is Charlotte's representation of Emily. I mention this, because all that I, a stranger, have been able to learn about her has not tended to give either me, or my readers, a pleasant impression of her. But we must remember how little we are acquainted with her, compared to that sister, who, out of her more intimate knowledge, says that she 'was genuinely good, and truly great'" (379). When we also recall that Shirley calls herself "Captain Keeldar" in that novel,[20] we find a new woman warrior whose ferocity *in propria persona,* as well as in fiction, draws the sting of charges of untoward aggression away from Charlotte. Yet Gaskell also uses the example of Emily to argue for extenuating circumstances and the need to withhold judgment of a person until intimacy has been established.[21]

These authorial strategies, subtly permeating the entirety of the two volumes, converge at once in a powerful passage that directly takes up the charge of coarseness near the biography's end:

> *This seems a fitting place to state how utterly unconscious she was of what was, by some, esteemed coarse in her writings. . . .I do not deny for myself the existence of coarseness here and there in her works, otherwise so entirely noble. I only ask those who read them to consider her life,—which has been openly laid bare before them,—and to say how it could be otherwise. She saw few men; and among these few were one or two with whom she had been acquainted since early girlhood,—who had shown her much friendliness and kindness,—through whose family she had received many pleasures,—for whose intellect she had a great respect,—but who talked before her, if not to her, with as little reticence as Rochester talked to Jane Eyre. Take this in connection with her poor brother's sad life, and the out-spoken people among whom she lived,—remember her strong feeling of the duty of representing life as it really is, not as it ought to be,—and then do her justice for all that she was, and all that she would have been (had God spared her), rather than*

(*LCB,* 495–96)

censure her because circumstances forced her to touch pitch, as it were,
and by it her hand was for a moment defiled. It was but skin-deep.
Every change in her life was purifying her; it hardly could raise her.
Again I cry, "If she had but lived!"

Metonymy, Gaskell insists, must not be mistaken for metaphoric totalization: coarseness was the external pitch Brontë touched, but it left no permanent or inward stain.

Gaskell deployed several other rhetorical interventions that worked to contain implications of feminine impropriety in Brontë. As a number of commentators have observed,[22] Gaskell again and again portrays Brontë's unremitting sense of duty to others, no matter the financial (*LCB,* 289, 384–85), emotional, physical, or professional costs to herself. To cite only the most prominent instances, Brontë rejects a marriage proposal from Nicolls when her father objects (491); she puts aside the writing of *Villette* just when she is emerging from protracted writer's block and forgoes attendance at the Royal Literary Fund dinner in London, which she had set her heart on, when her father falls ill and requires her nursing (408, 479–80). Brontë's unvarying observation of feminine duty, of course, is also the means by which Patrick Brontë can be judged a tyrannical patriarch; thus, as so often with Gaskell, what seems the closest conformity to domestic ideology also upends its claims.[23] The themes of duty and submission, moreover, make Brontë a victim rather than a combative revolutionary. Indeed, the biography is a catalog of unremitting sickness, solitude, and depression that Brontë not only endured but triumphed over to produce her last two novels. The triumph, though, exists only because she first enacted feminine sacrifice to duty.

Here, as throughout the biography, Gaskell interweaves the accounts of writer and woman,[24] even though she also gestures toward separating the two: "Henceforward Charlotte Brontë's existence becomes divided into two parallel currents—her life as Currer Bell, the author; her life as Charlotte Brontë, the woman. There were separate duties belonging to each character—not opposing each other; not impossible, but difficult to be reconciled" (*LCB,* 334). The assertion is characteristically evasive, suggesting stark separation only to note the possibility of convergence. This familiar passage is, moreover, explicitly linked to the gendering of authorship. The passage continues, "When a man becomes an author, it is probably merely a change of employment to him. . . .But no other can take up the quiet, regular duties of the daughter, the wife, or the mother, as well as she whom God has appointed to fill that particular place . . . nor can she drop the domestic charges devolving on her as an individual, for the exercise of the most splendid talents that were ever bestowed." Yet just when Gaskell seems to have capitulated to regimes of difference, she reallocates the realm of genius and achievement to women: "And yet she must not shrink from the extra responsibility implied by the very fact of her possessing such talents. She must not hide her gift in a napkin; it was meant for the use and service of others. In an humble and faithful spirit must she labour to do what is not impossible, or God would not have set her to do it" (334). Gaskell deftly evokes the whole domestic world that must not suffocate talent through the image of the napkin, associated with housewives' superintendence of household linens. At once separating yet also bridging personal and professional life, Gaskell acknowledges yet complicates the ideology of separate spheres. She takes up firmly differentiated, totalizing realms—the home, the public world—then dissolves the boundaries she identifies until juxtaposition replaces a static, atemporal representation of difference.

Less obtrusive than direct avowals of duty or the dilemmas of female authorship is another rhetorical strategy crucial to the biography. Gaskell consistently bridges assertions of fiery passion, intellect, ambition, and fame to the domestic in Brontë's life, celebrating the expansion and exercise of rare talents but enacting structural connections of these to domestic duty, piety, and selflessness as an implicit argument that female authorship posed no threat to feminine virtue.[25] An expression of irritability and ferocity during Brontë's time at Roe Head School, for example ("those little sallies of ridicule, . . . owing to my miserable and wretched touchiness of character, used formerly to make me wince, as if I had been touched with a hot iron; things that nobody else cares for, enter into my mind and rankle there like venom" [*LCB,* 164]), is represented as the result of temporary illness ("a temporary ailment") and is immediately succeeded by—and accommodated to—daughterly duty to her father (164–65). At the end of volume 1 of the biography, Gaskell juxtaposes the first mention of Brontë and her sisters in public discourse—a notice of their poems in the 4 July 1846 *Athenaeum*—with a letter in which Brontë subordinates self-interest to filial duty ("The right path is that which necessitates the greatest sacrifice of self-interest—which implies the greatest good to others") and another letter to her publishers expressing the "Bells'" desire to remain unknown (295–97). Even the memorable picture of the Brontë sisters pacing in their parlor "like restless wild animals" while discussing their art and future plans is neatly spliced onto their prim domestic routines (sewing, meal preparation, prayers) during daylight hours, the proprieties minimizing their feral prowls, their wildness suggesting how confining the domestic sphere could be (199).

The second volume presented particular challenges, insofar as it tracks the career of the author of *Jane Eyre*.[26] Gaskell again, however, accommodates the female writer at work to the sphere of domesticity. After the attack on Brontë by Elizabeth Rigby, who suggested in the *Quarterly Review* that the author of *Jane Eyre* was most likely a woman who had forfeited the right to respectable female companions, Brontë fiercely defended her right to her own artistic vision ("I must have my own way in the matter of writing"). Gaskell reports the rejoinder but then carefully constructs the domestic backdrop to the declaration: "At the time when this letter was written, both Tabby and the young servant whom they had to assist her were ill in bed; and, with the exception of occasional aid, Miss Brontë had all the household work to perform, as well as to nurse the two invalids" (*LCB*, 383). In a later episode Gaskell suggests the power to which Brontë's talent gave her access, since Brontë, the woman formerly denied the education allotted to Branwell, attracted admiration for her work from a young university student at Cambridge. He may have privileged access to higher learning, but it is she who instructs him: "Certainly it is 'something to me' that what I write should be acceptable to the feeling heart and refined intellect." Gaskell continues quoting from the letter, however, to include a passage in which Brontë veils her cultural authority by troping the dissemination of her texts in domestic terms: "If [my works] cannot make themselves at home in a thoughtful, sympathetic mind, and diffuse through its twilight a cheering, domestic glow, it is their fault. . . .If they *can,* and can find household altars in human hearts, they will fulfil the best design of their creation" (410).

Gaskell is even more oblique in handling the author's relationship to Harriet Martineau, one of the members of Brontë's proliferating literary network as her fame grew. Martineau, as noted earlier (and as the infamous caricature of her in *Fraser's* attests), was herself a highly problematic site of professionalism and femininity. Gaskell approaches the portrayal of their friendship by quoting a letter in which Brontë's assessment of Martineau models the strategy Gaskell pursues with Brontë:

> *She is certainly a woman of wonderful endowments, both intellectual and physical; and though I share few of her opinions, and regard her as fallible on certain points of judgment, I must still award her my sincerest esteem. The manner in which she combines the highest mental culture*
> (LCB, 438)   *with the nicest discharge of feminine duties filled me with admiration; while her affectionate kindness earned my gratitude. . . .I think her good and noble qualities far outweigh her defects. It is my habit to consider the individual apart from his (or her) reputation, practice independent of theory, natural disposition isolated from acquired opinions.*

Gaskell thus freely connects Brontë to a woman writer who was also a declared atheist and public authority on political economy; but she quotes Brontë admiring Martineau for her feminine virtues even more than for her writing and suggesting that all professional women need to be approached inductively rather than in overdetermined ideological terms.

A final instance of Gaskell's mediation of professionalism and femininity needs to be cited, since it involves Brontë's reply to a letter from Gaskell herself. The exchange establishes that the two novelists discussed feminist issues and adjudicated the merits of contemporary writers, active assertions of cultural authority; but the passages selected by Gaskell slide easily into domestic proprieties and the genre of female gossip: [27]

> *Of all the articles respecting which you question me, I have seen none, except that notable one in the "Westminster" on the Emancipation of Women. . . .Your words on this paper express my thoughts. Well-argued it is,—clear, logical,—but vast is the hiatus of omission; harsh the consequent jar on every finer chord of the soul. . . .I think the writer*
> (LCB, 458)   *forgets there is such a thing as self-sacrificing love and disinterested devotion. When I first read the paper, I thought it was the work of a powerful-minded, clear-headed woman, who had a hard, jealous heart, muscles of iron, and nerves of bend leather; of a woman who longed for power, and had never felt affection.*

The passage has figured in scholarship as the cause of offense given to J. S. Mill through its characterization of his wife, Harriet Taylor Mill.[28] But in the context of Gaskell's relation to print culture and implied readers, the passage also enacts women's relation to public authority and domesticity.

Gaskell's representations of Brontë's visits to London or her participation in literary life are also of particular interest, since these involve Brontë's penetration into public spaces. Most typically, Gaskell presents the public Brontë under the aegis of modesty and innocence, linking assertion and propriety. As often noted, Charlotte and Anne Brontë had literally to present their bodies in a public space to prove their separate authorship after an American publisher, presuming that Acton Bell's work was by the same hand as *Jane Eyre,* charged infringement of a publishing contract. Gaskell represents the sisters as truly innocents abroad, stumbling into the precincts of Paternoster Row ("a strange place, but they did not well know where else to go" [*LCB,* 345]) or failing to consider that they could hire a "conveyance" to take them to the publishing house rather than walking through the streets. When they arrive, their diminutive persons and subdued attire contrast humorously with the excitement and expectations their writing had stirred: "On reaching Mr Smith's, Charlotte put his own letter into his hands. . . . 'Where did you get this?' said he,—as if he could not believe that the two young ladies dressed in black, of slight figures and diminutive stature, looking pleased yet agitated, could be the embodied Currer and Acton Bell, for whom curiosity had been hunting so eagerly in vain" (345–46). Relishing the arch possibilities such material offered, a few pages later Gaskell expanded on the sisters' choice of hotel. The women placed themselves in what had earlier been the heart of the literary marketplace ("the resort of all the booksellers and publishers; and where the literary hacks, the critics, and even the wits, used to go in search of ideas or employment" [348]). More strikingly, they were the lone women guests in a public tavern "solely frequented by men" (349). It is rather a nice trope for women's incursion into privileged male domains that was soon to be accomplished by Brontë's fame as a novelist. But this aspect is muted by the sheer humor of the incident and by Gaskell's attributing their blunder to ignorance and family ties, since the daughters merely stayed where their father had stayed on earlier trips (349).

But Gaskell does not stop here. As in *Mary Barton,* when Mary's public display of her body in the courtroom and incursion into the streets of Liverpool are followed by physical suffering, hence purification, so here the unprecedented visit to London and display of the female authorial body in public leads temporarily to Charlotte's collapse: "When they returned back to their inn, poor Charlotte paid for the excitement of the interview [with Smith], which had wound up the agitation and hurry of the last twenty-four hours, by a racking headache and harassing sickness" (*LCB,* 346). Gaskell's active work in the episode is all the clearer, and more significant, because she expunged moments of playfulness and assertion from the Charlotte Brontë letter she otherwise relied on for her narration of Brontë's incursion into the literary marketplace. Alison Kershaw, who details Gaskell's mediation of Brontë's account, concludes, "As Brontë's identity as a woman is established before this male bastion of the publishing world, Gaskell is concerned that at the moment of revelation Smith should be impressed by her feminine modesty and that any hint of forthrightness be suppressed." [29] Yet Gaskell also chose to include, and elaborate, the process by which a private female became a public author—and survived the ordeal.

After *Shirley* was published, Brontë paid another visit to London and entered the whirl of literary London. Gaskell is careful not to present this excursion as a desire to capitalize on the public circulation of Brontë's name and fame. Rather, Charlotte's visit figures as a form of healing rather than displaying the body, and of daughterly duty: "She determined to take the evil in time, as much for her father's sake as for her own, and to go up to London and consult some physician there. It was not her first intention to visit anywhere; but the friendly urgency of her publishers prevailed" (*LCB,* 388–89). If she muffles Brontë's public role, however, Gaskell also underscores the public voices and persons surrounding her at this time. She carefully notes the favorable reviews of *Shirley* in the *Examiner* and *Standard,* in which Brontë took pleasure, and narrates her introduction to Thackeray. At a dinner hosted by her publisher with Thackeray and several other literary men, however, modesty rather than triumph dominates Gaskell's narration. Charlotte enters the dining room, sees the place of honor reserved for her next to her publisher, Mr. Smith, but deliberately ignores it to sit by the only other woman present at the dinner: "This slight action arose out of the same womanly seeking after protection on every occasion, when there was no moral duty involved in asserting her independence" (393).

Brontë's greatest public triumph comes when she attends a lecture given by Thackeray. As Brontë recounted in a letter, "I did not at all expect the great lecturer would know me or notice me under these circumstances, with admiring duchesses and countesses seated in rows before him; but he met me as I entered—shook hands—and took me to his mother, whom I had not before seen, and introduced me" (*LCB,* 446). The triumph is unmediated here (though the detail of Thackeray's mother softens Brontë's exultation in precedence over duchesses). But Gaskell overlays this with another account in which Brontë desires to avoid public recognition in the lecture hall (447) and quivers like a hunted animal when forced to exit by passing between spectators lined up to gaze on the author of *Jane Eyre*: "During this passage through the 'cream of society,' Miss Brontë's hand trembled to such a degree, that her companion feared lest she should turn faint and be unable to proceed" (448).

The care to present Brontë's publicity under the cloak of modesty might suggest similar awareness in Gaskell's own self-presentations in the biography. We have cited one of these, in which the writers' discussion of feminism modulates into domestic affection and gossip. Another of Brontë's letters that Gaskell selected for reprinting compared Martineau and Gaskell as writers, bringing Gaskell before her own readers not only as Brontë's friend[30] but also as a writer of public repute. Here as elsewhere Gaskell is scrupulously fair to the controversial Martineau, yet the letter also works, parallel to Gaskell's efforts on behalf of Brontë, to distance Gaskell from masculinity by troping strong artistic powers in terms of domestic goodness. Brontë writes:

> *About a fortnight ago, I received a letter from Miss Martineau; also a long letter, and treating precisely the same subjects on which yours dwelt. . . . It was interesting mentally to place the two documents side by side—to study the two aspects of mind. . . . Full striking was the difference; and the more striking because it was not the rough contrast of good and evil, but the more subtle opposition, the more delicate diversity of different kinds of good. The excellences of one nature resembled (I thought) that of some sovereign medicine—harsh, perhaps, to the taste, but potent to invigorate; the good of the other seemed more akin to the nourishing efficacy of our daily bread. It is not bitter; it is not lusciously sweet: it pleases, without flattering the palate; it sustains, without forcing the strength.*

(*LCB,* 455–56)

Gaskell also allows representations of herself as a public writer to appear in the last section of the biography, in part of course because only at this stage in Brontë's life had the two women become friends—though they became friends, one should remember, because their public careers as novelists prompted interest in each other. By this stage of the biography Gaskell has fully established her representation of Brontë as an artistic genius who is also a woman of supernal virtue. Hence Brontë's encomiums on Gaskell's work have aesthetic as well as moral authority, and they shield Gaskell's own fiction from charges of impropriety. These self-presentations, in other words, are a form of benign self-advertisement.[31]

To narrate the crucial convergence of the two women authors, Gaskell opts for self-citation, quoting from two separate letters, here presented as one,[32] to Catherine Winkworth and an unidentified correspondent (*LMG*, 123–27). The physical convergence of the two women is mirrored in a shifting, unstable "I" that is now the biographer, now the object of Brontë's utterance: "I was struck by Miss Brontë's careful examination of the shape of the clouds and the signs of the heavens, in which she read, as from a book, what the coming weather would be. I told her that I saw she must have a view equal in extent at her own home. She said that I was right, but that the character of the prospect from Haworth was very different; that I had no idea what a companion the sky became to any one living in solitude,—more than any inanimate object on earth,—more than the moors themselves" (*LCB*, 418). Physical, linguistic, and subjective boundaries blur in this central moment of the biography; if such merging signals the dawn of a literary friendship and documents a biographer's sympathetic identification with her subject (whose own comments on the moors have been extensively quoted to this point), it also discloses Gaskell's active presence in Brontë's life story.

This enactment of intersubjectivity leads to another form of self-advertisement, in which the brilliant but pure Brontë vouches for the worth of Gaskell's own writing. Here, for example, is Brontë on Gaskell's second novel: "Thank you for your letter; it was as pleasant as a quiet chat, as welcome as spring showers, as reviving as a friend's visit; in short, it was very like a page of 'Cranford'" (*LCB*, 504). Brontë's reaction to the sketch of *Ruth* Gaskell sent her is usually cited for Charlotte's protest against the death of Gaskell's heroine. But the excerpted letter seems equally important for its assertion that the novel is a virtuous one: "The sketch you give of your work (respecting which I am, of course, dumb) seems to me very noble; and its purpose may be as useful in practical result as it is high and just in theoretical tendency. Such a book may restore hope and energy to many" (474). Later Gaskell quotes Brontë's letter explaining that she has told her publisher to withhold *Villette* for two weeks to give *Ruth* a fair start with the public; besides grounding the women's professional lives in the affectionate friendship that prompted Brontë's extraordinarily generous gesture, the passage again draws on the ethos established for Brontë to vouch for the probity of *Ruth*. *Villette*, Brontë remarked, "has indeed no right to push itself before '*Ruth.*' There is a goodness, a philanthropic purpose, a social use in the latter, to which the former cannot for an instant pretend; nor can it claim precedence on the ground of surpassing power: I think it much quieter than 'Jane Eyre'" (492).

The passage also insists on the proximity of the two novelists' works, for as Brontë herself remarks, "I dare say, arrange as we may, we shall not be able wholly to prevent comparisons; it is the nature of some critics to be invidious; but we need not care: we can set them at defiance" (*LCB*, 492). Gaskell's awareness of their proximity, whether in domesticity or as objects of public attack, may well inform the other passage in the biography in which Gaskell explicitly takes up and repudiates the charge of coarseness against Brontë. This occurs in the familiar passage detailing Elizabeth Rigby's attack in the December 1848 *Quarterly Review*. Gaskell's voice rises in crescendo as she recounts the injustice of the snide implications:

> *Who is he that should say of an unknown woman: "She must be one who for some sufficient reason has long forfeited the society of her sex"? Is he one who has led a wild and struggling and isolated life,—seeing few but plain and outspoken Northerns, unskilled in the euphuisms which assist the polite world to skim over the mention of vice? Has he striven through long weeping years to* (360) *find excuses for the lapse of an only brother; and through daily contact with a poor lost profligate, been compelled into a certain familiarity with the vices that his soul abhors? Has he, through trials, close following in dread march through his household, sweeping the hearthstone bare of life and love, still striven hard for*

strength to say, "It is the Lord! let Him do what seemeth to Him
good"—and sometimes striven in vain, until the kindly Light re-
turned? If through all these dark waters the scornful reviewer have
passed clear, refined, free from stain,—with a soul that has never in all
its agonies, cried "lama sabachthani,"—still, even then let him pray
with the Publican rather than judge with the Pharisee.

Easson remarks, "In dealing with the review, we may feel Gaskell has
allowed *her* feelings to lead her into unworthy insults. . . .[and] she rises
embarrassingly through a series of rhetorical questions that culminate in
Charlotte as Christ in agony."[33] But the periodical context of the biography, as well as Gaskell's own self-presentation in the work itself, suggests
how far, in viewing Brontë's case, Gaskell might observe, "La femme,
c'est moi." Gaskell's evident engagement with Brontë's own plight in the
passage above may stem from indignant affection, but the voice is equally
plausible as that of the woman author attacked for *Ruth* whose defense of
Brontë is also self-defense.

The best gauge of the success of Gaskell's interventions in public
discourse on Brontë's—and her own—behalf is to be found in reviews
published before the lawsuit threatened by Lady Scott and Gaskell's letter
of retraction published 31 May 1857. After that date issues of accuracy
and reliability cloud the discourses of gender and authorship clear in the
earliest responses.[34] The *Saturday Review* notice of 4 April 1857 made ex-
plicit what was at stake in Gaskell's biography. It opened by asserting that
English women tended not to have lives worth relating since, as private
creatures, nothing happened to them. It then reminded readers of *the*
question regarding the author of *Jane Eyre:* "When the public heard that
the author of *Jane Eyre* was a plain little woman, the daughter of a cler-
gyman living in the remotest wilds of Yorkshire, it was natural to wonder
whence came this astonishing knowledge of the workings of fiery passion. Did she write from memory—or was she taught by the inspiration
of a creative mind? . . . It was an inquiry as legitimate as it was interesting,
how Charlotte Brontë came to draw the character of Mr. Rochester"
(*SR,* 4 April 1857, 313). This notice also revealed how successful Gaskell's
rhetorical strategies had proved: "Miss Brontë had, so far as is known to
her biographer, never felt anything like love when she wrote *Jane Eyre.*
She had never seen or known personally what she described. There
was no original of the character of Rochester. We may accept it as an

undoubted psychological fact that, by the mere force of genius, a young woman did really apprehend a phase of the human heart of a most complex and subtle kind" (313). Not only did Gaskell clear Brontë from the charges of coarseness or impropriety, but in doing so she also expanded the claims for genius in Brontë, who could create out of sheer brilliance rather than personal experience. Goodness and genius are here mutually constitutive.

The 4 April 1857 *Spectator* opened by emphasizing the story of the Brontës' childhood, their strange, eccentric father, their isolation, and their rich inward lives that underscored their genius. Taking Gaskell's lead, the reviewer displaced any suggestions of coarseness onto the Yorkshire landscape and culture rather than discerning them in Brontë herself: "Some influence may have come upon the Brontë girls from the rugged uncivilized character of the majority of the people in their father's parish; a plainness of speech and a fearlessness of thought which startled the readers of their novels" (*SP*, 373). Even more striking is the evidence that Gaskell had indeed rewritten the script of the daring author of *Jane Eyre* into a story of the dutiful, suffering woman in whom genius and goodness were inseparable:

> *It is impossible to read through Mrs. Gaskell's two volumes without a strong conviction that Charlotte Brontë was a woman as extraordinary by her character as by her genius. . . . One way and another, she gave mind and body no rest; spent herself lavishly for others—lavishly and even wastefully. The result was a confirmed state of suffering and ill-health, terribly aggravated by certain domestic circumstances, over which Mrs. Gaskell throws no veil, ruthlessly exposing them in her anxiety for the character of her heroine. . . . The profound pathos, the tragic interest of this book, lies in the exhibition of the terrible struggle that life was to a woman endowed with Charlotte Brontë's conscientiousness, affection for her family, and literary ambitions, and continually curbed and thrown back by physical wretchedness. Its moral is, the unconquerable strength of genius and goodness.*　(373–74)

Even the passing reference to reckless courage in Brontë's biographer, who dared expose secrets of the hearth, is absorbed to the stance of deep womanly sympathy as well as an artist's sense of truth.

The remarks of "Shirley" (Sir John Skelton) in the May 1857 *Fraser's* are notable for indicating that Gaskell's work allowed for emphasizing genius more than goodness in the continuum between the two her work had established, and for indicating how closely Gaskell and Brontë were linked in the public mind. Although noting Brontë's unwavering duty and long-suffering, Skelton opens by focusing on the works and the genius behind them, turning considerable attention to the achievement of Emily Brontë as well as that of Charlotte. Citing the biography's epigraph from *Aurora Leigh* (*F*, 576), Skelton then considers the charge of coarseness against *Jane Eyre* and defends the novel, Barrett Browning's poem, and Gaskell's *Ruth* as works that explore social ills while the authors themselves remain free from moral taint:

> *when a woman like Charlotte Brontë does try to evoke that mighty spirit of tragedy which lurks in the heart of every man, she is told that she is creating the horrible, and breaking artistic statutes more immutable than those of the Medes and Persians. . . . According to certain scrupulous zealots, everything is immoral in our present art—from* Marie *and* La Traviata, *to* Ruth, Jane Eyre, *and* Aurora Leigh— *which presumes to assert that society is not a mass of respectabilities, and that there are certain waifs and strays scattered about, who, as they have contrived to get into the world, require at least to be looked after till they leave it. . . . They cannot know how . . . purity and courage go hand in hand; how it is the most stainless conscience which is least afraid of impurity, as it is the last easily sullied by contact with the impure. . . .if* Aurora Leigh *is such a book, then* Jane Eyre *may be included in the class. . . .rudeness, indelicacy, masculine directness, are words that have been somewhat loosely applied to describe a fine and peculiar insight into the heart of man.*

(578)

Given Skelton's conviction that what has been blamed as coarseness is in fact imaginative and moral truth, he can invoke Gaskell's own "scandalous" novel, *Ruth,* as a warrant for Gaskell's qualifications to write a superb biography of Brontë—not because of their common scandal but owing to common feminine tenderness conjoined to artistic skill: "[Brontë's] is a life always womanly. And we are thankful that such a life—the life of the authoress of *Villette*—should have been written by the writer of *Ruth.* No one else could have paid so tender and discerning a tribute to the memory of Charlotte Brontë" (577).

Interestingly, to the degree that early reviews stressed domesticity more than genius in their appraisals of Brontë, they tended to deemphasize Gaskell's work as biographer, suggesting in yet another guise the presence of gender norms underlying Victorian authorship. Both the *Saturday Review* and *Spectator* notices, which hail the woman more than the artist in Brontë, tend to treat Gaskell as a transparent medium for conveying Brontë's story; the former allotted Gaskell a single sentence at the review's close ("Such a story does not lose anything of its pathos or its instructiveness when told by such a biographer as Mrs. Gaskell" [*SR*, 314]). Skelton, less committed to narrow definitions of female authorship, gives Gaskell more credit, not only as the author of *Ruth* but also as a shrewd and skillful biographer: "Mrs. Gaskell has done her work well. Her narrative is simple, direct, intelligible, unaffected. Her descriptions . . . are vivid and picturesque. . . . The extracts from the letters are excellently selected" (*F*, 577).

Henry Fothergill Chorley in the *Athenaeum* directly criticized bourgeois domestic ideology while also singling out Gaskell's artistry in shaping Brontë's life story. Having recounted some of the racier details of Yorkshire life presented by Gaskell at the biography's opening, Chorley observes: "Those who have ever thought of such wild, lawless doings as these, and of their consequences—overt crime or concealed vice—will pause over the writings of the sentimentalists ere they accept domestic happiness, superior content, and cheerful sense of duty as the prevailing spirit of middle-class life among persons of modest fortunes in England during the past half-century, in order that they may point to our island as a place now rotting under the wrecks and ruins of a healthier, simpler society" (*A*, 4 April 1857, 428). In this shrewd critique of what might be termed specious "family values," Chorley identifies the active work of gender ideology in reinforcing conservative regimes[35]—and resists it. He is not loath to characterize Patrick Brontë as a family tyrant or to contemplate the sad tale of Branwell, praising Gaskell's candor in relating the details: "Mrs. Gaskell has told the whole dismal story, without hesitation or suppression, too emphatically for any one dealing with it to forbear from comment" (428). His review opens, though, by considering the biography as a work of art. If he notes gender as a qualifying factor, he nonetheless counters reviews treating Gaskell's text as a transparent medium for disseminating another's story: "The story of a woman's life unfolded in this book is calculated to make the old feel young and the

young old. . . .By all, this book will be read with interest. As a work of
Art, we do not recollect a life of a woman by a woman so well exe-
cuted.—The materials were not large, and the difficulties of selection
were obvious" (427).

In constructing her narrative of Brontë's life, then, Gaskell can be
viewed as using her text to intervene in representations of Brontë first
circulated by the obituaries, which in turn had implicated Gaskell in
public discourse. Through a number of deft rhetorical strategies, from
metonymic displacements to mediations of authorial assertion, Gaskell
brilliantly established a continuum between professionalism and domestic
propriety so that readers could appropriate the narrative to their own
agendas or emphases but never lose the connection of virtue with artistic
genius.

Such efforts in the *Life of Charlotte Brontë* expose the constraints under which women authors achieved reputations and managed their appearances in the public sphere. Reading the *Life* in its periodical context
clarifies the energetic work performed by the biography in defending
Brontë and rewriting narratives of female authorship. We will further
illuminate the dynamics of gender in Gaskell's biography by turning to
a biography from the 1880s, James Anthony Froude's life of Thomas
Carlyle. The first two volumes of that biography, published in 1882, followed on the shock waves precipitated by the publication of *Reminiscences*
a month after Carlyle's death (at which time obituaries had tended to
verge on hagiography).[36] The *Reminiscences* revealed a splenetic Carlyle
awash in petty prejudice; *Thomas Carlyle: A History of the First Forty Years
of His Life, 1795–1835* (hereafter referred to as 1882) revealed Carlyle in
the guise of domestic tyrant. In Froude's account the brilliant and beautiful heiress Jane Welsh, blocked from marriage with Edward Irving[37] and
herself intent on a literary career, is forced to remove to a bleak, isolated
farmhouse and undertake menial labor to support Carlyle's efforts when
he insists on dwelling at Craigenputtock. Froude calls Jane variously a
"victim" as "of old in Aulis" (1882, 1:213) and a "slave": "Her life was
the dreariest of slaveries to household cares and toil. She was without
society. . . .Carlyle, intensely occupied with his thoughts and his writing,
was unable to bear the presence of a second person when busy at his desk.
He sat alone, walked alone, generally rode alone" (1882, 2:154). Froude
also takes care to emphasize repeatedly the sheer physical labor Jane

was forced to undertake: "The necessary imperfections of Scotch farm-servant girls had to be supplemented by Mrs. Carlyle herself. She baked the bread, she dressed the dinner or saw it dressed, she cleaned the rooms. Among her other accomplishments, she had to learn to milk the cows, in case the byre-woman should be out of the way, for fresh milk was the most essential article of Carlyle's diet. Nay, it might happen that she had to black the grates to the proper polish, or even scour the floors while Carlyle looked on encouragingly with his pipe" (1882, 2:27). The result was a heavy toll on Jane's health and nerves. Froude quotes a 10 February 1833 letter from Carlyle to his brother John averring that, though Jane is not particularly well, she "is at least not worse"; then, remarking that Carlyle "observed nothing, as through his life he never did observe any-thing, about her which called away his attention from his work and from what was round him," Froude quotes Jane's own postscript to the letter: "In truth, I am always so sick now, and so heartless, that I cannot apply myself to any mental effort without a push from necessity" (1882, 2:195).

We quote at length because the experience of Jane Carlyle—sub-jected to harrowing solitude not only geographically but also domestically because of a patriarch's selfish isolation, often suffering from deep depres-sion and physical weakness yet nonetheless forced to undertake strenuous physical labor considered inappropriate to bourgeois women—is so like Charlotte Brontë's own as described by Gaskell.[38] But in the story Froude tells, Jane Welsh Carlyle, a woman of undoubted artistic talent, is not the genius who must write against all odds. Carlyle is. Charlotte Brontë's distinction was to enact, as it were, the stories of both Thomas and Jane Carlyle: she was an artistic genius compelled to write but also a domestic drudge deprived of emotional support by her father and often forced to put domestic duty before her vocation as writer. The contrast highlights the immense privilege accorded male authors within the home and in narratives constructed to relay their stories. It is impossible to conceive of a Carlyle compelled by artistic vision yet also forced to postpone the next sentence of *Sartor* because he was called on to scour the kitchen floor.

Unlike Brontë, moreover, Carlyle had the privilege of acknowledg-ing literary ambition rather than being forced to cloak it under apparent self-subordination to others' needs. Froude excerpts Carlyle's 24 August 1833 journal, in which Carlyle declares, "Happily (this is probably my greatest happiness), the chief desire of my mind has again become to *write* a masterpiece, let it be acknowledged as such or not acknowledged" (1882, 2:207). Carlyle's aspirations are hedged about with doubt of accomplishment, but ambition itself is not problematical, in contrast to Brontë's presentation in Gaskell's biography.

If Gaskell's biography has at times been seen as overly complicit in repressive domestic ideologies,[39] Froude's 1882 volumes, paradoxically, can be read as feminist biography. His subject may be the career of a great man of letters, but the distinction of the 1882 volumes is their consistent appraisal of Carlyle from the standpoint of Jane Welsh Carlyle and her needs, desires, and experiences.[40] If Carlyle is clearly a writer of the highest order, a generous and loving family member with his siblings and parents, he is, according to Froude, "selfish" and "arrogant" when it comes to Jane.

Although recourse to hagiography and erasure of Jane's presence in obituaries immediately following Carlyle's death in 1881 might be construed as calling forth the revisionary voice of Froude's 1882 volumes, this was not so. As Waldo Dunn remarks, Froude had nearly completed them before Carlyle's death.[41] Once published, moreover, Froude's work, like Gaskell's, quickly became bogged down in a morass of charges of inaccuracy and, in Froude's case, questions of ethics as well. This element of the "Froude-Carlyle controversy" has received principal attention in scholarship.

But as Trev Broughton makes clear, the controversy revolved around crucial issues of gender as well: "The first phase of the Froude-Carlyle controversy (1880–1903) reflected, and reinforced, new relationships between representations of the Man of Letters as husband, the surveillance of the middle-class marriage, and the regulation of literary masculinity."[42] Broughton places Froude's work in the context not only of literary professionalism but also of the rise of companionate marriage as an ideal and new conceptions of marital cruelty circulated through divorce court hearings. Broughton seconds Mary Poovey's contention that the professional writer's relation to the literary marketplace was mediated at midcentury through positioning the writer in a private realm, in which the sacrifice of the bourgeois wife to sustain her husband's work was crucial.[43] Broughton, however, argues that the ideal of companionate marriage raised women's expectations about equal treatment in the private realm. For male hegemony within marriage and the literary marketplace to be maintained, in turn, it was necessary to curb the worst excesses, hence the investment of Froude and his readers in the surveillance of male genius within marriage. Broughton concurs with Phyllis Rose [44] that Froude ultimately represented the Carlyle marriage under the aegis of tragic irony, the great sage of penetrating vision being unable to see what was closest to him. Yet Broughton also notes that Froude's audiences resisted this strategy, wishing to assign blame to individuals (whether Carlyle or, in attempts to recuperate him, Jane Welsh Carlyle or Froude). Froude's careful, exhaustive presentation of minute detail from the two lives he chronicled, moreover, involved him as well as Carlyle in anxieties about masculinity. Minute details revealed Carlyle's unmanly pettiness and also suggested that Froude himself was unmanly in channeling serious biography toward the stuff of gossip. Yet the prevailing fixation on biographical details in the immediate aftermath of the biography and into the early twentieth century suggests to Broughton that the details themselves served some function. Broughton concludes that densely massed details centered the Froude-Carlyle controversy in the irreducible quiddities of a man of unique genius; by stressing both the details and the genius, readers could air the issues of companionate marriage yet exempt themselves from the implications of the Carlyles' specific case.

The periodical context of Froude's life of Carlyle, significantly, does not indicate public preoccupation with feminist views of authorship or marriage.[45] Reviews of the volume that began the controversy, the *Reminiscences,* focused less on marriage in questioning Carlyle's masculinity than on Carlyle's relation to other men and on his vitiated powers of masculine endurance.[46] Reviewers of *Reminiscences* were particularly incensed that Carlyle cast slurs on the beloved Elia and concluded that Carlyle was a petty, egocentric whiner who could not endure to have others praised or listened to when he was present. *Temple Bar* judged Carlyle by comparing his difficulties to those of Samuel Johnson, the latter "a more social and a more kindly man. . . .Though both men could be brusque enough, and both were impatient of a fool, there was no feminine bitterness in Johnson, such as is to be found in these Reminiscences, which, it must be admitted, lower Carlyle somewhat in the esteem and affection in which he has been held." A footnote to the sentence added, "Whilst Carlyle throughout his Reminiscences has scarce a good word for Hazlitt,

Lamb, and Wordsworth, or his more celebrated contemporaries, yet we find Dr. Johnson rejoicing in the public appreciation of Goldsmith, Richardson, and Savage" (*TB,* 62 [1881]: 24). Jane Welsh Carlyle figures in this review merely as an angel in the house: "[Her] magnanimous soul repressed itself that his soul might ride in safety" (29). The reviewer is even content that Carlyle should have attacked the woman of letters Harriet Martineau, whose own pettiness serves to fix Carlyle's as a distinctly feminine trait: "Carlyle's treatment of Harriet Martineau is more just. Her unbounded conceit and belief in herself, fostered by her foolish adorers, who lent themselves to blow out her fame, are let off gently enough, though he speaks of her 'scrubbyish . . . Socinian didactic little notes'. . . .Harriet Martineau, her sayings and doings and her conceits, are buried for ever under the sands of time" (27). It is when Carlyle violates the regulations governing a homosocial male literary circle, then, and when he represents himself as vulnerable to his environment and bodily ills, that he is termed "feminine" and unseated as sage.[47] James Cotter Morison, writing in the April 1881 *Fortnightly Review,* concluded that "the great preacher and prophet of heroes was not himself the hero we thought him" (*FR,* 457) because of the "constant depreciation of contemporaries, even acquaintances and friends" (458). He also singled out the "soft, shrinking, puling tone with which, on his own showing, [Carlyle] met the ills and even paltry discomforts of his life" (459).

When in 1883 Froude began the last installment of his biography, after he had seen the *Letters and Memorials of Jane Welsh Carlyle* through the press, he intervened, as Gaskell did with the Brontë biography and femininity, to indicate Carlyle's more active conformity with norms of masculinity.[48] Particularly in the first volume of 1884, Froude used a number of rhetorical strategies. Relative to 1882, Froude appears more selective in what he quoted from letters or Carlyle's journal, reprinting fewer shrill complaints. Thus, for example, when Froude relates that in June 1837 Carlyle "fled to Scotland fairly broken down . . . his strangely organised nervous system shattered" (1884, 1:93), Froude merely states the fact rather than quoting from a pertinent document, hushing querulous tones that would otherwise erupt into the text. Several letters, in contrast, represent a stoic Carlyle refusing to whine, as when, alone at Chelsea, he labored to complete the *French Revolution.* Carlyle writes a reasonably cheerful letter to his wife, after which Froude notes,

His heart was less light than he tried to make it appear. The jour-
nal of August 1 says:—

> *Have finished chapter i. (September) of my third volume,*
> *and gone idle a week after, till as usual I am now reduced to a*
> *caput mortuum again, and do this day begin my second chap-*   (1884, 1:65)
> *ter, to be called "Regicide." Jane in Dumfriesshire these three*
> *weeks or more, shattered with agitation. I see no one . . . for*
> *above two weeks; very dreary of outlook; one sole guiding star for*
> *me on earth, that of getting done with my book.*

Only a few pages after the excerpt above, Froude directly asserts Carlyle's
manliness:

> *Ten years before, he had formed large hopes of what he might do*
> *and become as a man of letters. He concluded now that he had*
> *failed, and the language in which he wrote about it is extremely*
> *manly.*
>
> Journal
>
> *October 23 [1836].—Nothing noted here for a long time. It*   (1884, 1:71)
> *has grown profitless, wearisome, to write or speak of one so sick,*
> *forlorn as myself. Chap. 3 (Girondins) finished about a week*
> *ago. Totally worthless, according to my feeling of it. I persist,*
> *nevertheless.*

Froude even brings the language of chivalry into play. After the publication—and triumph—of the *French Revolution* Carlyle restores himself
from his labors at his mother's house in Scotsbrig, at which point Froude
compares him to "Spenser's knight, sorely wounded in his fight with the
dragon, [who] fell back under the enchanted tree. . . .what that tree was
to the bleeding warrior, the poor Annadale [*sic*] farmhouse, its quiet innocence, and the affectionate kindred there, proved then as always to
Carlyle, for he too had been fighting dragons and been heavily beaten
upon" (1884, 1:96). Later Froude observes that "rustic as he was in habits,
dress, and complexion, he had a knightly, chivalrous temperament, and
fine natural courtesy" (1884, 1:215).

In keeping with this courtesy Froude took care to quote several excerpts in which Carlyle either praised or softened his censure of other
men. Connop Thirlwall, for example, is "very pleasant, free and easy. . . . a

most sarcastic, sceptical, but strong-hearted, strong-headed man, whom he had a real liking for" (1884, 1:142); Carlyle's first impression of Tennyson, so familiar it need not be quoted here, was also reprinted (1884, 1:163), and later Froude narrated Carlyle's growing admiration for Ruskin after *Unto This Last* began appearing (1884, 2:207–14). Froude did not cease recording Carlyle's complaints or self-regard in 1884, but in the later volumes these are softened, muted, and much more carefully situated in complex psychological currents and circumstances.

The catch-phrase of the 1882 volumes, taken from Carlyle's mother, "gey ill to live wi,'"[49] gave way in 1884, then, to a phrase drawn from Carlyle's own journal, "the nature of the beast." A woman's judgment gave way to knowing masculine self-assessment. In a crucial passage, in fact, Froude argued that the literary life Carlyle pursued exacerbated all his weaknesses, for the need to work alone meant he was never forced to learn to work with others (1884, 2:196–97). By implication, if Carlyle's writings had value, the temperament that made him difficult to live with had to be accepted as well.

In fact, in the 1884 volumes Carlyle emerges as truly heroic on two counts: the self-sacrifice of his reputation as penance for wrongs to Jane during their marriage and his completion of the *French Revolution*. As Froude relates, Carlyle deliberately amassed documents that would compromise his reputation after death because of grief for Jane and remorse over his treatment of her. Retroactively, the domestic tyrant of the 1882 volumes is recuperated as the man who sacrifices worldly reputation for the sake of love. The woman-centered biography of 1882, in which Carlyle is seen through the eyes of Jane, becomes an effect orchestrated by Carlyle from the beginning and a grand chivalric gesture for a lady love. The shift can also be construed as the triumph of conscience over sin: Carlyle's puritan conviction demanded that, insofar as he had sinned, he must stand in the pillory of public opinion. His bequeathing unflattering materials also validates the intellectual and man of letters, for it ratifies his own insistence that biography must present truth rather than sentimental cant.

The other great act of heroism is the rewriting of the burned volume of the *French Revolution*. When Carlyle's fortunes are at their lowest after the failure of *Sartor Resartus,* when his income dwindles to nothing in the face of editors' lack of interest, he writes his history in the heat of inspiration. When, in turn, his work of genius is burned and he is unable for the first time in his life to keep writing, he pulls himself together by iron will and heroic determination, rewrites the first volume, and produces a masterpiece.

But then this story is not so very different from the one Gaskell tells about Brontë's composition of *Jane Eyre*[50] and *Villette*. As Gaskell remarks of the former, "Among the dispiriting circumstances connected with her anxious visit to Manchester, Charlotte told me that her tale came back upon her hands, curtly rejected by some publisher, on the very day when her father was to submit to his operation. But she had the heart of Robert Bruce within her. . . .she began, in this time of care and depressing inquietude,—in those grey, weary, uniform streets, where all faces save that of her kind doctor, were strange and untouched with sunlight to her,—there and then, did the brave genius begin 'Jane Eyre'" (*LCB*, 305). Gaskell handles the composition of *Villette* with a more subdued palette; no invocation of storied heroes occurs in these pages, yet the account is hardly less heroic than that of Carlyle's completion of the *French Revolution*. Haunted by grief for the sisters whose deaths deprived her of emotional support and of fellow writers with whom she could discuss her work; struggling daily against crippling depression; fearful that her lingering cold might betoken consumption, and thus terrified of seeking medical advice; wracked by writer's block and a sense of guilt in being unable to finish what she had begun, Brontë nonetheless rallied and finished *Villette,* resisting meanwhile her father's behest that she give it a happy ending in an act of artistic integrity at odds with daughterly duty.

Literary heroism, it seemed, was not always expressed in accounts overdetermined by gender. Nor was genius. One expects to find Carlyle dubbed a genius or sage in reviews of the Froude biography. It is less expected to encounter John Skelton treating the author of *Jane Eyre* as a sage: "The curiosity of the public . . . was piqued as to who the unknown author might be, and many famous names were suggested. For no one dreamt that this strong Pythoness, or prophetess, with her sharp, ringing, oracular warnings—'conventionality is not morality; self-righteousness is not religion; to pluck the mask from the face of the Pharisee is not to lift an impious hand to the Crown of Thorns.'—could be the homely child of a rustic parsonage, the unpretending little girl called Charlotte Brontë by her friends" (*F,* May 1857, 576).

As reviews of Carlyle's *Reminiscences* and Froude's 1882 volume make clear, moreover, inscriptions of the body could engulf, and constrain, masculine as well as feminine authorship. Anxieties about the representation of Carlyle in *Reminiscences* exposed the constructedness of masculine norms, particularly the assumption that male skin functioned rather like armor,[51] forming an impermeable shield against the perils of the public sphere or against bodily pain or suffering. A number of reviews thus attributed Carlyle's display of spite, "nerves," and discomfort, as well as misanthropic prejudice, to his dyspepsia. As if enacting the central tenet of Carlyle's own "Characteristics," such reviews accommodated discomfiting symptoms to a form of illness that made the normally invisible masculine body at once highly visible and vulnerable. As well, Froude's efforts to mediate "feminine" pettiness in the 1882 volumes as he constructed the 1884 volumes clarifies how far masculinity, like femininity, was a construction that had to be vigorously maintained—and mystified.

Both the periodical context of Gaskell's *Life of Charlotte Brontë* and its relation to Froude's biography of Carlyle, then, illuminate the importance of gender and difference in the ideology of Victorian authorship. But the operation of difference was uneven and inconsistently applied. If Victorian authorship calls for critique, the *Life of Charlotte Brontë* and its periodical context suggest that a faint cheer is in order as well. Victorian authorship provided a space for Mrs. Gaskell's work as well as prompting its necessity.

Epilogue: "Cousin Phillis" and the Construction of "Mrs. Gaskell"

THE BODY OF GASKELL'S WORK was completed and shaped for the future by those who wrote her obituaries and who reviewed the entirety of her literary career. Among most London commentators, a text that emerged as embodying the greatest strength in Gaskell's maturity was "Cousin Phillis" (*Cornhill Magazine*, November 1863 to February 1864). But that choice sprang more from these readers' needs than from the story's artistry. Determining why this story rose to the top of nineteenth-century appraisals of Mrs. Gaskell's work takes us to our own conclusions about what this author has to offer the present century and the next.

Just as the *Cornhill*'s editor completed the text of *Wives and Daughters* using the author's notes, so the London obituary writers of 1866 took up Elizabeth Gaskell's life story in the periodical press, fixing her work in the larger literary history of her time. Unfortunately, no contemporary of equal power took on the task of representing Gaskell's achievements as she had done for Charlotte Brontë a decade earlier. In fact, in the January 1866 essay including the conclusion to *Wives and Daughters,* Frederick Greenwood sounded some of the key themes that would place Elizabeth Gaskell in a carefully limited role among the many literary figures of her age. Citing the formal qualities of "Cousin Phillis" ("the exquisite little story" [*C*, 13]), Greenwood used a word favored in subsequent obituaries: the *Englishwoman's Domestic Magazine* for March 1866 pointed to "her exquisite little cabinet picture of Cousin Phillis" (*CH*, 526), and Harriet Parr in the 1 April 1867 *British Quarterly Review* also praised "her last manner" in such things as "the exquisite short story of 'Cousin Phillis'" (*CH*, 534). This story survived modernism's devaluation of Mrs. Gaskell's work even though its achievement now seems far less than that of half a dozen other titles by the same author.

The *Cornhill's* editor, then, advanced a view of Gaskell that would continue for over one hundred years—as an author whose work captured in exquisite forms the idyllic charm of a lost era. Rather than crediting her powerful topical novels (*Mary Barton, Ruth, North and South*) or her moving psychological portraits (*Sylvia's Lovers, Wives and Daughters*), many Victorians preferred to remember her as the author of *Cranford* and "Cousin Phillis." When we realize that in 1989 John Sutherland wrote that this late short story still "is thought by many critics to be Gaskell's masterpiece," we must acknowledge that these Victorians' view had a long life (see also Winifred Gérin, who says that "Cousin Phillis" and *Wives and Daughters* are "the crowning works of her career").[1] Although in her last great work she had pictured a young woman, Molly, threading her way through many versions of Victorian womanhood, and though she herself had developed a voice that took a strong place among many making up a powerful literary industry, Elizabeth Gaskell's fiction turned, among dominant voices who constructed her culture's memory, into something comfortably reassuring rather than unsettling and potentially transforming.

In the *Cornhill* essay Greenwood allowed Gaskell the gift of taking readers away from unpleasant realities: "You feel yourself caught out of an abominable wicked world, crawling with selfishness and reeking with base passions, into one where there is much weakness, many mistakes, sufferings long and bitter, but where it is possible for people to live calm and wholesome lives; and, what is more, you feel that this is at least as real a world as the other" (*C,* January 1866, 13). This ability to imagine a better world, however, is distinguished from an analytical faculty. Greenwood writes that Gaskell dealt with "emotions and passions which have a living root in minds within the pale of salvation" and that they were more important than "the merely intellectual qualities" in the same late works. And he uses the fact of her death to silence dissent among his contemporaries: "Twenty years to come, that [intellectual quality] may be thought the important question of the two; in the presence of her grave we cannot think so" (13). In other words, says Greenwood, taking our cue from our own reading of her work, let us think of Mrs. Gaskell as someone with such superior feelings that careful thought is inappropriate in reviewing her accomplishments.

Henry Fothergill Chorley in the 18 November 1865 *Athenaeum* had praised *Wives and Daughters* in a similar way, allowing it little intellectual content when he referred to "that excellent, quiet story of country town life, involving no 'mission,' just wound up in the *Cornhill Magazine*" (*A, 690*). Thus many Victorians gave Gaskell a place in capturing fading goodness, but not in promoting future good by unsettling her audience. As more recent readers have asserted, however, the "calm and wholesome lives" pictured by Gaskell belong to a romanticized past, to a lost or even illusory order. The saccharine tone of George Barnett Smith in the February 1874 *Cornhill* reminds us that no such world ever existed: "The farm life of England was never drawn in sweeter, clearer colours. We can almost scent the hay-fields, and see the sun shedding its golden light upon their broad bosom, and upon the gardens and hedges. As we read, the melody of birds passes almost from a description into a reality, whilst the spirit which breathes through everything takes the willing senses captive, and fills them with an answering delight" (*C, 545*).[2]

Among those papers with less authority to confer cultural prestige upon writers[3] than principal London or Edinburgh journals, a refreshingly different view of Gaskell emerged. The "hometown" press in the north of England constructed a far less sentimental portrait of Gaskell in its obituaries. The writer ("M.") in the 17 November 1865 *Unitarian Herald,* published in Manchester, was closely connected to Gaskell, since the paper was cofounded by her husband William Gaskell.[4] However, true to Unitarian commitments to education and enlightened social roles for women,[5] this obituary passed up the opportunity to inscribe her as a minister's wife, instead beginning with her literary fame and offering this distinctly complicated view of her domestic role: "For many years after her marriage her life was mainly devoted to the instruction of her children (four daughters), whom she brought up most tenderly. She steadily and consistently objected to her time being considered as belonging in any way to her husband's congregation for the purposes of congregational visiting, and to being looked to for that leadership in congregational work which is too often expected of 'the minister's wife'" (*UH, 366*). The writer immediately noted, however, her indefatigable labor where she thought she could do good, especially on behalf of the poor, and remarked on Gaskell's role as teacher and mentor to working-class girls: "She was also much interested in the older girls at Lower Mosley-street Sunday School, and for several years carried out a plan of having them at her own house, once a month, on Sunday afternoons, when she read and talked with them, and, as one of these old pupils expressed it, 'seemed to divine what was in our hearts before we spoke it.' She also gave up Saturday evening for some time, for the purpose of teaching them geography and English history; and these afternoons and evenings are still held in cherished remembrance by those who attended them" (366). Rather than merely absorbing such social work to gendered roles of religious service and emotional labor, this obituary firmly linked Gaskell's social work and her literary work, commenting that "in all this work she was unconsciously acquiring that sympathetic insight into the character of our northern manufacturing poor, which has been one of the strongest elements of her literary success" (366).

Although noting others' views that either the *Life of Charlotte Brontë* or *Cranford* would be best remembered among her works, this writer clearly prefers *Mary Barton,* noting its role in establishing Gaskell's reputation and concluding the obituary by reiterating the link between literary and social labor: "It was but last Monday afternoon that we were reading the first few chapters of 'Mary Barton' to a group of poor women who meet every week for a few hours, at one of our mission stations. We little thought, as we noted their appreciation of its sketches of a life so familiar to them, how still the hand of its writer already was" (*UH,* 366–67). Here mission is central, as is the authorial hand that labors to produce literary work.

The secular *Manchester Guardian* began far more conventionally than the *Unitarian Herald,* noting at the outset "the death of Mrs. Gaskell, the wife of the respected minister of the Unitarian Chapel, Cross-street" (14 November 1865). But this obituary, like several others, singled out not *Cranford,* not even "Cousin Phillis," but the biography of Brontë as "her greatest work and that by which she will be longest known, . . . of which it has been said that no biography has equalled it since Boswell's 'Johnson.'" Noting the controversies surrounding the biography's publication, this obituary unexpectedly shifted to public scandal and *Cranford*—elsewhere the sine qua non of idyllic sweetness and nostalgia—remarking, "A similar feeling had been occasioned at an earlier period of Mrs. Gaskell's literary career, for in sketches entitled 'Cranford,' which appeared in *Household Words,* she had drawn portraits rather too accurately of some living personages."

The *Reader,* a liberal weekly founded in London in 1863 and directed toward an intellectual elite,[6] had recruited Gaskell as a contributor ("one of the earliest contributors to our pages, and her last contribution to THE READER was a review of Torrens's 'Lancashire's Lesson,' in the spring of the present year"). Its obituary singled out *Ruth* as her best novel, along with *Sylvia's Lovers,* and refused to separate pastoral from manufacturing settings in its assessment of her distinctive gifts: "The author of 'Ruth' and 'Sylvia's Lovers' could paint English life in its truest colours, and it is this, however fashion may change, that will make her works descend to posterity as a study both of genteel and manufacturing life of the reign of Queen Victoria, of which no other writer has given so vivid a picture" (*TR,* 18 November 1865, 572). Among those who knew her work best, then, and who had greatest proximity, Gaskell was a figure of complexity whose fiction, even at its sweetest and most inviting, could never be severed from its social context or effects.[7]

What appealed to reviewers in major London journals at the end of Gaskell's career were the nostalgic portraits of a vanishing village way of life attributed to *Cranford* and "Cousin Phillis." But also compelling was what they felt as the nostalgic representation of a Victorian type of female, the eternally prepubescent woman who dies (to all practical purposes) for love and of love. As that feminine stereotype was being undermined by characters in novels (*Romola*) and women in real life (Florence Nightingale), readers clung to comfortable figures of childhood innocence, of female virginity. But when we look more closely, Phillis Holman, like Elizabeth Gaskell herself, is more than the typical Victorian woman in this fine story.

The transformation of Phillis into what Gaskell's audience desired began, as was so often the case, with the restrictions of publication format established by Victorian editors and publishers. Jennifer Uglow notes that although "Cousin Phillis" has been called "Gaskell's most 'perfect' story,"[8] the work was actually cut short by George Smith, *Cornhill's* publisher. She had planned a lengthier conclusion in which Paul was to return years later to Hope Farm and find the older, mature Phillis working the land with advanced technical skill, having adopted several abandoned children. But only four numbers of the *Cornhill* were allowed Gaskell for telling this story, and she ended it rather abruptly with a sentence that merely foreshadows the heroine's recovery: Phillis claims, "We will go

back to the peace of the old days. I know we shall; I can, and I will!"
(CP, 354). The long-suffering Phillis who closes the tale in the magazine,
then, probably fit Victorian expectations better than a restored, recovered
independent woman would have. The limitations of publication space
became restrictions on authorial vision, just as Gaskell's own death cut
off her production at the height of her creative powers.

In many ways, what matters to those of us reading "Cousin Phillis"
more than a century later is what is missing in the text, what history now
allows readers to infer but toward which Gaskell could only gesture in
her own time. The father of the story's narrator, Paul Manning, admits
to his son, "Thou'rt not great shakes, I know, in th' inventing line; but
many a one gets on better without having fancies for something he does
not see and never has seen" (CP, 290). That is, the eyes through which
we view Phillis and her world are notable for lack of vision.[9] Later in the
story, the servant Betty also draws attention to Paul's inability to put into
words what he does see: "Not that you've got the gifts to do it [i.e., win
a woman's love], either; you're not great shakes to look at, neither for
figure, nor yet for face, and it would need be a deaf adder to be taken in
wi' your words, though there may be no great harm in 'em" (CP, 337).

That the narrator is working in areas that exceed his ability is underscored by his professional life. The new railroad line he is helping
build must go over "shaking, uncertain ground," which "was puzzling
our engineers—one end of the line going up as soon as the other was
weighted down" (CP, 263). Later he mentions the difficulties of "not
being able to find a steady bottom on the Heathbridge moss, over which
we wished to carry our line" (275). While the "progress of the line" is
being carried on "in the slow gradual way which suited the company
best, while trade was in a languid state, and money dear in the market"
(295), Paul, an apprentice who is less imaginative than his more famous
father, would not seem to be the ideal candidate for building Gaskell's
narrative on a challenging subject. He feels inferior to his father, to
Holdsworth, to Mr. Holman, and even to Phillis, who studies Latin and
could clearly have learned engineering (289). Thus his tentative narrative
switches from first-person singular to first-person plural (319) when he is
unsure or wishes to avoid responsibility.

Like the masculine narrator of "The Poor Clare" (*Household Words*,
1856, discussed in chapter 4), Paul works backward from a known position

to tell his story, making the task simpler with the outcome known: "I see her now—cousin Phillis" (CP, 266), he says of their first meeting. Suppressing his own romantic feelings for his cousin by citing her greater height, he had retreated at that time to the more comfortable, safe relationship of brother and sister (300). Still, his excessive guilt at having told Phillis that Holdsworth loved her (331–33) recalls the narrative tentativeness in *Mary Barton* and Mary Smith's confused emotions at writing the letter to Peter Jenkyns in *Cranford* (discussed in chapters 2 and 3). Taking the retrospective narrative stance, then, allows Paul to view his subject as static and unchanging, and thus under control—just as "Mrs. Gaskell" was for those who wrote her obituaries.

This narrator remains a cousin and friend to Phillis, so he does not dramatically shape her life; but the two conventional figures of authority, father and lover, do. Farmer and preacher, Mr. Holman ("whole man") represents the idealized, integrated life of an earlier time. He tells Holdsworth, "I dare say you railway gentlemen don't wind up the day with singing a psalm together . . . but it is not a bad practice—not a bad practice" (CP, 272). And his speech embodies the same value of harmony: "He had no notion of doing or saying things without a purpose" (265). Although the talented railroad engineer has a promising future, Holdsworth is a bit surprised at "trying to make one's words represent one's thoughts, instead of merely looking to their effect on others" (303). And Holman finds "a want of seriousness in [Holdsworth's] talk at times" (305), concluding that "his careless words were not always those of soberness and truth" (310).

Neither man, however, allows Phillis to grow from childhood to womanhood.[10] Holdsworth thinks of her as a sleeping princess: "I shall come back like a prince from Canada, and waken her to my love. I can't help hoping that it won't be difficult, eh, Paul?" (CP, 315). And he is put off by her bold action of rescuing his surveying equipment in a sudden storm (309), typically resorting to insincere language ("badinage" [309]). Holman sees his daughter who loses her hope of married love as "a sleeping child" (347), even though he articulates a theoretical (if conventional) view of a woman's needs: "She'd forget 'em [Latin and Greek], if she'd a houseful of children" (291). Holman also appreciates Phillis's support for his preaching when it reinforces the typical roles of the sexes: "But, at any rate, father, you do good to the women, and perhaps they repeat what you have said to them to their husbands and children?" (284). Although he helps his daughter read, he does not recognize her need for self-expression, insisting, "The love of dress is a temptation and a snare" (285).

For all the gaps in Paul's account of his cousin Phillis, his creator, Elizabeth Gaskell, left enough clues for her readers to build a larger story of one Victorian woman. If Paul is no "great shakes . . . in the inventing line," Gaskell's "fancy" was, as this study attests, enormous. She produced six major novels, several important novellas, and more than twenty fine short stories. Anne Thackeray Ritchie in an 1891 preface to *Cranford* summed up her life with references to "Cousin Phillis" and other works: "It remains for readers of this later time to see how nobly she held her own among the masters of her craft. 'She has done what none of us could do,' said George Sand to Lord Houghton; 'she has written novels which excite the deepest interest in men of the world, and yet which every girl will be the better for reading'" (569). Although we consider Anne Thackeray Ritchie's assessment restricted by the cultural definitions imposed on her predecessor, "Mrs. Gaskell," the work accomplished by this body of material is expanding, deepening, and—most important of all—continuing.

Notes

Introduction

1. Ffrench, *Mrs. Gaskell,* 107.
2. Jordan and Patten, "Introduction," 1, 13, 14.
3. Uglow, *Elizabeth Gaskell,* ix.
4. Bonaparte, *Gypsy-Bachelor of Manchester,* 221–22.

I. Standing in the Cornhill

1. See Ong, "Writer's Audience," 9–21.
2. See Hughes and Lund, *Victorian Serial,* 9–12.
3. See Skilton and Miles, "Introduction," 26–28.
4. Julian Wolfreys makes a similar point, noting "Gaskell's anticipation, and inclusion, of several differing, often contradictory, ideological voices in the space of a single text. Gaskell gathers into her writing many positions and situations that are broadly political, often mutually contradictory; and she does so not through an active gesture of gathering but through the act of desistance. She desists from critique, from the sounding of authoritative voice, so as to leave the possibility of silence in which there can be heard various political discourses. Gaskell's texts do not attempt to avoid the snares of traditional modes of thought; such evasion, she realizes, is impossible (this is one of the truths of Elizabeth Gaskell). However, in the fact of formal structures of thinking, Gaskell's desistance opens gaps through which dissidence is enunciated" (*Being English,* 81).
5. See Schor, *Scheherezade in the Marketplace,* 182.
6. See Poovey, *Proper Lady,* 36; Marcus, "Profession of Author," 207–10.
7. See also Wright, *Elizabeth Gaskell,* 246.
8. Among such readers, at least on one occasion, was Elizabeth Gaskell herself. Her 23 December 1859 letter to George Smith, after the first number of the *Cornhill* appeared, concludes, "I extremely like & admire Framley Parsonage,—& the Idle Boy; and the Inaugural Address. I like Lovel the Widower, only (perhaps because I am stupid), it is a little confusing on account of its discursiveness,—and V's verses; and oh shame! I have not read the sensible & improving articles. So a merry Xmas to you & yours" (*LMG,* 596).
9. See also Brake, *Subjugated Knowledges,* 66, 71.
10. Coral Lansbury says: "The title of the novel expresses the limitations of this society for women: there are only two recognized roles for middle-class women, that of a daughter or that of a wife—the latter conferring a small measure of indepen-

dence. . . .therefore spinsters and widows are anomalous figures" (*Elizabeth Gaskell,* 109). See also Homans, *Bearing the Word,* 251.

11. See Stoneman, *Elizabeth Gaskell,* 176–77; Colby, *"Some Appointed Work,"* 90. On the multiplicity implied by the title, see also Buchanan, "Mothers and Daughters," passim, and Davis, "Feminist Critics," 521.

12. Some of the more famous instances of resistant invalidism, of course, include Florence Nightingale after Scutari, Elizabeth Barrett, and Isabella Bird (who rose from her sickbed to become an indefatigable traveler).

13. See Stoneman, *Elizabeth Gaskell,* 174–76, for the feminist implications of Hyacinth's indirection and calculation. See also Davis, "Feminist Critics," 522–24.

14. See Lansbury, *Elizabeth Gaskell,* 108, and Stoneman, *Elizabeth Gaskell,* 178.

15. John Kucich presents a more skeptical approach to the relationship of Osborne and Roger, discerning in Gaskell's representation a horror of sexual inversion that helps maintain social and political hierarchies: "Her dogmatic polarization of sexuality limits the terms in which she can imagine transgression against middle-class ideology" ("Transgression," 187; see also 188).

16. A point made by students in English 7483, Victorian Women Writers, Texas Christian University, spring 1994.

17. Compare Henry James, who in his review of the novel linked the time of reading to bodily presence within the world of fiction: "So delicately, so elaborately, so artistically, so truthfully, and heartily is the story wrought out, that the hours given to its perusal seem like hours actually spent, in the flesh as well as the spirit, among the scenes and people described, in the atmosphere of their motives, feelings, traditions, associations" (*CH,* 463). For a contrasting view of Molly's successive scenes before the mirror, see Homans, *Bearing the Word,* 257–65.

18. Johnson, *Charles Dickens,* 1:197. Patricia Yaeger notes that textual discontinuities echo interruptions women writers endured when forced to lay aside manuscripts for domestic duties, inscribing the rhythms of the writing woman's body in the text ("Violence in the Sitting Room," 210).

19. See also Schor, *Scheherezade in the Marketplace,* 208–9.

II. Narrative Authority

1. Easson notes that in terms of the social problem novel Gaskell "was remarkably early in the field" (*Elizabeth Gaskell,* 62), and he places *Mary Barton* within the context of similar work of the 1840s. Fryckstedt, *Elizabeth Gaskell's Mary Barton,* provides a detailed placement of Gaskell's *Mary Barton* (and *Ruth*) within the context of conditions in industrial England, the tenets of Unitarianism, and literary predecessors.

2. As Hilary Schor's brilliant study of Gaskell shows (*Scheherezade in the Marketplace*), questions about authority, especially for a woman writer, pervade Gaskell's work. The issue of credibility was raised in the 13 March 1852 chapters of *Cranford* with an unjustified ringing of a warning bell, the same event we will discuss in greater detail as it occurred in *Sylvia's Lovers.* One of the letters written by Miss Deborah Jenkyns in 1805, when she was visiting friends near Newcastle-upon-Tyne, evokes the fear of an imagined invasion by Napoleon. Villagers, she writes, were told to flee "to Alston Moor (a wild hilly piece of ground between Northumberland and Cumberland)" when they heard "the church bells [ringing] in a particular and ominous manner"

(*CR*, 48). And "this warning-summons was actually given" one day, creating "the breathless shock, the hurry and alarm" of panic before it is learned it had all been a false alarm. Although the idea that Napoleon was planning to capture outlying villages is part of this work's gentle humor, we can still see Gaskell concerned with the question of what voice should be heeded in critical moments, the stance and style of those who would speak to society.

3. Lansbury finds the narrative tone "conciliatory," the voice of someone "so mealy-mouthed and platitudinous that the reader's teeth are set on edge" (*Elizabeth Gaskell*, 10), but she attributes this to Gaskell's radically sympathetic treatment of workers. Easson also finds the work's tone confused: "Two forms—tragic poem and 'condition of England' novel—are in conflict" (*Elizabeth Gaskell*, 76). Felber pursues a similar argument: "It is, then, the ideological irresolution of the narrator, seemingly inconsonant with her emphasis on the gravity of the problem, as well as a pseudo-romance structure, evading the situation dramatized, which create the oft-criticized tension in *Mary Barton*" ("Gaskell's Industrial Novels," 69). Wheeler proposes *William Langshawe, the Cotton Lord* (1842) by Mrs. Elizabeth Stone as an important model for the plot of *Mary Barton*, and this reliance on another's work might also have contributed to narrative uncertainty. Marjorie Stone, however, argues that "through her rhetorical and narrative strategies, [Gaskell] subverts the hegemony of middle-class discourse that empowers her to speak" ("Bakhtinian Polyphony," 176). Flint also sees the uncertain authorial tone as in some ways productive: "The deliberate destabilizing of the author's voiced 'authority' is counterbalanced by a careful manipulation of the reader to a position where no concrete solutions to social problems may be offered" (19). Gallagher, though, finds that Gaskell's "criticism of false conventions does not succeed in deflecting attention from the absence of a stable, self-assured narrative posture" (*Industrial Reformation*, 68).

4. Brooks, *Reading for the Plot*, 61. As Brooks also notes, the "generally anti-industrial and antitechnological attitude of most nineteenth-century poets and novelists is more and more matched by a fascination with engines and forces" (45); thus Gaskell's commitment to Manchester grew to include both love and hate. Whereas depictions of working-class conditions like the Davenports' cellar show Gaskell's negative reaction to her own experience of Manchester, Easson finds "a sense of pride in the Industrial Revolution as manifested in Manchester, a pride that finds expression in Gaskell's depiction of Manchester life, of Manchester people and customs, of cotton and its power and its wealth" ("Elizabeth Gaskell," 709).

5. Stone, "Bakhtinian Polyphony," 192.

6. Gaskell's letter to Chapman on 10 July 1848 also reveals uncertainty: "If you think the book requires such a preface I will try to concoct it; but at present, I have no idea what to say" (*LMG*, 58). Before *Mary Barton* Gaskell had attempted only some short works, most published by her friends the Howitts. An understandable tentativeness from a beginning writer surely contributed to the narrator's repeated admissions in early chapters of "I do not know" (*MB*, 40, 79, 91–92). The need to know, however, was great in the troubled times of the novel's events and of its publication, when cities like Gaskell's own Manchester daily feared workers' rebellion.

7. As Easson explains, Gaskell's extensive outline of the work "divides the novel into the common three-volume form (it actually appeared in two); apart from names and minor details, it corresponds substantially to the finished work" (*Elizabeth Gaskell*, 73).

8. Bodenheimer, "Private Grief," also links Mary's action to Gaskell's own brave act of writing.

9. See Bodenheimer, "Private Grief," 208. Schor sees this change as part of the movement from John Barton's story to Mary Barton's: "In Gaskell's disavowal of authorial aggression, we can see her carving out for herself other territory (that of earnestness and truth) and reinserting herself—as a sympathetic authority—into the story" (*Scheherezade in the Marketplace*, 22).

10. Jordan, "Spectres and Scorpions," 58. Kestner, who reviews male characterization in "condition of England" novels leading up to *Mary Barton*, finds that Gaskell too focuses on male psychology: Mary's "function in the novel is more structural than contextual" ("Men in Female Condition," 94). Kalikoff, on the other hand, includes Mary among those "female heroes who transcend popular stereotypes" under the hands of female novelists ("Falling Woman," 366); Schor (*Scheherezade in the Marketplace*, 15) and Lansbury (*Elizabeth Gaskell*, 20) see Mary as central to the novel. Stone notes Mary's association with epic and tragic figures ("Bakhtinian Polyphony," 189).

11. Mary's lack of status is revealed in key scenes like the Carson's mill fire, where Jem appears as hero. Mary cannot see directly to report on or understand events: "Oh, tell us what you see?" begs Mary of "a tall man who could over look the crowd" (*MB*, 89). Caught in the crowd and unable to flee the terrible scene, even at times "sick with the close ramming of confinement" (89), Mary depends on the narration of others to learn the workers' fates: she "longed to faint, and be insensible, to escape from the oppressing misery of her sensation" (90). From this position of silence and negation, Mary will eventually grow to speak in court for her lover's innocence; but to take on that role she must first collect the necessary papers.

12. Uglow finds in the valentine a sign of the novel's many dualities: "father and daughter," "death and love," "people and place" (*Elizabeth Gaskell*, 206).

13. Anderson discusses the rich textual identity of the wadding used by John Barton: "Barton's shot fires not only a bullet but a counter-representation, a sympathetic social ballad by one of his own" (*Tainted Souls*, 123).

14. Craik explores the importance of knowledge for all characters in *Mary Barton*, finding "a growing reverence for and thirst for knowledge in the more practical sense of education, through literacy, not as a means to or mark of social status . . . but in order to understand their world and its workings" ("Lore, Learning and Wisdom," 21). Yeazell, however, argues that Mary avoids "reflection" on her father's crime even as she seeks evidence of Jem's innocence because "the novelist shared in her heroine's anxiety. . . .To the degree that Gaskell too loved John Barton she joined with his daughter in turning aside from the contemplation of his crime" ("Why Political Novels Have Heroines," 133). Like other Victorian novelists, then, according to Yeazell, Gaskell "covers" a story of political violence with the familiar courtship narrative.

     The argument that Mary Barton is an early type of the famous Victorian figure of the detective might be one small part of an answer to Anne Humpherys's complaint that there has been "obsessive" critical attention among Victorian scholars to "a handful of canonized texts by three male writers—Charles Dickens, Wilkie Collins, and Arthur Conan Doyle" ("Who's Doing It?" 259). She hopes for "a thorough recovery and serious analysis of the dozens of other texts that contributed to the shape of this enduring and problematic figure" of the detective (272).

15. Uglow notes: "The novel constantly returns to the difficulty of speaking. Again and again the characters fail to find the words they need" (*Elizabeth Gaskell*, 202); but

Schor does not see Mary's inability to speak as negative: "A significant number of moments of real understanding in the novel come precisely from (or in) silence" (*Scheherezade in the Marketplace*, 18).

16. Gaskell explores a similar situation of reluctant testimony during the time she began *Sylvia's Lovers*. In "The Crooked Branch," published in the extra Christmas number of the 1859 *All the Year Round,* Hester Huntroyd is compelled to testify that one of the three burglars who broke into her house is her own son Benjamin, whom she loves even though he has become "a bad, hard, flippant young man" (CB, 206). The cousin intended for Benjamin, Bessy Rose, fears having to endure a similar questioning in court: "No one knew how she apprehended lest she should have to say that Benjamin had been of the gang" (233). The lawyer who must dig out the truth in this case repeatedly regrets the situation he must place the mother in: "My lord, I am compelled to ask these painful questions" he says to the judge (236). Like Hester Huntroyd, who "is stricken with paralysis" (238) after her testimony, and like Mary, who collapses at the trial, the narrator of *Mary Barton* reveals an uncomfortableness about the role of questioner or seeker of the truth. That voice seeks documentation as underpinning for authority.

17. Other characters in the novel struggle to know what has occurred or is occurring. Job "*knew* nothing" (*MB,* 363; emphasis added) of Mary's success in reaching Will Wilson on the *John Cropper;* Jem's mother says, "Not a bit would I fret if folk would but *know* him to be innocent—as I do" (370; emphasis added); and Jem explains to his mother that his love for Mary will not change his feelings for her: "Mother! you know all this while, *you know* I can never forget any kindness you've ever done for me" (409; Gaskell's emphasis). John Barton must face a terrible truth: "But now he *knew* that he had killed a man, and a brother,—now he *knew* that no good thing could come out of this evil" (436; emphasis added). The father of the murdered Carson also moves in the last chapters of the novel toward a supreme knowledge in Gaskell's world. When he sees "a rough, rude errand boy" (437) inadvertently knock down a young girl from Carson's class, he takes in the girl's plea to her nurse, "*He did not know what he was doing*" (438; Gaskell's emphasis). When Carson recognizes that she has echoed John Barton's words, "I did not know what I was doing" (438), Carson recalls Christ's statement on the cross—"They know not what they do" (439)—and eventually comes to forgive John Barton. Terence Wright explains: "The incident of Mr. Carson's 'conversion' is the climax of a pattern of Christian and Biblical reference that informs the whole book" (*Elizabeth Gaskell,* 35). Gallagher says of Gaskell's use of Christian thought, "The novel we have been reading is finally resolved by the introduction of a different book, the Bible. The narrator finds relief from the multiple reinterpretations of John Barton's story by superimposing the ending as well as the meaning of the Gospel onto her novel" (*Industrial Reformation,* 87).

18. The narrator's own effort to put things "into words" that accurately reflect what has happened is shadowed by a number of other characters such as Job, whose taxonomy of insects (with names attached) would constitute a kind of fictional world. And Esther, doomed herself always to stay in the dark, nevertheless tries to bring some things to light in order that the full world be recognized. She appears before John Barton (*MB,* 170) and Jem Wilson (210) hoping to convince them to keep Mary away from Henry Carson. And later, disguised as a "mechanic's wife" (293), she puts in front of Mary evidence of her folly in listening to such a man.

19. Craik, *Elizabeth Gaskell,* 9.

20. See Easson, "Sentiment of Feeling," 71.

21. Robyn R. Warhol, who has proposed a theory of the "engaging narrator" in nineteenth-century fiction, explains the purpose of such first-person addresses: engaging narrators "intrude to remind their narratees—who, in their texts, should stand for the actual readers—that the fictions reflect real-world conditions for which the readers should take active responsibility after putting aside the book" ("Towards a Theory," 815).

22. This blurring of narrator and narrated is further represented by the public performances of the blind Margaret, who is viewed by an audience she cannot herself see. Those who come to hear her sing can determine her identity, but she is denied an equal power. Margaret's voice, immaterial but strong, is another version of the narrator's. The accordion Will purchases for Margaret (*MB*, 246), for instance, is one more step toward presence, like the strategies Gaskell uses to give her voice increasing strength as the novel moves forward. Witte has studied the role of Will Wilson as "the model spokesman for Carlyle's transcendental synthesis between the eye and ear" ("Transcendental Eye and Ear," 257) and considers Margaret's voice and her audience's response as part of the larger pattern of possible reform in Gaskell.

23. As Deborah Epstein Nord remarks, "The repetition of . . . exposure—of being looked at on the street and assessed as an object of sexual interest—and the variation on it Gaskell used to explain the genesis of *Mary Barton* suggest its importance in the creation of her identity as urban novelist, as public woman, and as social critic" (*Walking the Victorian Streets,* 144). Nord's chapter on Gaskell also notes the decisive shift in Mary's agency in the course of the novel:

    (154) After the murder . . . Mary is transformed from the passive subject of discussions of her sexual virtue and proper role to the active agent of her own fate. The efforts of those around her in the early part of the novel to keep her out of the public eye, to tie her safely to private domestic space, are totally defeated in the second half. Her ascendancy in the story marks an awakening of consciousness and purpose that reproduces the workers' earlier mobilization. Like them, she must go beyond even the public sphere of work and engage in the wider world of politics and law. To the extent that she is the workers' double—that they are parallel victims of Carson's callousness and arrogance—she seems to vindicate them as she exonerates Jem and herself.

    For Nord, the sexual plot of the novel is inseparable from the theme of "class antagonism" (150).

24. Uglow, *Elizabeth Gaskell,* 214, 216; see also Spencer, *Elizabeth Gaskell,* 50.

25. Amanda Anderson provides perhaps the most detailed study of Esther's role in the novel, seeing important links between John Barton and his sister-in-law, who are in the end buried together (*Tainted Souls,* 125). Bick explains how Esther helps Mary become active rather than passive ("'Take Her up Tenderly,'" 20), where Stoneman has drawn attention to Esther's importance in the novel as an echo of Mary's mother: "The 'mother's voice' speaks in the public world only through men—not only the male characters of the novel but also the male writers whose 'language' defines its parameters" (*Elizabeth Gaskell,* 85). Valverde discusses the importance of Esther and clothes: "Gaskell's view is that, though the fallen woman may be the object of

sympathy and pity, she cannot leave her moral stain behind with her finery" ("Love of Finery," 171).

26. Flint states that *Sylvia's Lovers* "is a novel which directs the reader's attention to instinctive rather than reasoned emotions: feelings which are perennially difficult to explain or justify" (*Elizabeth Gaskell*, 49). Lansbury says: "There is simply no place for books or writing in a society that lives and entertains itself with stories told by the fire, or snatches of gossip at market day in Monkshaven" (*Elizabeth Gaskell*, 99). Stoneman has linked Gaskell's exploration of illiterate culture to "the growing impact of evolutionary theory" (*Elizabeth Gaskell*, 141) after Darwin's *Origin of Species* (1859). Spencer says that "Gaskell's attitude to the simplicity of her characters is ambivalent" (*Elizabeth Gaskell*, 102), but Shaw reminds us: "Interest in 'low life' amongst middle-class readers and reviewers may have had its limits" ("Elizabeth Gaskell," 51).

27. Brooks, *Reading*, 39.

28. Nancy Armstrong, *Desire and Domestic Fiction: A Political History of the Novel* (New York: Oxford Univ. Press, 1987), 23.

29. Terence Wright says: "The ocean, and the moorland which is never far from its piping, salt winds, are both symbols of freedom for Sylvia" (*Elizabeth Gaskell*, 179).

30. Easson says, "The natural scene plays its part in the relationship between sea and moorland, between fishing town and farm, between character and action, establishing a world where even the dweller inland is aware of the sea" (*Elizabeth Gaskell*, 171).

31. Sanders explores the specific religious doctrines represented in Monkshaven's church at the top of the long flight of stairs ("Varieties of Religious Experience," 16). And Terence Wright discusses the symbolic power in Gaskell's description of stairs and church (*Elizabeth Gaskell*, 165–67).

32. Contemporary critics are finding increasing subtlety in Gaskell's heroine. Shaw, for instance, terms Sylvia's growth "psychologically subtle, and one of the great satisfactions of the novel" ("Elizabeth Gaskell," 52). Krueger argues that a key speech by Sylvia six chapters from the end exposes the falseness of male-centered "history": "By reading the attempts to romanticize her experience for what they are—disciplinary structures deployed against her—Sylvia refuses to become the tragic heroine of history, or, indeed, the villain" ("'Speaking Like a Woman,'" 149). And Uglow explores the implications of Sylvia's being drawn to the violent nature of men, aspects of personality hinted at in the names of Robson and Kinraid (*Elizabeth Gaskell*, 517).

33. See Shaw, "Elizabeth Gaskell," 46.

34. See Sharps, *Mrs. Gaskell's Observation*, 403.

35. Uglow notes that Daniel's and Charley's sea tales are borrowed from a source, but that Gaskell adapts them to her own purposes: "The whaling stories of Daniel and Kinraid are a male genre, where the ship which holds them (and, in Gaskell's telling, the whales they hunt) are also gendered as female" (*Elizabeth Gaskell*, 517).

36. See Flint, *Elizabeth Gaskell*, 50.

37. Uglow, *Elizabeth Gaskell*, 499. See also Bonaparte, *Gypsy-Bachelor*, 200–201, who sees Gaskell as reluctant to write the chapter on Sylvia's marriage to Philip.

38. Schor, *Scheherezade in the Marketplace*, 163.

39. Others have commented on the narrative voice of this novel. Schor finds strength in "the voice of storytelling" (*Scheherezade in the Marketplace*, 181), especially in the final chapter. And Craik concludes: "The position of the narrator and the personality revealed become equally absorbed into the texture [of the novel] as a whole" (*Elizabeth*

Gaskell, 147). Krueger says, "Gaskell uses a third-person omniscient narrator en-dowed with the apparent authority of historical hindsight that characterizes Dickens's or George Eliot's narrators" ("'Speaking Like a Woman,'" 141); however, she goes on to suggest that other features of the text undercut traditional narrative authority.

40. Easson explains how the historical perspective shapes response: "The reader, wiser through a standpoint which is broader and advanced in time, can see as they [the characters] cannot the end to which the characters must come" (*Elizabeth Gaskell,* 162). Lansbury observes: "*Sylvia's Lovers* is an historical novel that speaks from the past to address contemporary issues" (*Elizabeth Gaskell,* 94–95). Rignall, however, sug-gests that authors' confidence in the accessibility of the past and its meaning shrinks as the century advances, with Gaskell less sure of historical wisdom than predecessors like Scott ("Historical Double"). Krueger finds in *Sylvia's Lovers* a "profound despair over women writers' power to represent women when the very conventions gov-erning historical writing served to silence and discipline them" ("'Speaking Like a Woman,'" 139). And Spencer makes a similar point: "The narrative's own revelations of how history is distorted in the telling make it more difficult for the reader to pay the tribute of implicit trust demanded by the traditional omniscient narrator" (*Eliza-beth Gaskell,* 115).

41. Not all reviewers thought she handled this well, however; the 28 Feb. 1863 *Reader* called "the storming of St. Jean d'Acre . . . the only too ambitious passage in the book" (*CH,* 439).

42. See Uglow, *Elizabeth Gaskell,* 482–85.

43. Many scholars have discussed the importance of the central character to the novel's total effect. Easson, for instance, says, "Sylvia is the undoubted centre of the novel" (*Elizabeth Gaskell,* 172) and explores her role as tragic heroine. Lansbury also links Sylvia's character to the novel's major themes: "So often in *Sylvia's Lovers* feeling is a more direct path to the truth than any amount of rational thought" (*Elizabeth Gaskell,* 96).

44. The narrator confidently presents the emotional life of other characters as well. Of Hester Rose, for instance, we read: "To her, an on-looker, the course of married life [with Philip and Sylvia], which should lead to perfect happiness, seemed too plain! Alas! it is often so! and the resisting forces which make all such harmony and delight impossible are not recognized by the bystanders, hardly by the actors" (*SL,* 395). Masculine hearts are also dissected with authority: "It is an old story, an ascertained fact, that, even in the most tender and stable masculine natures, at the supremest season of their lives, there is room for other thoughts and passions than such as are connected with love" (357). Sometimes Gaskell's voice mixes male and female realms to present emotions, as when Donkin, the male tailor, provides gossip for Daniel Robson: "'Well,' said [Daniel] at last; 'a mought be a young man a-goin' a wooin', by t' pains thou'st taken for t' match my oud clothes. I don't care if they're patched wi' scarlet, a tell thee; so as you'lt work away at thy tale wi' thy tongue, same time as thou works at thy needle wi' thy fingers'" (52). Trapped at home like many women, Rob-son finds his desire for information satisfied by a man whose craft resembles a story-teller's, knitting together "small pieces of various coloured cloth, cut out of old coats and waistcoats, and similar garments."

45. See Easson, "Introduction," *CH,* 39.

46. Rignall, "Historical Double," 27.

47. Rignall, "Historical Double," for instance, discusses Charley and Philip as another of the doubles often found in historical novels. Schor notes the connections growing out of linked primary characters: "The novel encloses the relations between the three central characters within larger circles of desire that draw in other characters as well" (*Scheherezade in the Marketplace,* 156).

48. Stoneman sees alternation in the passing of generations: "In *Sylvia's Lovers* there is an 'authentic' recognition of physical cycles when, after her lovers have come and gone, Sylvia sits on the bed supporting both her dying mother and her baby" (*Elizabeth Gaskell,* 158).

III. Left Documents and Illegitimate Children

1. Scarry, *Body in Pain,* 234; Scarry, "Introduction," xi.
2. Bonaparte, *Gypsy-Bachelor,* 161.
3. Lund, "Elizabeth Gaskell's Virgins," relates Peter to Frederick Hale in *North and South,* Charley Kinraid in *Sylvia's Lovers,* and Osborne Hamley in *Wives and Daughters.*
4. Felicia Bonaparte has discussed this tendency to continue exploration of a subject from one work into another: "What Gaskell leaves undone in one [work] she feels compelled to do in the next. The fall that Mary does not complete [in *Mary Barton*] is thus passed on to other characters, not only in the novel itself but to the heroine of 'Lizzie Leigh,' the story to which Gaskell turned after she had finished the novel" (*Gypsy-Bachelor,* 81; see also Lansbury, *Elizabeth Gaskell,* 52). Angus Easson explains how Gaskell's treatment of the fallen woman in *Ruth* departs from previous works: "Unlike earlier writers, Gaskell insists upon placing Ruth at the center of the novel. . . . The subject is before us all the time, so if distasteful it cannot be avoided" (*Elizabeth Gaskell,* 113). Bick concurs: "Gaskell's audacity . . . in tackling the subject of the fallen woman—a subject which exposed raw nerves in the Victorian reading public—should be recognized" ("'Take Her up Tenderly,'" 17).
5. George Henry Lewes in *Westminster Review* (1 Apr. 1853) calls *Ruth* "a sermon, and of the wisest, but its teaching is unostentatious" (*CH,* 270). And John Malcolm Ludlow in *North British Review* (May 1853) claimed it contained "a purpose not ticketed in the shape of a moral, but inwoven with the whole texture of the book" (*CH,* 276). Other reviewers, however, found the novel too didactic.
6. Fitzwilliam, "Politics," explains how money and gender roles are tightly intertwined in this family history, noting that Lizzie's fall causes a loss of value for the family in the marketplace. Mulvihill explains that Mrs. Leigh's household reflects careful management of resources: "The Leigh home in 'Lizzy Leigh,' [was] 'exquisitely clean and neat, even in outside appearance'; threshold, window, and window-sill were outward signs of some spirit of purity within" ("Economies of Living," 342–43).
7. Thompson, "Faith of Our Mothers," 24.
8. Gaskell says in the same letter that "Wm has composedly buttoned it [20£] in his pocket. He has promised I may have some money for the Refuge" (*LMG,* 252), that is, the effort to help fallen women. Gérin, among others, states that this tongue-in-cheek remark does not mean her husband controlled her money (*Elizabeth Gaskell,* 107–8). Thompson interestingly links the problematic money Lizzie Leigh's daughter leaves for her baby to the amount Elizabeth Gaskell was paid by Dickens ("Faith of Our Mothers," 25–26). That this story appeared under Dickens's name in the

American *Harper's* later the same year and that Dickens's name appears as "Conductor" on each page of *Household Words* (Uglow, *Elizabeth Gaskell,* 251) further shows how Gaskell had to struggle for control of her material in the established system of literary effort and reward.

9. Anderson, *Tainted Souls,* 128.
10. Stoneman, *Elizabeth Gaskell,* 101–2.
11. Lansbury, *Elizabeth Gaskell,* 23.
12. See Anderson, *Tainted Souls,* 129; Lansbury, *Elizabeth Gaskell,* 31–32.
13. Lansbury notes how Gaskell "concealed her subversive opinions of society in a traditional mode made inoffensive by constant biblical reference" (*Elizabeth Gaskell,* 33). Anderson observes that, nonetheless, "the novel seeks to demonstrate that sexual lapses don't destroy fallen women, discourse does" (*Tainted Souls,* 130). And Schor says that the "questioning of inherited languages [in *Ruth*] marks her [Gaskell's] movement from reader to writer—from daughter to self-created author" (*Scheherezade in the Marketplace,* 79).

   Frank Buxton, the young hero in Gaskell's "The Moorland Cottage" (Christmas 1850), is tempted to abandon a system where money and "inherited language" have the defining power experienced by Ruth. He urges his lover to flee the country with him: "My heart aches about the mysterious corruptions and evils of an old state of society such as we have in England.—What do you say, Maggie? Would you go [to Australia]?" (MC, 61). The heroine, however, counters with a philosophy Elizabeth Gaskell herself followed: "Don't you think it would be braver to stay, and endure much depression and anxiety of mind, for the sake of the good those always can do who see evils clearly. . . .Then, if all the good and thoughtful men run away from us to some new country, what are we to do with our poor, dear Old England?" (61).
14. Hapke shows that in Gaskell women like Faith and Sally are crucial to the rescue of fallen women ("He Stoops to Conquer," 19–20), a situation she finds common to female Victorian novelists but not male, who more often credit only men.
15. See Lansbury, *Elizabeth Gaskell,* 28.
16. Flint has also noted that "Benson's planned funeral sermon remains unpreached; the headstone to her grave uninscribed." Thus, Flint concludes, "Leonard's blank statement of grief to Bradshaw . . . demands our internalization of the emotion behind" (*Elizabeth Gaskell,* 24–25). Schor too finds this silence in Gaskell's text significant: "A novel like *Ruth* can comment only through what it leaves out" (*Scheherezade in the Marketplace,* 78). Stoneman argues that "the emotionalism of her funeral signals a general faltering of ideology, its inability to 'interpret' the 'dumb and unshaped' feelings people have about Ruth" (*Elizabeth Gaskell,* 117). Bonaparte has seen the heroine's death as the novel's only possible solution to her dilemma: "Gaskell needed to kill Ruth, not to punish her but to free her" (*Gypsy-Bachelor,* 129; see also Fryckstedt, *Elizabeth Gaskell's Mary Barton,* 165).
17. Schor, *Scheherezade in the Marketplace,* 77; Uglow, *Elizabeth Gaskell,* 341.
18. Schor puts the case even more strongly: "The martyring of the heroine may be, as I have suggested, a slap in the face of her readers . . . but it also has a harshness to it that suggests Gaskell's deeper hostility to Victorian mores and to the demands of polite readers—to the way, in a sense, novelists are made" (*Scheherezade in the Marketplace,* 75).
19. Easson, speaking of *Ruth,* explains why the three-volume form was important in this

period: "The story falls roughly into three parts, corresponding to volume division. . . .The three-volume novel was the established form for any hoping to be bought in large numbers of the circulating libraries" (*Elizabeth Gaskell,* 109). John Relly Beard (*Tait's Edinburgh Magazine,* April 1853) separated the first two volumes from the last: "The book now before us is remarkable for harmonious consistency. During the first two volumes at least, the fate of poor Ruth is the interest ever present with us; and other occurrences only as affecting this" (*CH,* 258).

20. Uglow, *Elizabeth Gaskell,* 278. Uglow also reports that during this break from *Ruth's* composition Gaskell wrote "The Old Nurse's Story" (*Household Words,* 1852), reworking the principal themes of this period. In the powerful ghost story, a woman had been betrayed by her sister and, with her daughter, is turned out of the house by their father. After their deaths, father, daughter, and granddaughter haunt the isolated manor house and surrounding countryside. Although not "fallen," Maude Furnivall had married a visiting musician, "all unknown to any one" (*ONS,* 50) and later gave birth secretly to a daughter. Her repentant sister's desperate final plea—"Oh, father! father! spare the little, innocent child!" (55)—is Gaskell's message to unforgiving fathers in this tale and in *Ruth.*

21. Nina Auerbach has provocatively traced the unusual nature of *Cranford* to a significant event near the time of its composition, Gaskell's meeting the Brontë sisters: "She was inflamed by the story of the beleaguered sisters, a good deal of which seeped into and animated the genteel exclusiveness of Cranford before a biography proper seemed conceivable" (*Communities of Women,* 91). Gillooly, on the other hand, argues: "The familiar yet peculiar world of the novel—its nostalgic, utopian community—is fashioned upon childhood memories viewed from a psychological distance" ("Humor as Daughterly Defense," 883). Tim Dolin has perceptively argued that "*Cranford* is removed from the central issues of Victorianism yet, almost from the day of its publication, it has occupied a privileged place in representations of the Victorian" ("*Cranford* and the Victorian Collection," 203). Stoneman says that "although the 'cooperative female community' [in *Cranford*] is admirable, it is not triumphant. All it can do is to make the best of the little space allowed it" (*Elizabeth Gaskell,* 91).

22. Yarrow, "Chronology of *Cranford,*" 29. According to Uglow, Gaskell had nearly completed volume 1 of her novel when she composed the first episode about the little village of Cranford in the fall of 1851. She continued publishing stories about Cranford in Dickens's journal until the last months of 1852, when she concentrated on the final volume of *Ruth,* the whole of which appeared in January 1853. The final parts of *Cranford* then appeared in the spring of 1853. Uglow concludes that the richness of Elizabeth Gaskell's work derives from the full texture of her professional and personal life, "from the very fullness of the daily life which constricted her writing time . . . overlapping circles, drawn by a compass whose point is fixed in a central circle of Elizabeth's family, marriage and faith" (*Elizabeth Gaskell,* 309).

23. Gaskell writes to John Forster: "Shall I tell you a Cranfordism. An old lady a Mrs Frances Wright said to one of my cousins 'I have never been able to spell since I lost my teeth'" (*LMG,* 290; 17 May 1854). Patricia Meyer Spacks calls the imagination "the seat of vivid life for all the Cranford group" (*Gossip,* 184). Wendy Craik says that Gaskell's work "demonstrates that the freer the novelist becomes of the pattern, the more the part that men's and women's relations play in everyday life can be revealed, and revealed with greater nuances of feeling" ("'Man, Vain Man,'" 64).

24. Miller notes how both characters and author "pick up that [material] culture and manipulate it to particular ends" ("Fragments," 95). Miller also deftly places Gaskell's treatment within contemporary Victorian debate about questions of financial liability: "Taking up the sequestered sphere of the private and displaying its apparent distance from the discourse of liability, Gaskell demonstrates both its implication in and its active resistance to that discourse" ("Subjectivity Ltd.," 141). Spacks discusses both fashion and finance in the novel: "Cranford female society deprecates the power of money. Its members happily wear (and establish conventions for valuing) outmoded fashions" (*Gossip,* 185).
25. See, for instance, Easson, *Elizabeth Gaskell,* 106.
26. As Schor explains in considering Gaskell as contributor to Dickens's magazine, "Literary daughters are not given the language they need; rather, they are given languages, often dead languages, that mediate their experience for them" (*Scheherezade in the Marketplace,* 94). Miller says that the residents of Cranford both comply with and resist conventional restrictions: "Like goods, language is a *donné,* structuring behavior while, at the same time, being available for manipulation" ("Fragments," 96).
27. Stiles sees Leonard as Christlike, Ruth as "a madonna" ("Grace, Redemption and the 'Fallen Woman,'" 63–64).
28. Dolin has also suggested that Peter represents one extreme of the Victorian woman, "the fallen woman" ("*Cranford* and the Victorian Collection," 197), whereas Recchio argues that Peter as woman works "to satirize Miss Deborah's voluntary sterility" ("Cranford and 'The Lawe of Kynde,'" 24). Hyde, on the other hand, points out that the violent reaction of Peter's father could be to cross-dressing, not hints of pregnancy or illegitimacy: "Peter would be displaying the monstrous propensity for which preachers had denounced the Elizabethan theatres" ("'Poor Frederick' and 'Poor Peter,'" 23).
29. Gillooly has noted that—as is so often the case in this novel—there is an echo of the flung pillow in Peter's fantastic tale of a cherubim's falling from above, shot by accident in the high Himalayas ("Humor as Daughterly Defense," 159).
30. The character of the narrator has attracted interest since her creation. The *Examiner* (23 July 1853) found that "Miss Mary Smith cannot help revealing not a little of her own character in making so free with the characters of her friends"—she is "shrewd," "penetrating," "critical," "knowing" (*CH,* 197). More recently Boone says, "She too is an unmarried woman, and her spinster status leaves her entirely empathetic toward her subject matter; spiritually she is one of the Cranford single women, never an entirely objective commentator" (*Tradition Counter Tradition,* 297). In a detailed study of her identity, Carse writes: "In Mary, Elizabeth Gaskell created not simply a convenient narrator but a character who could feel, judge, and articulate the value of Cranford; in making her a 'well-to-do and happy young woman,' Gaskell gave Mary qualities that circumstances of their background deny the older women" ("Penchant for Narrative," 328).
31. Mulvihill interprets this string- and paper-saving passage within a psychological framework: "The needs they [such obsessions] serve may be real or nominal, but as arrangements they are formally equivalent and stem from fundamental human economic behaviors reaching far beyond Cranford's tiny sphere" ("Economies of Living," 347). Terence Wright says: "Ridiculous as these examples [of private economy] are, they clearly are much more the matters by which people live than are stocks and

shares, mortgages and columns of figures, as the behavior of the gentleman with the bank-book shows" (*Elizabeth Gaskell,* 134).

32. Gillooly has also studied connections between Mary and Peter, suggesting that both have been made to play subservient roles in Cranford society. Thus it satisfies Mary's sense of justice to call Peter back to his rightful place ("Humor as Daughterly Defense," 896).

33. Gillooly, "Humor as Daughterly Defense," 890.

34. Dolin has also found "Mary's long pause at the post-box" (*"Cranford* and the Victorian Collection," 203) a key moment in the novel, where the many female collections embody a distinctive quality of life.

35. Collin says the novel's composition and publication history is "a story of erratic stops and starts" ("Composition and Publication," 59). Critics have proposed a number of structural principles governing the form of the novel. Boone, for example, says, "If *Cranford*'s narrative structure is cohesive, its unifying principles derive more from the circumscribed status associated with spinsterhood than from precepts of conventional narrative linearity" (*Tradition Counter Tradition,* 296). Gérin notes that "the style of *Cranford* resembles far more the style of her letters than any of her other fictions" (*Elizabeth Gaskell,* 124). And Miller explains how "Gaskell carefully interweaves stories of detection and financial failure in two linear plots. These narratives, however, coexist with a more cyclical movement, an alternative narrative form which emerges out of and represents the routines of everyday life" ("Fragments," 91). Griffith debates the genre of *Cranford,* terming it "a short fiction series" ("What Kind of Book Is *Cranford?*" 57), which he characterizes as "periodically published at a leisurely pace, never writing to a close, content with casual repetition" (58).

36. Bonaparte states: "Every so often, however, [Mary Smith] feels the need to get away to Cranford. And this is the very need that drives Gaskell herself to write the tale" (*Gypsy-Bachelor,* 156). And Uglow explains that "her subject had pulled her back" (*Elizabeth Gaskell,* 284) after the first episode.

IV. Textual/Sexual Pleasure and Serial Publication

1. Easson, *Elizabeth Gaskell,* 88. Lansbury says that serialization was "a mode of publication that she detested, scrambling to fit the work into twenty separate numbers, instead of the twenty-two that she insisted Dickens had promised her" (*Elizabeth Gaskell,* 36). Elsie Michie explores the gendered characterizations that inform such approaches to the Dickens-Gaskell relationship (*Outside the Pale,* 83–88, 110) and (though in different terms than we offer) also discusses Gaskell's resistance to Dickens's editorial control of her work (95–98).

2. Homans, *Bearing the Word,* 229. Still, it is notable that Homans detects in the final part of the story not emphatic closure but indications of an ongoing story: "The story closes with a telescoped account of their [Lizzie's and her mother's] lives afterward, in which mother and daughter continue their stand outside patriarchy and patriliny" (232). See also Julian Wolfreys: "I comprehend Gaskell's writing primarily to be episodic and exemplary, rather than narrative and linear" (*Being English,* 82).

3. Gérin, *Elizabeth Gaskell,* 124. According to Showalter, *Cranford* "probably" depicts "an Amazon Utopia" ("Feminist Criticism," 31).

4. As Gérin explains and we reiterate in chapter 3, the nine-month gap in *Cranford*'s

serialization was most likely occasioned by Gaskell's turning from this story to the composition of *Ruth,* issued as a whole novel in January 1853, after which *Cranford* resumed.

5. Winnett, "Coming Unstrung," 515.

6. Winnett, "Coming Unstrung," 509.

7. Norman Feltes, *Modes of Production,* has provided the fullest assessment of the serial's effects from a Marxist perspective; see also Mary Poovey's chapter on Dickens and the serial, in which she offsets the author's greater connection with a reading audience against the serial's imposition of alienated labor conditions on the author (*Uneven Developments,* 104).

8. Tuchman, *Edging Women Out,* 209. Compare Elaine Showalter's model for gyno-centric criticism, one that never loses sight of the appearance of women's writing within dominant social structures: "No publication is fully independent from the economic and political pressures of the male-dominated society. . . . women's writing is a 'double-voiced discourse' that always embodies the social, literary, and cultural heritage of both the muted and the dominant" ("Feminist Criticism," 31). As she notes later, "A gynocentric criticism would also situate women writers with respect to the variables of literary culture, such as modes of production and distribution, relations of author and audience, relations of high to popular art, and hierarchies of genre" (32−33). The serial is relevant to all the categories Showalter cites.

9. See Tuchman, *Edging Women Out,* 7, and Martineau, *Autobiography,* 2:117. Women were major producers of fiction before the 1840s, of course; Showalter, working from J. M. S. Tompkins's study, points out that women wrote most eighteenth-century epistolary novels (*Literature of Their Own,* 17). But mass markets did not develop until well into the nineteenth century. For further evidence that women functioned as ma-jor forces in the production and consumption of nineteenth-century fiction, see Showalter, *Literature of Their Own,* 20−21; Klingopulos, "Literary Scene," 71; Helsin-ger, Sheets, and Veeder, *Woman Question,* 3:8; and Tuchman, *Edging Women Out.*

10. Tuchman, *Edging Women Out,* 53. By the 1880s, however, this pattern had changed, and Tuchman explains that women were more likely to use male pseudonyms (54). Many novels accepted by Macmillan were first serialized in *Macmillan's Magazine,* though in the discussion Tuchman does not always distinguish serialized fiction from novels published only as three-deckers.

11. Howard, *Rattlin,* 230. See also 233, where female readers are again addressed. When the novel was published in volume form, it was renamed *Rattlin, the Reefer.*

12. Quoted in Skilton, "Introduction," xi.

13. Hughes and Lund, *Victorian Serial,* 8.

14. Nightingale, *Cassandra,* 32. See also Helsinger, Sheets, and Veeder, *Woman Question,* 3:10, 12, and Spender, *Writing or the Sex?* 127−30, for the dilemma of interruption for women writers.

 Michael Apple's remarks about twentieth-century romance novels and soap op-eras (themselves serials) might well apply to nineteenth-century serial fiction: "One of the benefits of romance novels is that they enable women to control their own pleasure. In much the same ways as soap operas on television are geared to the tem-poral and emotional structure of household labor, and thus are more contradictory than their critics allow for, so too do romance novels allow for a more complex set of meanings than we might imagine" ("Series Editor's Introduction," xii). Apple cites Dorothy Hobson, *Crossroads,* in support of his point about soap operas.

15. Quoted in Murray, *Strong-Minded Women,* 84, 88. Short stories, of course, could have responded to the demand for reading in restricted units of time, but short stories feature the gathering and dispersal of narrative energy in a single burst rather than the slowly accreting and intimate form of the serial novel—itself a form defined by its interruptions in the text (see Hughes and Lund, *Victorian Serial,* 2).

16. Quoted in Helsinger, Sheets, and Veeder, *Woman Question,* 2:83 (see also Poovey, *Uneven Developments,* 7).

17. See Showalter and Showalter, "Victorian Women and Menstruation," 42; Helsinger, Sheets, and Veeder, *Woman Question,* 2:86–88, 104; Maudsley quoted in Murray, *Strong-Minded Women,* 221; Martineau, *Autobiography,* 1:258.

18. See Murray, *Strong-Minded Women,* 211, and Spender, *Writing or the Sex?* 113, 117.

19. Haight, *George Eliot,* 205.

20. Showalter, *Literature of Their Own,* 15.

21. Cixous, "Sorties," 87, 88. Jelinek, "Introduction," 17. We are particularly interested in the analogy between the serial and notions of feminine form as process oriented and open. However, the serial's enfolding of silence into the text—the nonverbal spaces between parts are a fundamental part of the form—might usefully be examined in relation to the notion of the preverbal (the "semiotic," according to Julia Kristeva) that has been identified with the feminine in the work of Lacan and related theorists.

22. Beetham, "Towards a Theory," 27, 28–29; see also Poovey, *Uneven Developments,* 104.

23. Du Plessis, in Eagleton, *Feminist Literary Theory,* 228. Le Guin, "Carrier Bag Theory," 169, 170. Compare Susan Morgan, who argues that nineteenth-century British heroines embody the virtues of change and connectedness so often celebrated in fiction: "These heroines represented the fictional transformation of religious values into secular values, of Christianity into femininity, of eternity into history, of fixity into change. The novels argue that a sense of history is a precondition for any social or individual progress. That sense of history, including the sense that character means character in process, self is self in time, celebrates qualities of connectedness the culture has traditionally undervalued and labeled as feminine" (*Sisters in Time,* 17). Note our arguments above regarding the serial's potential for "connectedness" on the part of both writer and reader.

24. Tuchman, *Edging Women Out,* 7–8, 188. See Hughes and Lund, "Linear Stories," and *Victorian Serial,* 229–74, for discussions of changes in aesthetic values at the end of the nineteenth century.

25. Lansbury and David, among others, have discussed this eroticism. Schor, importantly, explores the means by which the erotic and industrial plots complement and complicate, rather than oppose, each other (see, for example, *Scheherezade in the Marketplace,* 128, 144–45).

26. See Radway, *Reading the Romance,* 65–67.

27. Radway, *Reading the Romance,* 65, 54, 77. Just as Margaret Hale is displaced from her family homes in London and Helstone at the novel's outset, so the ideal romance, according to Radway's study, "begins with its heroine's removal from a familiar, comfortable realm usually associated with her childhood and family" (Ibid., 134), a move that allows the heroine to adopt unconventionally assertive behavior and to encounter the hero.

28. Radway, *Reading the Romance,* 81, 64–65, 105. The practice of romance reading described by Radway differs in one significant way from serial reading: the readers

Radway interviewed "do not like to return to reality without experiencing the resolution of the narrative," and many consumers read the ending before they purchase a romance (59). A serial is defined by enforced interruption and by the withholding of narrative resolution. Yet, like serial readers, Radway's romance readers express the desire to participate in characters' ongoing lives through new "installments": "[Readers] wish that more authors would write sequels to stories in order to follow the lives of particularly striking minor characters" (109).

29. Ann Barr Snitow, "Mass Market Romance," 146. Snitow also suggests that the romance deals with the only adventure permitted middle-class women (the seeking of a marriage mate) and yet ends before arriving at material that suggests prosaic, intractable realities the reader may be all too familiar with—the realities of marriage.

30. Cixous indicates the regressive politics of such desire, which she perceives as a masculinist strategy: "The good woman [in patriarchy], therefore, is the one who 'resists' long enough for him to feel both his power over her and his desire . . . to give him the pleasure of enjoying, without too many obstacles, the return to himself which he, grown greater—reassured in his own eyes, is making" ("Sorties," 79–80). But John Thornton does not return to his single, same self as a result of desire; like Margaret himself, he changes over the course of the novel, spurred in part by his vulnerability to Margaret's attacks or praise.

31. In Paroissien, *Selected Letters of Charles Dickens,* 320, 322. In a 26 July 1854 letter discussing five later installments, Dickens again explains his idea of parts structure by stressing how each must "close" (322).

32. Collin, "Composition," 70; Paroissien, *Selected Letters of Charles Dickens,* 323n.

33. Philip Collins compares the parts endings proposed by Dickens with the conclusions of installments actually published, which presumably were approved by Mrs. Gaskell (*Dickens and Crime,* 89–91). Vann explains that Dickens was guided not only by his notion of effective parts structure for fiction but by concern for the overall shape of each issue of *Household Words* ("Dickens, Charles Lever and Mrs. Gaskell," 67).

34. Paroissien, *Selected Letters of Charles Dickens,* 320.

35. Collins, *Dickens and Crime,* 274.

36. Dodsworth, "Introduction," 7.

37. This swerve from labor relations to romance has received considerable attention in cultural analyses of Gaskell's work. See Gallagher, *Industrial Reformation,* 148–49.

38. Gaskell's emphasis on social relations and characters' contexts is evident in the title she preferred. Her choice for the novel's title was *Margaret Hale,* which roots the story in personal circumstance; Dickens's choice of title, which prevailed, emphasizes conflict, abstraction, and ideological issues that rest on but supersede given individuals.

39. Letter of 20 August 1854, in Paroissien, *Selected Letters of Charles Dickens,* 323 (Dickens's emphasis).

40. Bodenheimer's analysis of the novel's structure is similar: "In its every situation, whether industrial politics or emotional life, traditional views and stances break down into confusing new ones, which are rendered in all the pain of mistakenness and conflict that real human change entails" ("*North and South,*" 282).

41. Easson concludes: "If [Margaret and Thornton] begin as standing in some sort for north and south, they end by merging to form an entity, though any allegorical blending is pretty remote in the actuality of their love" (*Elizabeth Gaskell,* 95).

42. Cited in Collin, "Composition," 88. Bodenheimer argues, "It may be that the dif-

ficulty of ending [the novel] had something to do with the stubbornly open presentation of character and social change in the main part of the story" ("*North and South*," 301).

43. Lansbury argues that "this moment of understanding gathers up all time, past, present, and future, in a single decision" (*Elizabeth Gaskell*, 41).

44. Letter of January 1855 cited in Gérin, *Elizabeth Gaskell*, 154. Lansbury says, "Now Gaskell had no objection to Dickens abbreviating her work; what she would not accept were his attempts to cast her vision of reality into a Dickensian frame. . . . Indeed, her perception of truth was founded upon a depreciation of external forms better to elucidate and define the inner workings of the personality. . . . Nothing could be farther from Dickens's 'circle of stage fire,' and characters who live in memory by means of a single gesture" (*Elizabeth Gaskell*, 36). David says that Gaskell wrote this novel "feeling perhaps that her woman's knowledge was not the 'correct knowledge,' and it was a painful experience for her, marked by what she felt were unreasonable demands for the compression and speedy production necessary for its serialization in *Household Words,* easily managed by its editor, but incompatible with her more leisurely methods of composition" (*Fictions of Resolution*, 9).

45. Although not all of Mrs. Gaskell's letters to Dickens about serialization have survived, Dorothy Collin argues, "It may be shown that disregard was not [Gaskell's] attitude to serial divisions in the case of *North and South*" ("Composition," 73). Collin also notes: "There is evidence that the disagreement between Dickens and Mrs. Gaskell was bruited abroad at least among the circle of her correspondents" (74).

46. Uglow, *Elizabeth Gaskell*, 395, 448.

47. Edgar Wright, "Introduction," xiv; Uglow, *Elizabeth Gaskell*, 468, 460.

48. "Lois the Witch" appeared in three parts (1859) and "A Dark Night's Work" in eight (1863), both in Dickens's *All the Year Round.*

49. Lewis, "Introduction," ix, x.

50. Uglow, *Elizabeth Gaskell*, 536; Lewis, "Introduction," x.

V. Engendered Lives

1. Ross, "Honoring the Woman as Writer," 26. See also Easson, *Elizabeth Gaskell*, 152, and Warhol, "Towards a Theory," passim.

2. See Pollard, *Mrs. Gaskell*, 143, and Easson, *Elizabeth Gaskell*, 135.

3. Pollard, *Mrs. Gaskell*, 142–43; Easson, *Elizabeth Gaskell*, 150; Heilbrun, *Writing "A Woman's Life,"* 22, and Spencer, *Elizabeth Gaskell*, 70–71; Lansbury, *Elizabeth Gaskell: The Novel of Social Crisis*, 146; Uglow, *Elizabeth Gaskell*, 407; Ross, "Honoring the Woman as Writer," 25–38; and Peterson, "'No Finger Posts,'" 35.

4. Scholars frequently assert Gaskell's personal investment in the biography and her representation of the woman writer. See, e.g., Lansbury, *Elizabeth Gaskell*, 130, and Colby, *"Some Appointed Work to Do,"* 75–87. We emphasize the embedding of this personal stake in public discourses that touched on Gaskell's reputation as well as that of Brontë.

5. L. A. Marchand, historian of the *Athenaeum*, dates substantive obituaries in that periodical from the advent of Dilke's editorship in 1830 and notes the extensive use made of *Athenaeum* obituaries by contributors to the *Dictionary of National Biography* (*Athenaeum*, 60–61).

6. Whitman, *Come to Judgment,* xiii–xiv.

7. Brooks, *Reading for the Plot,* 22, 29. To support his linking of plot to the "discourse of Mortality," Brooks cites Walter Benjamin ("Death . . . is the sanction of everything that the storyteller can tell") and Jean Paul Sartre ("In telling everything is transformed by the structuring presence of the end to come, and narrative in fact proceeds 'in the reverse'; or, as Sartre puts it in respect to autobiographical narration in *Les Mots,* in order to tell his story in terms of the meaning it would acquire only at the end, 'I became my own obituary'") (*Reading for the Plot,* 22).

8. See Poovey, *Proper Lady,* 35–36, and Nord, *Walking the Victorian Streets,* 12 and passim.

9. Gérin, *Elizabeth Gaskell,* 415.

10. The 6 June 1855 issue of *Harper's New Monthly Magazine* also linked Brontë and Gaskell: "Among the female writers of a time so affluent in works of female genius, Charlotte Brontë was, in England at least, the most eminent and powerful. Her only peer in many points was Mrs. Gaskell, the author of 'Mary Barton,' 'Ruth,' 'Cranford,' and 'North and South.' But their genius was very different; and they were peers without being rivals" (*HJ,* 128).

    We should note that at the end of her *Blackwood's* essay Oliphant announces the recent death of Brontë and acknowledges the hostile edge of the essay's criticism of her work: "Since writing the above, we have heard of an event which will give to some of its comments an air of harsh and untimely criticism" (*B,* 568). But if her last word is that no other novelist is worthy to succeed Brontë in the literary world, Oliphant also resolutely refuses to retract her previous statements.

11. Shelston, "Introduction," 14.

12. Sharps, *Mrs. Gaskell's Observation,* 576–77. Robinson, "Elizabeth Gaskell," suggests that Catherine Winkworth wrote the obituary, though the plausible reasons he marshals against Gaskell's authorship also apply to Winkworth—who, like Gaskell, was a friend of Brontë's (Gérin, *Elizabeth Gaskell,* 525) and was not likely to have spelled the name of Brontë's husband incorrectly (it is given as "Nicol" in the obituary) or recycled an inaccurate story about the marriage of Brontë's parents. Robinson's alternative suggestion, that Winkworth could have "freely allowed the letter to circulate and did not herself object to someone else making use of it, or that it fell into someone else's hands in an accidental fashion and they had even fewer scruples about consulting its author or recipient before publishing its contents" (397), seems far more plausible.

    Juliet Barker, it should be noted, assigns responsibility for the *Sharpe's* obituary to Gaskell (*Brontës,* 780–81), whom she aligns with "other scandalmongers" (792). In Barker's view Gaskell gravely distorted the lives and characters of Patrick Brontë, Branwell Brontë, and Arthur Nicolls; and in creating the Brontë "myth," Barker contends, Gaskell undermined accurate representation of Charlotte's literary production and her relations with her family (xviii–xix).

13. Robinson, "Elizabeth Gaskell," 396.

14. Other obituaries occupied a middle ground between Martineau's domesticated Brontë and the transgressive Brontë presented by Oliphant. The *Manchester Guardian* obituary, reprinted in the *Times* (6 April 1855, 6), stressed the author more than the daughter or wife, an author marked by "lasting reputation," "great power of conception," and "vigorous portrayal of character." The *Illustrated London News* likewise emphasized the author and sister more than the wife and daughter (14 April 1855,

363). The *Literary Gazette* first announced the loss of "an author of lasting reputation" at her "father's house at Haworth" in the 7 April 1855 number (219). In the 14 April 1855 issue, however, the journal transformed Brontë into a character in a romance novel, representing Patrick Brontë as blocking agent to a courtship plot until the incumbency of Haworth was settled on Nicolls (235).

15. Gaskell remarked on Arnold's poem in a 5 May 1855 letter to John Greenwood, observing the poet's "falling into the same mistake Miss Martineau did" (*LMG*, 342). The "mistake" concerned placing the burial site in the churchyard rather than in the church itself.

16. Ross, "Honoring the Woman as Writer," 34. See Uglow, *Elizabeth Gaskell*, 256, 327, and Sanders, "Introduction," viii–ix.

17. Ross, "Honoring the Woman as Writer, 32; Lansbury, *Elizabeth Gaskell: The Novel of Social Crisis*, 143.

18. Pollard, *Mrs. Gaskell*, 155; Easson, *Elizabeth Gaskell*, 154. See also Homans, *Bearing the Word*, 237.

19. Scholars have often noted Gaskell's inability to understand Emily Brontë (e.g., Easson, *Elizabeth Gaskell*, 153). We suggest that the stance of incomprehension has a rhetorical thrust, that it "purifies" Charlotte's character by allowing Emily's to be brought into question.

20. See, for example, Brontë, *Shirley*, 160, 214–15.

21. Easson considers this last orientation a defining stance in the biography as a whole (*Elizabeth Gaskell*, 150–51).

22. See, for example, Easson, *Elizabeth Gaskell*, 150, 155.

23. See Colby, *"Some Appointed Work to Do,"* 78, and Uglow, *Elizabeth Gaskell*, 310.

24. Ross, "Honoring the Woman as Writer," 28–29; Colby, *"Some Appointed Work to Do,"* 75–87; Uglow, *Elizabeth Gaskell*, 407.

25. Colby, *"Some Appointed Work to Do,"* 78. The following letter cited in Barker's biography indicates the degree of Gaskell's selection among the range of voices in Brontë's correspondence: "[Do] you think this chapter [in *Shirley*] will tender the work liable to severe handling by the press? Is it because knowing as you now do the identity of "Currer Bell"—this scene strikes you as unfeminine—? Is it because it is intrinsically defective and inferior—? I am afraid the two first reasons would not weigh with me—the last would" (*Brontës*, 586–87). Nowhere is Brontë represented in Gaskell's text as rejecting the claims of femininity.

26. Linda Peterson (personal communication) remarks that the second opens with Brontë as author: the first, domestic volume ushers in a volume devoted to the public author.

27. For a contrasting account of the two novelists' relation to gossip and Gaskell's degree of identification with Brontë, see D'Albertis, "'Bookmaking,'" 14–16 and passim.

28. See, for example, Pollard, *Mrs. Gaskell*, 165.

29. Kershaw, "Business of a Woman's Life," 20; see also 18–19. See Nord, *Walking the Victorian Streets*, 156–57, on Mary Barton's public display of her body.

30. Ross, "Honoring the Woman as Writer," 29.

31. See Marcus, "Profession of Author," 207, 213–17.

32. See Shelston, in *LCB*, 607n. 1.

33. Easson, *Elizabeth Gaskell*, 148.

34. Of course the debate about Gaskell's credibility was itself subject to gendered notions of authorship. But emerging doubts about the accuracy of her research preempted a

focus on the lineaments of the biography itself. Harriet Martineau's reaction in the July 1857 *Westminster Review* indicates how assessment of the narrative might be derailed by anxieties about credibility: "Of Mrs. Gaskell's share in this matter a few weeks since [before the publication of her retraction] we would gladly have said much. She herself will now desire that we should say as little as possible" (*WR*, 295).

35. See Poovey, *Uneven Developments*, 2ff.

36. See also Trela, "Froude on the Carlyles," 181. An exception was that in the 7 February 1881 *Times*, which gave a far more detailed, and complex, account than those cited, for example, in the *Critical Heritage*.

37. The marriage was blocked by Irving's prior engagement with another, from which he was not released. See Trela, "Froude on the Carlyles," 181–82.

38. One wishes it were possible to know Jane's own thoughts on reading Gaskell's biography, assuming she did so. The Duke edition of Carlyle letters for 1857, however, has not yet appeared.

39. See Spencer, *Elizabeth Gaskell*, 71–72.

40. Feminist biography understood in these terms is discussed by Iles, "Introduction," 1. See also Broughton, "Froude-Carlyle Embroilment," 564.

41. Dunn, *Froude and Carlyle*, 16.

42. Broughton, "Froude-Carlyle Embroilment," 552.

43. See also Poovey, *Uneven Developments*, 89–125.

44. Rose, *Parallel Lives*, 257.

45. Our findings parallel those of Dale Trela: "The real picture is . . . complex. Although many reviewers [of the 1881 *Reminiscences*] were offended by the private details of married life, others were not" ("Froude on the Carlyles," 183). Trela cites an 1883 *North American Review* essay written by a woman (Gail Hamilton) in which a feminist critique of Carlyle as husband and public writer is central. We confine our focus to British reviews of Froude's life and editions of Carlyle material. The 31 March 1883 *Times* review of *Letters and Memorials of Jane Welsh Carlyle* (1883) is one of the British notices indicating ongoing speculation about and concern with the Carlyle marriage.

46. The 12 February 1881 obituary of Carlyle in the *Athenaeum* indicates in its closing paragraphs just why so much was at stake in the represented masculinity of Carlyle in the *Reminiscences*:

(*A*, 235)

> One of the best epigrams about Carlyle has been written by Mr. John Morley.
> "Carlylism is the male of Byronism," he says. "It is Byronism with thew and sinew, bass pipe and shaggy bosom. There is the same grievous complaint against the time and its men and its spirits, something even of the same contemptuous despair, the same sense of the puniness of man in the centre of a cruel and frowning universe; but there is in Carlylism a deliverance from it all, indeed, the only deliverance possible. Its despair is a despair without misery. Labour in a high spirit, duty done, and right service performed in fortitudinous temper,—here was, not indeed a way out, but a way of erect living within."

47. See Sussman's chapter on Carlyle (chap. 1) in *Victorian Masculinities*.

48. Dunn, *James Anthony Froude*, 493, records Froude's involvement with Jane Welsh Carlyle's letters. K. J. Fielding observes a shifting "tone" between the first and second installments of the biography ("Froude and Carlyle," 257). As Broughton notes ("Froude-Carlyle Embroilment," 553), Froude was himself implicated in the charge

of unmanliness, his dilemma as biographer mirroring Carlyle's own infringement of gender codes. See also Broughton's "Froude: The 'Painful Appendix,'" 65–80.

49. As the 15 April 1882 *Academy* remarked in a notice of *Thomas Carlyle: A History of the First Forty Years of His Life, 1795–1835,* "Old Mrs. Carlyle's description of her son as 'gey ill to live wi' suggests itself in these volumes almost as often as 'wae's me' in the *Reminiscences*" (*A*, 260).
50. Easson, *Elizabeth Gaskell,* 151.
51. See Klaus Theweleit, in Kestner, *Masculinities in Victorian Painting,* 98.

Epilogue

1. Sutherland, *Stanford Companion to Victorian Fiction,* 240; Gérin, *Elizabeth Gaskell,* 230.
2. For a critique of such romanticized visions of farm life, see Raymond Williams's *Country and the City,* 182–96.
3. Bourdieu, *Field of Cultural Production,* 42.
4. Uglow, *Elizabeth Gaskell,* 497.
5. Lansbury, *Elizabeth Gaskell: The Novel of Social Crisis,* 12–13.
6. Byrne, "*Reader,*" 346.
7. Obituaries in other papers lacking the cultural authority to fix literary histories of Gaskell also diverged from the accounts in the *Cornhill,* the *Athenaeum,* or *Macmillan's.* In a number of obituaries it is "The Moorland Cottage" as much as *Cranford* that is associated with charm and rusticity. In one obituary the short story was called merely a "simple" Christmas story (*Press,* 18 Nov. 1865, 1117), in another a "pretty" one (*Round Table* [New York], 9 Dec. 1865, 220). In the *Press* obituary and several others *Cranford* is identified only as "some sketches of life in a village . . . contributed to 'Household Words'" (*PR,* 1117). Gaskell's role as active contributor to periodicals was repeatedly noted in obituaries.
8. Uglow, *Elizabeth Gaskell,* 551.
9. See also Spencer, *Elizabeth Gaskell,* 127, and Wolfreys, *Being English,* 95–97.
10. Uglow, *Elizabeth Gaskell,* 548–49.

Bibliography

Works by Elizabeth Gaskell

Note on editions cited: In the interest of using texts easily accessible to our own readers, we have opted to cite modern, single-volume editions even when referring to serial parts published by Gaskell.

"Christmas Storms and Sunshine." 1865. In *"The Moorland Cottage" and Other Stories,* ed. Suzanne Lewis, 111–21. New York: Oxford Univ. Press, 1995.

"Cousin Phillis." 1863–64. In *"Cousin Phillis" and Other Tales,* ed. Angus Easson, 259–354. New York: Oxford Univ. Press, 1981.

Cranford. 1851–53. Ed. Elizabeth Porges Watson. New York: Oxford Univ. Press, 1972.

"The Crooked Branch." 1859. In *"Cousin Phillis" and Other Tales,* ed. Angus Easson, 195–238. New York: Oxford Univ. Press, 1981.

"A Dark Night's Work." 1863. In *"A Dark Night's Work" and Other Stories,* ed. Suzanne Lewis, 1–166. New York: Oxford Univ. Press, 1992.

"The Doom of the Griffiths." 1858. In *"My Lady Ludlow" and Other Stories,* ed. Edgar Wright, 229–69. New York: Oxford Univ. Press, 1989.

"The Heart of John Middleton." 1850. In *"The Moorland Cottage" and Other Stories,* ed. Suzanne Lewis, 145–65. New York: Oxford Univ. Press, 1995.

The Letters of Mrs. Gaskell. Ed. J. A. V. Chapple and Arthur Pollard. Cambridge: Harvard Univ. Press, 1967.

The Life of Charlotte Brontë. 1857. Ed. Alan Shelston. London: Penguin, 1975.

"Lizzie Leigh." 1855. In *"Cousin Phillis" and Other Tales,* ed. Angus Easson, 1–32. New York: Oxford Univ. Press, 1981.

Mary Barton. 1848. Ed. Stephen Gill. New York: Penguin, 1970.

"The Moorland Cottage." 1850. In *"The Moorland Cottage" and Other Stories,* ed. Suzanne Lewis, 3–100. New York: Oxford Univ. Press, 1995.

My Lady Ludlow. 1858. In *"My Lady Ludlow" and Other Stories,* ed. Edgar Wright, 1–210. New York: Oxford Univ. Press, 1989.

North and South. 1854–55. Ed. Dorothy Collin. Harmondsworth GB: Penguin, 1970.

"The Old Nurse's Story." 1852. In *"Cousin Phillis" and Other Tales,* ed. Angus Easson, 35–56. New York: Oxford Univ. Press, 1981.

"The Poor Clare." 1856. In *"My Lady Ludlow" and Other Stories,* ed. Edgar Wright, 271–333. New York: Oxford Univ. Press, 1989.

Ruth. 1853. Ed. Alan Shelston. New York: Oxford Univ. Press 1985.

Sylvia's Lovers. 1863. Ed. Andrew Sanders. New York: Oxford Univ. Press, 1982.

Wives and Daughters: An Every-Day Story. 1864–66. Ed. Angus Easson. New York: Oxford Univ. Press, 1987.

Contemporary and Secondary Works

Anderson, Amanda. *Tainted Souls and Painted Faces: The Rhetoric of Fallenness in Victorian Culture.* Ithaca: Cornell Univ. Press, 1993.

Apple, Michael W. "Series Editor's Introduction." In *Becoming a Woman through Romance,* by Linda K. Christian-Smith, ix–xiv. New York: Routledge, 1990.

A[rnold, Matthew]. "Haworth Churchyard, April, 1855." *Fraser's Magazine* 51 (May 1856): 527–30.

Auerbach, Nina. *Communities of Women: An Idea in Fiction.* Cambridge: Harvard Univ. Press, 1978.

Barker, Juliet. *The Brontës.* London: Weidenfeld & Nicholson, 1994.

Beetham, Margaret. "Towards a Theory of the Periodical as a Publishing Genre." In *Investigating Victorian Journalism,* ed. Laurel Brake, Aled Jones, and Lionel Madden, 19–32. New York: St. Martin's Press, 1990.

Belenky, Mary Field, Blythe McVicker Clinchy, Nancy Rule Goldberger, and Jill Mattuck Tarule. *Women's Ways of Knowing: The Development of Self, Voice, and Mind.* New York: Basic Books, 1986.

Bick, Suzanne. "'Take Her up Tenderly': Elizabeth Gaskell's Treatment of the Fallen Woman." *Essays in Arts and Sciences* 18 (1989): 17–27.

Bodenheimer, Rosemarie. "*North and South:* A Permanent State of Change." *Nineteenth Century Fiction* 34 (1979): 281–301.

———. "Private Grief and Public Acts in *Mary Barton.*" *Dickens Studies Annual: Essays on Victorian Fiction* 9 (1981): 195–216.

Bonaparte, Felicia. *The Gypsy-Bachelor of Manchester: The Life of Mrs. Gaskell's Demon.* Charlottesville: Univ. Press of Virginia, 1992.

Boone, Joseph Allen. *Tradition Counter Tradition: Love and the Form of Fiction.* Women in Culture and Society. Chicago: Univ. of Chicago Press, 1987.

Bourdieu, Pierre. *The Field of Cultural Production.* Ed. Randall Johnson. New York: Columbia Univ. Press, 1993.

Brake, Laurel. *Subjugated Knowledges: Journalism, Gender and Literature in the Nineteenth Century.* New York: New York Univ. Press, 1994.

Brontë, Charlotte. *Shirley.* London: J. M. Dent, 1908.

The Brontës: The Critical Heritage. Ed. Miriam Allott. Boston: Routledge & Kegan Paul, 1974.

Brooks, Peter. *Reading for the Plot: Design and Intention in Narrative.* New York: Alfred A. Knopf, 1984.

Broughton, Trev. "Froude: The 'Painful Appendix.'" *Carlyle Studies Annual* 15 (1995): 65–80.

———."The Froude-Carlyle Embroilment: Married Life as a Literary Problem." *Victorian Studies* 38, no. 4 (1995): 551–85.

Buchanan, Laurie. "Mothers and Daughters in Elizabeth Gaskell's *Wives and Daughters:* In a Woman's World." *Midwest Quarterly* 31, no. 4 (1990): 499–513.

Byrne, John F. "*The Reader.*" In *British Literary Magazines: The Victorian and Edwardian Age, 1837–1913,* ed. Alvin Sullivan, 346–51. Westport CT: Greenwood Press, 1984.

Carse, Wendy K. "A Penchant for Narrative: 'Mary Smith' in Elizabeth Gaskell's *Cranford.*" *Journal of Narrative Technique* 20, no. 3 (1990): 318–30.

Cixous, Hélène. "Sorties." In *The Newly Born Woman,* by Hélène Cixous and Catherine

Clement, trans. Betsy Wing, 63–132. Minneapolis: Univ. of Minneapolis Press, 1986.

Colby, Robin B. *"Some Appointed Work to Do": Women and Vocation in the Fiction of Elizabeth Gaskell*. Westport CT: Greenwood Press, 1995.

Collin, Dorothy M. "The Composition and Publication of Elizabeth Gaskell's *Cranford*." *Bulletin of the John Rylands University Library of Manchester* 69 (1986): 59–95.

———. "The Composition of Mrs. Gaskell's *North and South*." *Bulletin of the John Rylands University Library of Manchester* 54 (1971): 67–93.

Collins, Philip. *Dickens and Crime*. Bloomington: Indiana Univ. Press, 1968.

Collins, Wilkie. *Armadale*. *Cornhill Magazine*, November 1864–June 1866.

Coultrap-McQuin, Susan. *Doing Literary Business: American Women Writers in the Nineteenth Century*. Chapel Hill: Univ. of North Carolina Press, 1990.

Craik, Wendy. *Elizabeth Gaskell and the English Provincial Novel*. London: Methuen, 1975.

———. "Lore, Learning and Wisdom: Workers and Education in *Mary Barton* and *North and South*." *Gaskell Society Journal* 2 (1988): 13–33.

———. "'Man, Vain Man' in Susan Ferrier, Margaret Oliphant and Elizabeth Gaskell." *Gaskell Society Journal* 9 (1995): 55–65.

D'Albertis, Deirdre. "'Bookmaking out of the Remains of the Dead': Elizabeth Gaskell's *The Life of Charlotte Brontë*." *Victorian Studies* 39, no. 1 (1995): 1–31.

David, Deirdre. *Fictions of Resolution in Three Victorian Novels*. New York: Columbia Univ. Press, 1981.

Davis, Deanna L. "Feminist Critics and Literary Mothers: Daughters Reading Elizabeth Gaskell." *Signs* 17, no. 3 (1992): 507–32.

Dodsworth, Martin. "Introduction." In *North and South*, by Elizabeth Gaskell, ed. Dorothy Collin, 7–26. Harmondsworth GB: Penguin, 1970.

Dolin, Tim. "*Cranford* and the Victorian Collection." *Victorian Studies* 36, no. 2 (1993): 179–206.

Dunn, Waldo H. *Froude and Carlyle: A Study of the Froude-Carlyle Controversy*. New York: Longmans, Green, 1930.

———. *James Anthony Froude: A Biography*. Oxford: Clarendon Press, 1961.

Eagleton, Mary, ed. *Feminist Literary Theory: A Reader*. Oxford: Basil Blackwell, 1986.

Easson, Angus. *Elizabeth Gaskell*. Boston: Routledge & Kegan Paul, 1979.

———. "Elizabeth Gaskell and the Novel of Local Pride." *Bulletin of the John Rylands University Library of Manchester* 67, no. 2 (1985): 688–709.

———. "The Sentiment of Feeling: Emotions and Objects in Elizabeth Gaskell." *Gaskell Society Journal* 4 (1990): 64–78.

Eliot, George. *Romola*. *Cornhill Magazine*, July 1862–August 1863.

Elizabeth Gaskell: The Critical Heritage. Ed. Angus Easson. Critical Heritage. New York: Routledge, 1991.

Felber, Lynette. "Gaskell's Industrial Novels: Ideology and Formal Incongruence in *Mary Barton* and *North and South*. *Clio* 18, no. 1 (1988): 55–72.

Feltes, Norman. *Modes of Production of Victorian Novels*. Chicago: Univ. of Chicago Press, 1986.

Ffrench, Yvonne. *Mrs. Gaskell*. London: Home & Van Thal, 1949.

Fielding, K. J. "Froude and Carlyle: Some New Considerations." In *Carlyle Past and Present: A Collection of New Essays,* ed. K. J. Fielding and Roger L. Tarr, 239–69. New York: Barnes & Noble, 1976.

Fitzwilliam, Marie. "The Politics behind the Angel: Separate Spheres in Elizabeth Gaskell's *Lizzie Leigh*." *Gaskell Society Journal* 8 (1994): 15–27.

Flint, Kate. *Elizabeth Gaskell*. Writers and Their Work. Plymouth: Northcote House, 1995.

Froude, James Anthony. *Thomas Carlyle: A History of the First Forty Years of His Life, 1795–1835*. 2 vols. New York: Harper, 1882.

———. *Thomas Carlyle: A History of His Life in London, 1834–1881*. 2 vols. New York: Charles Scribner's Sons, 1884.

Fryckstedt, Monica Correa. *Elizabeth Gaskell's Mary Barton and Ruth: A Challenge to Christian England*. Stockholm: Almqvist & Wiksell, 1982.

Gallagher, Catherine. *The Industrial Reformation of English Fiction: Social Discourse and Narrative Form, 1832–1867*. Chicago: Univ. of Chicago Press, 1985.

Gérin, Winifred. *Elizabeth Gaskell: A Biography*. Oxford: Clarendon Press, 1976.

Gillooly, Eileen. "Humor as Daughterly Defense in *Cranford*." *ELH* 59 (1992): 883–910.

Greenwood, Frederick. *Margaret Denzil's History (Annotated by Her Husband)*. *Cornhill Magazine,* November 1863–October 1864.

Griffith, George V. "What Kind of Book Is *Cranford?*" *Ariel* 14 (1983): 53–65.

Haight, Gordon S. *George Eliot: A Biography*. New York: Oxford Univ. Press, 1968.

Hapke, Laura. "He Stoops to Conquer: Redeeming the Fallen Woman in the Fiction of Dickens, Gaskell and Their Contemporaries." *Victorian Newsletter* 69 (1986): 16–22.

Heilbrun, Carolyn G. *Writing "A Woman's Life."* New York: W. W. Norton, 1988.

Helsinger, Elizabeth K., Robin Lauterbach Sheets, and William Veeder. *The Woman Question: Society and Literature in Britain and America, 1837–1883*. 3 vols. Chicago: Univ. of Chicago Press, 1983.

Hobson, Dorothy. *Crossroads: The Diary of a Soap Opera*. London: Methuen, 1982.

Homans, Margaret. *Bearing the Word: Language and Female Experience in Nineteenth-Century Women's Writing*. Chicago: Univ. of Chicago Press, 1986.

Howard, Edward. *Rattlin, the Reefer*. Ed. Arthur Howse. Oxford: Oxford Univ. Press, 1971.

Hughes, Linda K., and Michael Lund. "Linear Stories and Circular Visions: The Decline of the Victorian Serial." In *Chaos and Order: Complex Dynamics in Literature and Science,* ed. N. Katherine Hayles, 167–94. Chicago: Univ. of Chicago Press, 1991.

———. *The Victorian Serial*. Charlottesville: Univ. Press of Virginia, 1991.

Humpherys, Anne. "Who's Doing It? Fifteen Years of Work on Victorian Detective Fiction." *Dickens Studies Annual* 24 (1996): 259–74.

Hyde, William J. "'Poor Frederick' and 'Poor Peter': Elizabeth Gaskell's Fraternal Deviants." *Gaskell Society Journal* 9 (1995): 21–16.

Iles, Teresa. "Introduction." In *All Sides of the Subject: Women and Biography,* ed. Teresa Iles. New York: Teachers College Press, 1992.

Jelinek, Estelle C. "Introduction: Women's Autobiography and the Male Tradition." In *Women's Autobiography: Essays in Criticism,* ed. Estelle C. Jelinek, 1–20. Bloomington: Indiana Univ. Press, 1980.

Johnson, Edgar. *Charles Dickens: His Tragedy and Triumph*. 2 vols. New York: Simon & Schuster, 1952.

Jordan, Elaine. "Spectres and Scorpions: Allusion and Confusion in *Mary Barton*." *Literature and History* 7, no. 1 (1981): 48–61.

Jordan, John O., and Robert L. Patten. "Introduction: Publishing History as Hypertext."

In *Literature in the Marketplace: Nineteenth-Century British Publishing and Reading Practices*, 1–18. Cambridge Studies in Nineteenth-Century Literature and Culture 5. Cambridge: Cambridge Univ. Press, 1995.

Kalikoff, Beth. "The Falling Woman in Three Victorian Novels." *Studies in the Novel* 19 (1987): 357–67.

Karl, Frederick R. *An Age of Fiction: The Nineteenth Century British Novel.* New York: Noonday Press, 1964.

Kershaw, Alison. "The Business of a Woman's Life: Elizabeth Gaskell's *Life of Charlotte Brontë.*" *Brontë Society Transactions* 20 (1990): 11–24.

Kestner, Joseph A. *Masculinities in Victorian Painting.* Aldershot GB: Scolar Press, 1995.

———. "Men in Female Condition of England Novels." *Women and Literature* 2 (1982): 77–99.

Klingopulos, G. D. "The Literary Scene." 1958. In *From Dickens to Hardy,* ed. Boris Ford, 59–116. Harmondsworth GB: Penguin, 1972.

Krueger, Christine L. "'Speaking Like a Woman': How to Have the Last Word in *Sylvia's Lovers.*" In *Famous Last Words: Changes in Gender and Narrative Closure,* ed. Alison Booth, afterword by U. C. Knoepflmacher, 135–53. Charlottesville: Univ. Press of Virginia, 1993.

Kucich, John. "Transgression and Sexual Difference in Elizabeth Gaskell's Novels." *TSLL* 32, no. 2 (1990): 187–213.

Lansbury, Coral. *Elizabeth Gaskell.* Boston: Twayne, 1984.

———. *Elizabeth Gaskell: The Novel of Social Crisis.* New York: Barnes & Noble, 1975.

Leavis, F. R. *The Great Tradition: George Eliot, Henry James, Joseph Conrad.* New York: George W. Stewart, 1948.

Le Guin, Ursula K. "The Carrier Bag Theory of Fiction." 1986. In *Dancing at the Edge of the World,* 165–70. New York: Grove Press, 1989.

Lewis, Suzanne. "Introduction." In *"A Dark Night's Work" and Other Stories,* ed. Suzanne Lewis. New York: Oxford Univ. Press, 1992.

Lund, Michael. "Elizabeth Gaskell's Virgins." *Australasian Victorian Studies Journal* 1 (1995): 51–57.

Marchand, Leslie A. *The Athenaeum: A Mirror of Victorian Culture.* Chapel Hill: Univ. of North Carolina Press, 1941.

Marcus, Sharon. "The Profession of Author: Abstraction, Advertising, and *Jane Eyre.*" *PMLA* 110, no. 2 (1995): 206–19.

Martineau, Harriet. *Autobiography.* 2 vols. London: Virago Press, 1983.

Michie, Elsie B. *Outside the Pale: Cultural Exclusion, Gender Difference, and the Victorian Woman Writer.* Ithaca: Cornell Univ. Press, 1993.

Miller, Andrew. "The Fragments and Small Opportunities of *Cranford.*" *Genre* 25 (1992): 91–111.

———. "Subjectivity Ltd: The Discourse of Liability on the Joint Stock Companies Act of 1856 and Gaskell's *Cranford.*" *ELH* 61 (1994): 139–57.

Morgan, Susan. *Sisters in Time: Imagining Gender in Nineteenth Century British Fiction.* New York: Oxford Univ. Press, 1989.

Mulvihill, James. "Economies of Living in Elizabeth Gaskell's *Cranford.*" *Nineteenth-Century Literature* 50 (1995): 337–56.

Murray, Janet, ed. *Strong-Minded Women and Other Lost Voices from Nineteenth Century England.* New York: Pantheon, 1982.

Nightingale, Florence. *Cassandra.* New York: Feminist Press, 1979.

Nord, Deborah Epstein. *Walking the Victorian Streets: Women, Representations, and the City.* Ithaca: Cornell Univ. Press, 1995.

Ong, Walter J. "The Writer's Audience Is Always a Fiction." *PMLA* 90 (1975): 9–21.

Paroissien, David, ed. *Selected Letters of Charles Dickens.* Boston: Twayne, 1985.

Peterson, Linda H. " 'No Finger Posts—No Guides': Victorian Women Writers and the Paths to Fame." In *A Struggle for Fame: Victorian Women Artists and Authors,* by Susan Press Casteras and Linda H. Peterson, 325–47. New Haven: Yale Center for British Art, 1994.

Pollard, Arthur. *Mrs. Gaskell: Novelist and Biographer.* Manchester: Manchester Univ. Press, 1965.

Poovey, Mary. *The Proper Lady and the Woman Writer: Ideology as Style in the Works of Mary Wollstonecraft, Mary Shelley, and Jane Austen.* Chicago: Univ. of Chicago Press, 1984.

———. *Uneven Developments: The Ideological Work of Gender in Mid-Victorian England.* Chicago: Univ. of Chicago Press, 1988.

Radway, Janice A. *Reading the Romance: Women, Patriarchy, and Popular Literature.* Chapel Hill: Univ. of North Carolina Press, 1984.

Recchio, Thomas E. "Cranford and 'The Lawe of Kynde.' " *Gaskell Society Journal* 1 (1987): 10–26.

Rignall, J. M. "The Historical Double: *Waverley, Sylvia's Lovers, The Trumpet-Major.*" *Essays in Criticism* 34, no. 1 (1981): 14–32.

Robinson, Dennis. "Elizabeth Gaskell and 'A Few Words about "Jane Eyre." ' " *Notes and Queries,* 1976, 396–98.

Rose, Phyllis. *Parallel Lives: Five Victorian Marriages.* New York: Alfred A. Knopf, 1983.

Ross, Ann Marie. "Honoring the Woman as Writer: Elizabeth Gaskell's *Life of Charlotte Brontë.*" *Nineteenth-Century Prose,* special issue on Victorian biography, ed. John Powell, 22, no. 2 (1995): 25–38.

Sanders, Andrew. "Introduction." In *Sylvia's Lovers,* by Elizabeth Gaskell, vii–xvi. New York: Oxford Univ. Press, 1982.

———. "Varieties of Religious Experience in *Sylvia's Lovers.*" *Gaskell Society Journal* 6 (1992): 15–24.

Scarry, Elaine. *The Body in Pain: The Making and Unmaking of the World.* New York: Oxford Univ. Press, 1985.

———. "Introduction." In *Literature and the Body: Essays on Populations and Persons,* ed. Elaine Scarry. Selected Papers from the English Institute, n.s., no. 12. Baltimore: Johns Hopkins Univ. Press, 1988.

Schor, Hilary M. *Scheherezade in the Marketplace: Elizabeth Gaskell and the Victorian Novel.* New York: Oxford Univ. Press, 1992.

Sharps, John G. *Mrs. Gaskell's Observation and Invention: A Study of her Non-biographic Works.* Fontwell GB: Linden Press, 1970.

Shaw, Marion. "Elizabeth Gaskell, Tennyson and the Fatal Return: *Sylvia's Lovers* and *Enoch Arden.*" *Gaskell Society Journal* 9 (1995): 43–54.

Shelston, Alan. "Introduction." In *The Life of Charlotte Brontë,* by Elizabeth Gaskell, ed. Alan Shelston, 9–37. London: Penguin, 1975.

Showalter, Elaine. "Feminist Criticism in the Wilderness." In *Writing and Sexual Difference,* ed. Elizabeth Abel, 9–35. Chicago: Univ. of Chicago Press, 1982.

————. *A Literature of Their Own: British Women Novelists from Brontë to Lessing.* Princeton: Princeton Univ. Press, 1977.

Showalter, Elaine, and English Showalter. "Victorian Women and Menstruation." In *Suffer and Be Still,* ed. Martha Vicinus, 38–44. Bloomington: Indiana Univ. Press, 1972.

Skilton, David. "Introduction." In *Lady Audley's Secret,* by Mary Elizabeth Braddon, vii–xxiii. New York: Oxford Univ. Press, 1987.

Skilton, David, and Peter Miles. "Introduction." In *Framley Parsonage,* ed. Anthony Trollope. New York: Penguin, 1984.

Snitow, Ann Barr. "Mass Market Romance: Pornography for Women Is Different." *Radical History Review* 20 (1979): 141–61.

Spacks, Patricia Meyer. *Gossip.* Chicago: Univ. of Chicago Press, 1986.

Spencer, Jane. *Elizabeth Gaskell.* Women Writers. London: Macmillan, 1993.

————. "*Mary Barton* and Thomas Carlyle." *Gaskell Society Journal* 2 (1988): 1–12.

Spender, Dale. *The Writing or the Sex? or Why You Don't Have to Read Women's Writing to Know It's No Good.* Athene Series. New York: Pergamon Press, 1989.

Stiles, Peter. "Grace, Redemption and the 'Fallen Woman': *Ruth* and *Tess of the D'Urbervilles.*" *Gaskell Society Journal* 6 (1992): 58–66.

Stone, Marjorie. "Bakhtinian Polyphony in *Mary Barton:* Class, Gender, and the Textual Voice." *Dickens Studies Annual* 20 (1991): 175–200.

Stoneman, Patsy. *Elizabeth Gaskell.* Key Women Writers. Brighton, Sussex: Harvester Press, 1987.

Sussman, Herbert. *Victorian Masculinities: Manhood and Masculine Poetics in Early Victorian Literature and Art.* Cambridge: Cambridge Univ. Press, 1995.

Sutherland, John. *The Stanford Companion to Victorian Fiction.* Stanford: Stanford Univ. Press, 1989.

Thackeray, William Makepeace. *Denis Duval. Cornhill Magazine,* March 1864–June 1864.

Thompson, Joanne. "Faith of Our Mothers: Elizabeth Gaskell's 'Lizzie Leigh.' " *Victorian Newsletter* 78 (1990): 22–26.

Trela, D. J. "Froude on the Carlyles: The Victorian Debate over Biography." In *Victorian Scandals: Representations of Gender and Class,* ed. Kristine Ottesen Garrigan, 180–206. Athens: Ohio Univ. Press, 1992.

Trollope, Anthony. *Framley Parsonage. Cornhill Magazine,* January 1860–April 1861.

Tuchman, Gaye, with Nina E. Fortin. *Edging Women Out: Victorian Novelists, Publishers, and Social Change.* New Haven: Yale Univ. Press, 1989.

Uglow, Jenny. *Elizabeth Gaskell: A Habit of Stories.* New York: Farrar, Straus & Giroux, 1993.

Valverde, Mariana. "The Love of Finery: Fashion and the Fallen Woman in Nineteenth-Century Social Discourse." *Victorian Studies* 32, no. 2 (1989): 169–188.

Vann, J. Don. "Dickens, Charles Lever and Mrs. Gaskell." *Victorian Periodicals Review* 22, no. 2 (1989): 64–71.

Warhol, Robyn R. "Towards a Theory of the Engaging Narrator: Earnest Interventions in Gaskell, Stowe, and Eliot." *PMLA* 101, no. 5 (1986): 811–18.

Wheeler, Michael. "Two Tales of Manchester Life." *Gaskell Society Journal* 3 (1989): 6–28.

Whitman, Alden. *Come to Judgment.* New York: Viking Press, 1980.

Williams, Raymond. *The Country and the City.* New York: Oxford Univ. Press, 1973.

Winnett, Susan. "Coming Unstrung: Women, Men, Narrative, and Principles of Pleasure." *PMLA* 105 (1990): 505–18.

Witte, Sarah E. "The Transcendental Eye and Ear in Mrs. Gaskell's *Mary Barton.*" *Durham University Journal* 80, no. 2 (1988): 257–63.

Wolfreys, Julian. *Being English: Narratives, Idioms, and Performances of National Identity from Coleridge to Trollope.* Albany: State Univ. of New York Press, 1994.

Wright, Edgar. "Introduction." In *"My Lady Ludlow" and Other Stories,* ed. Edgar Wright. New York: Oxford Univ. Press, 1989.

Wright, Terence. *Elizabeth Gaskell: Realism, Gender, Values.* New York: St. Martin's Press, 1995.

Yaeger, Patricia. "Violence in the Sitting Room: *Wuthering Heights* and the Woman's Novel." *Genre* 21 (1988): 203–9.

Yarrow, Press J. "The Chronology of *Cranford.*" *Gaskell Society Journal* 1 (1987): 27–29.

Yeazell, Ruth Bernard. "Why Political Novels Have Heroines: *Sybil, Mary Barton,* and *Felix Holt.*" *Novel: A Forum on Fiction* 18, no. 2 (1985): 126–44.

Index

Victorian Literature and Culture Series

———··◁≫▷··———

DANIEL ALBRIGHT
Tennyson: The Muses' Tug-o-War

DAVID G. RIEDE
Matthew Arnold and the Betrayal of Language

ANTHONY WINNER
Culture and Irony: Studies in Joseph Conrad's Major Novels

JAMES RICHARDSON
Vanishing Lives: Style in Tennyson, D. G. Rossetti, Swinburne, and Yeats

JEROME J. MCGANN, EDITOR
Victorian Connections

ANTONY H. HARRISON
Victorian Poets and Romantic Poems: Intertextuality and Ideology

E. WARWICK SLINN
The Discourse of Self in Victorian Poetry

LINDA K. HUGHES AND MICHAEL LUND
The Victorian Serial

ANNA LEONOWENS
The Romance of the Harem
Edited by Susan Morgan

ALAN FISCHLER
Modified Rapture: Comedy in W. S. Gilbert's Savoy Operas

EMILY SHORE
Journal of Emily Shore
Edited by Barbara Timm Gates

RICHARD MAXWELL
The Mysteries of Paris and London

FELICIA BONAPARTE
The Gypsy-Bachelor of Manchester: The Life of Mrs. Gaskell's Demon

PETER L. SHILLINGSBURG
Pegasus in Harness: Victorian Publishing and W. M. Thackeray

ANGELA LEIGHTON
Victorian Women Poets: Writing against the Heart

ALLAN C. DOOLEY
Author and Printer in Victorian England

SIMON GATRELL
Thomas Hardy and the Proper Study of Mankind

JEFFREY SKOBLOW
Paradise Dislocated: Morris, Politics, Art

MATTHEW ROWLINSON
Tennyson's Fixations: Psychoanalysis and the Topics of the Early Poetry

BEVERLY SEATON
The Language of Flowers: A History

BARRY MILLIGAN
Pleasures and Pains: Opium and the Orient in Nineteenth-Century British Culture

GINGER S. FROST
Promises Broken: Courtship, Class, and Gender in Victorian England

LINDA DOWLING
The Vulgarization of Art: The Victorians and Aesthetic Democracy

TRICIA LOOTENS
Lost Saints: Silence, Gender, and Victorian Literary Canonization

MATTHEW ARNOLD
The Letters of Matthew Arnold, vols. 1–3
Edited by Cecil Y. Lang

EDWARD FITZGERALD
Edward FitzGerald, Rubáiyát of Omar Khayyám: *A Critical Edition*
Edited by Christopher Decker

CHRISTINA ROSSETTI
The Letters of Christina Rossetti, vols. 1–2
Edited by Antony H. Harrison

BARBARA LEAH HARMON
The Feminine Political Novel in Victorian England

JOHN RUSKIN
The Genius of John Ruskin: Selections from His Writings
Edited by John D. Rosenberg

ANTONY H. HARRISON
Victorian Poets and the Politics of Culture: Discourse and Ideology

JUDITH STODDART
Negotiating a Nation: Ruskin's Fors Clavigera *in the Late Victorian Culture Wars*

LINDA K. HUGHES AND MICHAEL LUND
Victorian Publishing and Mrs. Gaskell's Work